Philipp D. Riekert

Venture Governance

GABLER EDITION WISSENSCHAFT

Philipp D. Riekert

Venture Governance

Venture Capital-backed Startups in Silicon Valley and Tokyo

Mit einem Geleitwort von Prof. Dr. Dr. h.c. mult. Horst Albach

Deutscher Universitäts-Verlag

Bibliografische Information Der Deutschen Bibliothek
Die Deutsche Bibliothek verzeichnet diese Publikation in der Deutschen Nationalbibliografie; detaillierte bibliografische Daten sind im Internet über <http://dnb.ddb.de> abrufbar.

Dissertation Wissenschaftliche Hochschule für Unternehmensführung (WHU)
Vallendar, 2003

1. Auflage Oktober 2004

Lektorat: Brigitte Siegel / Ingrid Walther

Der Deutsche Universitäts-Verlag ist ein Unternehmen von
Springer Science+Business Media.
www.duv.de

Umschlaggestaltung: Regine Zimmer, Dipl.-Designerin, Frankfurt/Main

Gedruckt auf säurefreiem und chlorfrei gebleichtem Papier

ISBN-13:978-3-8244-7991-7 e-ISBN-13:978-3-322-81660-3
DOI: 10.1007/978-3-322-81660-3

Geleitwort

Wer sich mit dem Thema "Corporate Governance" beschäftigt, denkt zumeist an die Führungsstrukturen in großen, börsennotierten Unternehmen. Er fragt sich nach den Vorkommnissen der letzten Jahre, ob der Aufsichtsrat von einem Kontrollorgan zum Selbstbedienungsladen geworden ist. Solche Diskussionen sind wichtig, weil sie dem Schutz uninformierter oder schlecht informierter Anleger von Kapital an den nationalen und internationalen Börsen dienen. Selbst diejenigen Anleger, die sich über die Kurssteigerungen bei Übernahmeschlachten freuen, mögen sich fragen, ob sie nicht noch mehr bekommen hätten, wenn sich die Vorstände und Aufsichtsräte nicht unkontrolliert hohe "Erfolgsprämien" gewährt hätten. Und so mancher mag seine Aktien eines Unternehmens verkaufen, wenn er erfährt, wie der Vorstandsvorsitzende dieses Unternehmens sich im Aufsichtsrat eines anderen verhält.

All diese Fragen sind weit über den konkreten Anlaß hinaus wichtig. Sie berühren die Glaubwürdigkeit des Kapitalmarkts und ganz grundsätzlich des marktwirtschaftlichen Systems.

Nicht minder wichtig sind die Probleme der Corporate Governance in der mittelständischen Wirtschaft und besonders im Familienunternehmen. Hier reichen die Themen vom "lästigen Gesellschafter" bis zum familienfremden Beirat. Die "Kleine Aktiengesellschaft" ist eine bedeutende Weiterentwicklung des Rechts der Corporate Governance in Familienunternehmen gewesen.

Die Erfahrungen, welche in jungen Unternehmen während der Zeit der "Venture Bubble" gemacht wurden, zeigen, daß die Corporate Governance auch bei neu gegründeten Unternehmen eine zentrale Rolle spielt. Hier geht es im allgemeinen um den Einfluß des Venture Capitalist auf die Führung des jungen Unternehmens oder um die Publizität des jungen Unternehmens. Der Aufsichtsrat ist weniger deutsches Kontrollorgan denn amerikanischer Board. Einen interessanten Vergleich der Corporate Governance in deutschen und amerikanischen Unternehmen haben Samwer und Finger vorgelegt. Hier vergleicht Riekert die Corporate Governance von Start-Up-Unternehmen im Silicon Valley und in Tokyo.

Der Vergleich wird in vier Abschnitten durchgeführt. Der erste Abschnitt behandelt die allgemeinen Grundlagen, die Firma, die Corporate Governance sowie die methodischen Grundlagen für einen Vergleich von Corporate Governance Strukturen. Das ist ein intellektuell höchst anregender Abschnitt.

Der zweite Abschnitt behandelt das Modell der Corporate Governance von Start-Up-Firmen im Silicon Valley. Die Ausführungen von Riekert sind methodisch klar und sehr informativ. Im Mittelpunkt steht die These, daß es zwei Arten von Start-Up-Unternehmen im Silicon Valley gibt. Das Unterscheidungsmerkmal ist die Rolle des Venture Kapitalisten. Im ersten Modell übernimmt der Risiko-Kapitalist das normale unternehmerische Risiko des Eigenkapitalgebers, im zweiten Modell dagegen ist er der eigentliche Übernehmer des unternehmerischen Risikos und nicht der Gründer. In diesem Modell ermöglicht es der Venture-Kapitalist risikoscheuen Trägern von Humankapital, also vor allem Wissenschaftlern, ihre Ideen in einem Wagnisunternehmen umzusetzen. Riekert entwickelt aus seinen empirischen Erhebungen ein Corporate Governance Modell für Wagnisunternehmen, das große Beachtung nicht nur bei gründungswilligen Studenten, Absolventen und wissenschaftlichen Mitarbeitern von Universitäten und Fachhochschulen finden sollte, sondern auch bei Gründungszentren und Patentverwertungsgremien in den Hochschulen.

Japanische Start-Up-Unternehmen werden im dritten Abschnitt vorgestellt. Mit diesem Abschnitt hat Riekert eine Pionierleistung vollbracht. Es schmälert die bedeutenden Arbeiten von Kiyonari über japanische Venture Capital-Firmen nicht, wenn ich sage, daß es bisher keine Untersuchung von Start-Up-Unternehmen in Japan gibt. Fragebogen und Fallstudien bilden das methodische Handwerkszeug, mit dem Riekert diesen Forschungsgegenstand erschließt. Der Autor kristallisiert die Hauptmerkmale der japanischen Corporate Governance heraus und entwickelt die Elemente einer Theorie der japanischen Corporate Governance.

Die wichtigsten Ergebnisse der Arbeit von Riekert lassen sich wie folgt zusammenfassen. Methodisch kann man das Eigentum an Start-Up-Unternehmen als ein Bündel von Ansprüchen auf die Cash-Flow-Ströme und die Kontrollrechte im Unternehmen verstehen. Wird Wagniskapital zur Finanzierung herangezogen, werden die Ansprüche auf Cash Flows und auf Kontrolle de facto geteilt. Die Investoren erhalten keinerlei Kontrollrechte und haben auch keinen Markt, auf dem sie ihr Investment verteidigen könnten. Die Kontrollrechte liegen bei Gründern. Daher gibt es Konflikte zwischen den Gründern und den Venture Capitalists um den richtigen Zeitpunkt für den Börsengang. Eine Alternative stellt das vom Venture Capitalist kontrollierte Venture Business dar. Der Venture Capitalist bleibt Monitor des Führungsteams im Venture Business und behält das Recht, die Ressourcenverteilung zu beeinflussen. Das Silicon-Valley-Modell 2 entspricht dieser Variante der Corporate Governance in Start-Up-Unternehmen. Der Gründer kann sich auf die Unternehmerfunktion konzentrieren und Humankapital mobilisieren, der Venture Capitalist übt die Governance aus und professionalisiert das Management. Das Tokyo-Modell ist dagegen noch dem traditionellen Begriff des Wagnis-Unternehmers verhaftet, also dem Modell 1. Das Gründungsrisiko wird durch Venture Capitalists gemildert, ist aber nicht wie im Modell 2 für den Gründer praktisch ganz ausgeschlossen.

Riekert vertritt die These, daß das Silicon-Valley-Modell (Modell 2) die überlegene Form der Corporate Governance in Start-Up-Unternehmen darstellt. Das erklärt auch, warum japanische Unternehmensgründer ihr Venture Capital vorwiegend in den USA beschaffen.

Die japanischen Venture Capitalists sind auf eine so umfassende Rolle, wie sie das Modell 2 verlangt, offenbar nicht eingestellt und auch nicht vorbereitet.

Mein herzlicher Dank gebührt meinem Kollegen Professor Dr. Akihiro Okumura von der Keio University Graduate School of Business Administration für seine wertvolle Mitbetreuung der Arbeit von Philipp Riekert. Er hat mich auch in meinem Urteil bestärkt, daß es Riekert gelungen ist, zur Entwicklung einer Theorie der Vergleichenden Corporate Governance maßgeblich beizutragen.

Horst Albach

Preface

In preparing this study, I greatly benefited from being able to spend time in two extremely favorable research environments, Stanford University in Palo Alto and Keio University in Tokyo.

From 1997 to 1999, I received support by the German National Merit Foundation to pursue two years of postgraduate studies at Stanford University's Center for East Asian Studies on an ERP Scholarship. During my time at Stanford, Masahiko Aoki served as my academic advisor and the work in his seminars on Comparative Institutional Analysis profoundly shaped my thinking and the theoretical framework adopted in this study. Together with other Japan-related and Entrepreneuship-related resources at Stanford, such as the Asia Pacific Research Center led by Dan Okimoto, the Stanford Project on Emerging Companies (in particular Thomas Hellmann's work on venture capital and entrepreneuship), other resources at the Graduate School of Business, as well as the hands-on start-up classes with venture capital practitioners in the Engineering Department, this provided an extremely stimulating work environment. Much of this study's theoretical framework as well as the empirical research on Silicon Valley was completed during this period at Stanford.

In June 1999, after graduating from Stanford with a M.A. in East Asian Studies, I moved to Japan, to become a Visiting Researcher at Keio University's Graduate School of Business Administration (KBS), supported by the DaimlerChrysler East Asia Scholarship. I do owe a great deal of gratitute to Akihiro Okumura, who invited me to Keio and who served as my academic advisor there. His endless support enabled me to quickly identify the right contacts and build the personal network required to pursue my empirical research program in Tokyo. Many others at KBS were helpful too and assisted me in pursuing this field research. Jiro Kokuryo's central position among Internet entrepreneurs helped to establish many contacts and numerous KBS students (special thanks to Makoto Suzuki) gave valuable advice and provided perspective.

I am very grateful to the more than one hundred individuals (founders, financiers, employees of startups) who provided their time for research interviews in the course of my case studies. Many of them I followed over a period of more than two years, during which some enjoyed great success in their business ventures and others had to cope with existential backlashes. For letting me observe their ups and downs I do owe them great respect and gratitude.

During the entire period of preparing this study, I did receive the patient support of my academic advisor Horst Albach, WHU Koblenz - Otto Beisheim Graduate School of Management. His broad and international perspective and his particular expertise in the areas of comparative corporate governance, entrepreneurship and venture capital is unique and was essential for enabling me to pursue a research program whose challenge was its consciously chosen broad setup.

Philipp Riekert

Table of Contents

List of Figures

List of Tables

Chapter 1. Introduction

1. 1. Thesis

The thesis of this dissertation is that modern, venture capital-backed startup ventures are characterized by an innovative governance system that makes them distinct from traditional archetypes of business venturing and allows the realization of an enlarged array of business opportunities. In Silicon Valley, this 'venture governance' system enables innovation incorporated in new firms by addressing the governance challenges faced by human capital and information-intensive organizations that operate under high uncertainty. However, the practice of startup venture capital in Silicon Valley is embedded in a complex set of (regional) institutions. Emerging startup venture capital in Japan operates in a different environment and conceptual differences between startup venture capital in Silicon Valley and Tokyo can be identified.

1. 2. Empirical Motivation

Startup venture capital in the U.S. has a fifty-year history and generates attractive long-term returns to investors (see Figure 1). Venture capital firms as specialized financial intermediaries are regarded as an indispensable source of finance for high-risk business opportunities. Over the last several decades, venture capital in the United Stated has experienced cyclical, but over the long-term consistent growth from a cottage industry into a major asset class approaching $100 billion in annual commitments. At the same time, classic venture capital is still regarded as, by and large, peculiar to several regions in the United

States and was still mostly noted for its lack or absence in other major developed countries, such as Japan.[1] Why is that?

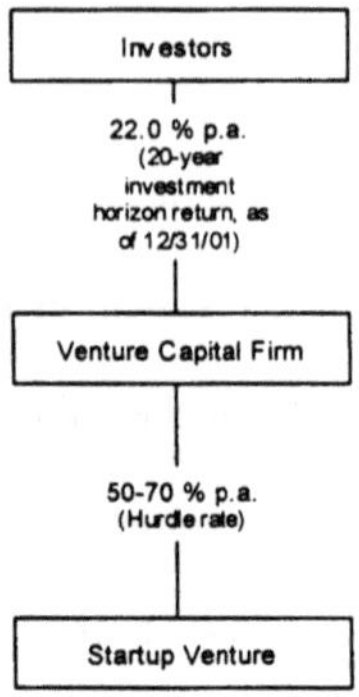

Figure 1: U.S. Startup Venture Capital, Hurdle Rate and Long-run Return to Investor[2]

This question has gained importance in mature industrialized economies, because recent years have seen tremendous change in the roles and functions that newly-established firms play in the economy. It has been argued that startups are especially important for innovation of the non-incremental type because established firms are unlikely to start totally new things.[3] A U.S. Commerce Department study sustains this view and finds that "95 % of all radical innovations since WWII have come from new and small companies, rather than large, established ones."[4] The importance of small companies is also reflected in their contribution to new job creation. During the 1980s, Fortune 500 companies lost 4 million jobs, while at the same time firms with less than 100 employees added 16 million jobs.[5]

---

1 Joseph W. Bartlett (1999), *Fundamentals of Venture Capital*, Lanham: Madison Books, p. 2.

2 Venture Economics. James L. Plummer (1987), "QED Report on Venture Capital Financial Analysis," Palo Alto: QED Research.

3 OECD (1996b), "Venture Capital and Innovation," OCDE/GD(96)168, Paris: OECD.

4 William D. Bygrave and Jeffry A. Timmons (1992), *Venture Capital at the Crossroads*, Boston: Harvard Business School Press, p. 65.

5 Paul A. Gompers (1994), "The Rise and Fall of Venture Capital," *Business and Economic History*, Vol. 23, No. 2, Winter 1994: 1-26, p. 1. Cf. OECD (1998). *Small Business, Job Creation and Growth*. Paris: OECD.

To be sure, venture capital-backed startup companies represent only a tiny segment of newly established companies. However, their contribution to innovation and growth in the U.S. is disproportionate. Using patenting activity as a proxy, Samuel Kortum and Joshua Lerner provide clear evidence that venture capital spurs innovation. They estimate that venture capital accounts for more than 10% of industrial innovation in the U.S. and find that it is more efficient in spurring innovation than corporate R&D.[6] Most prominently in the Silicon Valley region of the United States, but also in other major economies, many newly established venture capital-backed companies have developed into major corporations, gave birth to entire new industries, and make large contributions to innovation and economic growth. As a result, Silicon Valley and its highly developed venture capital system that supports these innovative startup ventures has become the envy of the world.

During the second half of the 1990s, booming equity markets and the perceived business opportunities arising from the commercialization of information technology and the Internet brought along an unparalleled international wave of business startups and venture capital activity. Whether the talk was of "startups," "ventures," and "Silicon Valley equity culture" in the US, or "Bitvalley" and "Netto-benchaa-kigyou" in Japan; venture capital and the rise of the startup venture seemed to have turned into a global phenomenon, spreading from the United States to Europe and Japan.

Japan, like some Western European countries, has long had its own indigenous venture capital industry. The promotion of startup businesses and venture capital has been a prime objective of public policy. Conscious efforts to learn from the U.S. venture capital model were undertaken, regulatory obstacles were eliminated, and the industry experienced remarkable growth and record investment volumes in 2000. Yet, the Japanese venture capital

---

6 Samuel Kortum and Joshua Lerner (2000), "Assessing the Contribution of Venture Capital to Innovation,"

industry is still very small compared to the U.S. and more importantly, as this study will show, there are major structural differences between the practice of venture capital in the U.S. and Japan.

These differences need to be seen against the background of deep-seated structural differences in the corporate governance of U.S. and Japanese firms. Corporate executives in both countries have found very different answers to the most fundamental questions regarding the concept of the firm and whose interests it should serve. A survey by Masaru Yoshimori shows that most Japanese managers (97.1%) think that the company exists for the interest of all stakeholders, whereas most American managers (75.6%) think that it exists primarily for the interest of shareholders. As a result, Japanese managers (97.2%) give the maintenance of stable employment priority over dividend payments, while U.S. managers (89.2%) find it more important to pay dividends, even if this requires laying off a number of employees.[7] Hiroyuki Itami describes the underlying Japanese concept of the firm as 'employee sovereignty', and puts it in contrast with the American concept of 'shareholder sovereignty'.[8] Venture capitalists are financially motivated equity investors, therefore structural differences of this kind are pertinent to them and call for a comparative analysis of the functioning of venture capital and the corporate governance of the companies that are financed by venture capitalists in both countries.

Any analysis of venture capital should keep in mind that the 'big money' venture capital model of entrepreneurship, although capturing a disproportionate share of attention, is by no

---

Mimeo, Harvard University.

7 Masaru Yoshimori (1995), "Whose Company Is It? The Concept of Corporation in Japan and the West," *Long Range Planning*, 28: 33-44.

8 Hiroyuki Itami (1999), "Concept of the Firm and Corporate Governance in Japan," *Mimeo*, Hitotsubashi University. Cf. Yoshiro Miwa (1997), "The Economics of Corporate Governance in Japan," *Working Paper*, University of Tokyo.

means a very common way of building a great company.[9] Even in the Unites States, where the venture capital industry is best developed, less than one percent of all newly established companies is funded by venture capitalists and even among the Inc. 500 group of high-growth private companies only few do work according to this model.[10] On the other hand, in some regions, and for the development of some new industries such as semiconductors, the Internet or biotechnology, venture capital appears to have been indispensable, and from a long-term perspective, the venture capital industry shows consistent growth.

Consequently, venture capital can be characterized as a) being not for everyone, b) being indispensable for some, and c) experiencing strong long-term growth. These characteristics suggests that a closer look at the startup companies that operate with venture capital funding is necessary to understand the industry. Unfortunately, understanding of the workings of venture capitalists and the companies they fund remains partial. Venture capital-backed startups take a different approach from the traditional low-budget startup. But what is characterizing this type of company? Are we just giving new names to an old phenomenon of outstanding innovative entrepreneurs who are able to convince financiers of their business, or are we seeing fundamental structural change in the organization of economic activity? Are we observing the re-rise of the Schumpeterian entrepreneur and the demise of the large corporation, or are we experiencing the evolution of a new organizational form of modern business venturing?

Seen through the lens of traditional concepts, some characteristics of modern venture activity seem to be noteworthy, or even odd, and call for a theory-grounded examination. A case in point is the concept of the entrepreneur. Some modern entrepreneurs appear to assume

---

9 Howard H. Stevenson, Michael J. Roberts, Irving H. Grousbeck, and Amar V. Bhidé (1999), *New Business Ventures and the Entrepreneur*, 5th edition, Boston: Irwin/MacGraw-Hill, p. 169. Mark Van Osnabrugge and

functions that are very different from those that have traditionally been regarded as characteristic of or even essential for an entrepreneur. To illustrate this point, let us have a brief look at the stories of two undisputedly successful entrepreneurs: Konosuke Matsushita and Jim Clark.

The Individual Entrepreneur: Konosuke Matsushita

> Konosuke Matsushita was born in 1894, the youngest of eight children of a land-owning farmer in Wakayama prefecture. At the age of four, his father loses home and farmlands in speculation on the rice exchange market. After trying one job after the other without success and seeing his three oldest children die of influenza within a short period, the father decides to support the family by finding work in Osaka. At the age of nine, Konosuke Matsushita follows his father to Osaka in order to become an apprentice at a manufacturer of charcoal heaters. When the shop moves to another part of the town he is handed over to a bicycle shop – a modern trade at the time – where he continues to work for six years. His father encourages him to endure the hardships of apprenticeship in order to learn about business and eventually become independent. Impressed by the newly constructed electric train and pondering the future of bicycles, Matsushita decides at the age of fifteen to "pursue a career in the field of electricity."[11] He joins the Osaka Electric Light Company, where he engages in wiring projects, and quickly rises in the ranks of the fast growing company, eventually becoming its youngest inspector. Increasingly bored with this more relaxed position, he becomes possessed of the idea of realizing a new socket design that he had proposed to his company but that had been rejected. At the age of 22 he leaves his employer to set up his own company and produce sockets according to his own design. He convinces two former co-workers and the younger brother of his wife to join his venture. Scratching together all his wealth of 100 Yen as capital and without knowing the manufacturing method of the socket isolation material, Matsushita launches the venture in his 13-square-meter apartment. After some struggling, they are able to find somebody who tells them the key know-how that they need, and also manage to borrow another 100 Yen from a frugally saving friend. Three months after Matsushita had left his previous position they succeed in the production of the first socket. However, sales of the new product turn out to be elusive, and after four months the company is left with no capital and total revenues of just 10 Yen. At that point, being without any prospect of making the business survive, his two associates leave the company, and Matsushita is left with neither money nor a saleable product. Only Matsushita, his wife, and her fifteen-year-old brother, Toshio Iue, are determined to struggle on.[12] Luckily,

---

Robert J. Robinson (1999a), "Do Venture Capitalists Behave Differently When Investing In High Tech Ventures?" *Working Paper*, Harvard Business School, March 1999.

10 Ibid., p. 170.

11 Konosuke Matsushita (1988), *Quest for Prosperity*, Tokyo: PHP Institute, p. 20.

12 Toshio Iue later founded Sanyo Electric Co., Ltd.

just at that time, they are approached by a parts wholesaler and offered a subcontracting order that does not require much capital and promises a significant profit. Continuing to create cash flow through subcontracting orders, Matsushita is able to finance expansion and the development of new products. An attachment plug that offers slight improvements and a 30% lower price than competitors', and later a two-way socket, lay the foundation for Matsushita as a "manufacturer of innovative products at reasonable prices." [13] From these foundations until Matsushita's death in 1989, the business grows to a company generating $42 billion in revenues with brands such as National, Panasonic, and Technics, and employing almost 200,000 people in 130 countries, making it the nineteenth largest industrial corporation in the Fortune 500 ranking.[14]

Konosuke Matsushita introduced many innovative management and marketing techniques and is regarded as the prototypical Japanese self-made entrepreneur.[15] He served as the company's president until 1961, as chairman until 1973, and thereafter continued to be an executive advisor to the company.[16]

The Serial Entrepreneur: Jim Clark

Jim Clark grows up in the 1950s in Plainview, Texas. His mother works in a doctor's office and supports her three children on a mere $300 a month, his father performs odd jobs and is a violent alcoholic.[17] After being suspended from school, Clark joins the Navy, studies for his high school equivalency, eventually earning a doctorate in computer science. In 1982 he starts his first company, Silicon Graphics, with venture capital backing and together with some of his students, commercializing a revolutionary 3-D graphics technology that he develops as an associate professor at Stanford University. The company goes public in 1986 and becomes a billion-dollar company.[18] However, after disenchantment with outside investors, whom he deemed had left him with too small a stake in the company's equity (5% at IPO),[19] and conflicts with the professional management that they had brought in, Clark leaves the company in 1994. [20] Together with Marc Andreessen, he establishes Netscape Communications to produce the browser that will trigger the commercial use of the Internet.[21] Thanks to his success with

---

13 Matsushita (1988), op. cit., p. 55.

14 Matsushita Electric Industrial Co., Ltd. Annual Report 1989 (for the year ending March 31, 1989).

15 John P. Kotter (1996), *Matsushita Leadership: Lessons from the 20th Century's Most Remarkable Entrepreneur,* New York: Free Press. Togo Sheba (1969), *Konosuke Matsushita*, Tokyo: Rengo Press.

16 For Matsushita's philosophical thoughts see: Konosuke Matsushita (1982), *Thoughts on Man*, Tokyo: PHP Institute. (Japanese: *Ningen wo Kangaeru*, Tokyo: PHP Institute, 1975.)

17 Evantheia Schibsted (1999), "The Triple Crown Winner," *Business 2.0*, June 1999, available at URL: http://www.business2.com, retrieved: March 21, 2000.

18 Michael Goldberg (1994a), "Fire in the Valley," *Wired Digital Archive*, January 1994, available at URL: http://www.wired.com, retrieved: March 20, 1999.

19 Schibsted (1999), op. cit.

20 Michael Goldberg (1994b), "Why Jim Clark Loves Mosaic," *Wired Digital Archive*, October 1994, available at URL: http://www.wired.com, retrieved: March 20, 1999.

21 Gary Wolfe (1994), "The (Second Phase of the) Revolution Has Begun," *Wired Digital Archive*, October 1994, available at URL: http://www.wired.com, retrieved: March 20, 1999.

> Silicon Graphics, this time investors are eager to invest in his company. Clark decides to invest $5 million (roughly one third of his net worth at the time) himself, and raises capital from prestigious venture capital firm Kleiner Perkins Caufield and Byers at a valuation that is unheard of at the time. With the help of their venture capitalist, John Doerr, Netscape assembles a professional management team with five vice presidents and a CEO.[22] Soon after, Netscape, as a barely established and loss-making company, goes public in what can be called the first Internet IPO, making Clark the first Internet paper billionaire. After leaving Netscape, Clark sets up Healtheon in 1996 with the mission to network the inefficient health care system, again creating a faithful following of the most prestigious investors, lawyers, executives and engineers in Silicon Valley.[23] In February 1999, Healtheon goes public and becomes the third multibillion company founded by Jim Clark.[24] Since then, he has founded and served as chairman of the board of two more companies (MyCFO.com and Shutterfly.com) that are still privately held and funded by first-rank Silicon Valley venture capital investors, and recently joined a venture capital partnership himself.[25]
>
> With Silicon Graphics, Netscape, and Healtheon, Jim Clark became the first person in the world to create three different multibillion-dollar technology companies, and at the same time the prototype of the Silicon Valley "serial entrepreneur."

Obviously, these two remarkable entrepreneurs could not have been placed in more different circumstances. They operate at different times, in different countries, and in different industries, so it is little wonder that their stories bear few commonalities. However, a not so self-evident difference concerns the role that each of them as a person assumes within the firm as an organization.

Konosuke Matsushita committed from the outset his entire human and financial resources to his company, being inventor, capitalist, manager, technologist, and laborer in personal union. In order to obtain resource commitments he had to rely on ties of kinship or friendship,

---

22 John Brockman (1997), "John Doerr: The Coach," *Edge*, available at URL: http://www.edge.org, retrieved: March 28, 2000.

23 Jayne Garrison (1998), "Doctor Stock," *Wired Digital Archive*, October 1998, available at URL: http://www.wired.com, retrieved: March 20, 1999.

24 John Naughton (1999), "The Billion Dollar Man who put us on the Web," *The Guardian*, December 19, 1999, available at URL: http://www.newsunlimited.co.uk, retrieved: March 21, 2000. Larry Kanter (1999), "Jim Clark," *Salon.com*, November 24, 1999, available at URL: http://www.salon.com, retrieved: March 21, 2000.

25 See the company websites at http://www.mycfo.com and http://www.shutterfly.com.

and he had to concentrate on generating cash flow to finance growth. He remained associated with his company until his death.

Jim Clark on the other hand has established at least five different companies operating in quite different areas. Even after he had acquired personal wealth, he had his startups bankrolled by venture capitalists. The more he built his reputation as a successful entrepreneur, the more he chose to reduce his own involvement in the company. In his more recent startups his role was limited to initiating the business, setting the strategic direction, and gathering specialized human and financial resources, basically reducing his own involvement to the act of bringing them together. Most recently, he actually became a venture capitalist with the Barksdale Group.[26]

This brief comparison was meant to illustrate that there is a wide spectrum of forms of business venturing, with the functions associated with the person called entrepreneur being very different. Moreover, business venturing of the type that Jim Clark is pursuing would not have been possible in the environment that Konosuke Matsushita was operating in. To understand the governance system that enables this modern type of venture capital-backed business venturing and place it in the framework of economic theory is the objective of this dissertation. In doing so, an informed comparative analysis of venture capital-backed business venturing becomes possible.

1. 3. Methodology

Existing comparative studies have related the availability of startup venture capital in different countries to the structure of national financial systems, capital markets and their

---

[26] Schibsted (1999), op. cit.

influence on the supply of venture capital.[27] Different studies have pointed out that the peculiar legal structure of U.S. venture capital organizations enables the supply of funds in situations characterized by high uncertainty and information asymmetries.[28] Still other authors tried to integrate a variety of theories and have proposed to approach the determination of industry size by using a supply and demand framework, regarding the number of promising businesses that seek venture capital as constituting the demand for VC and the volume of available funds constituting the supply.[29] This framework suffers from the technical problem that the 'price' in this market, which would be the investors' expected rate of return, cannot be measured. Yet, a more fundamental problem of this approach is that supply and demand factors can hardly be separated.[30] For example the return in equity markets can be expected to have both supply and demand side effects, because it influences how investors structure their portfolio (supply side factor) and is probably a proxy for entrepreneurial opportunities (demand effect), as well. Nevertheless, the explicit

---

27 Cf. Bernard S. Black and Ronald J. Gilson (1998), "Venture Capital and the Structure of Capital Markets: Banks versus Stock Markets," *Journal of Financial Economics*, 47: 243-277. Franklin Allen and Douglas Gale (2000), *Comparing Financial Systems*, Cambridge: MIT Press. OECD (1995), *National Systems for Financing Innovation*, Paris: OECD. Manfred J.M. Neuman (1997), "Wagniskapital," Gutachten des Wissenschaftlichen Beirats beim Bundesministerium für Wirtschaft [Report of the Council of Academic Advisers to the German Ministry of Economics], May 23, 1997, Bonn: Bundesministerium für Wirtschaft [German Ministry of Economics]. OECD (1997), "Special Feature: Shareholder Value and the Market in Corporate Control in OECD Countries," *Financial Market Trends*, No. 69, February 1998: 15-37. OECD (1996a), "Special Feature: Venture Capital in OECD Countries," *Financial Market Trends*, No. 62, February 1996: 15-39.

28 Cf. Patrick R. Liles (1977), *Sustaining the Venture Capital Firm*, Cambridge, Mass.: Management Analysis Center. William A. Sahlman (1990), "The Structure and Governance of Venture-Capital Organizations," *Journal of Financial Economics*, 27: 473-521. William A. Sahlman (1992), "Aspects of Financial Contracting in Venture Capital," William A. Sahlman, and Howard H. Stevenson (eds.), *The Entrepreneurial Venture*, Boston: Harvard Business School Publications: 222-242. Thomas Hellmann (1998a), "The Allocation of Control Rights in Venture Capital Contracts," *Rand Journal of Economics*, Vol. 29, No. 1, Spring 1998: 57-76. Daniel M. Cable, and Scott Shane (1997), "A Prisoner's Dilemma Approach to Entrepreneur-Venture Capitalist Relationships," *Academy of Management Review*, Vol. 22, No.1: 142-175.

29 Cf. James Porterba (1989), "Venture Capital and Capital Gains Taxation," Lawrence Summers (ed.), *Tax Policy and the Economy*, Cambridge: MIT Press. Paul A. Gompers, and Joshua Lerner (1998a), "What Drives Venture Capital Fundraising?" *Working Paper*, Harvard University, August 1998. Paul Gompers and Joshua Lerner (2000), "Money Chasing Deals? The Impact of Fund Inflows on Private Equity Valuations," *Journal of Financial Economics*, 55: 281-325.

30 Thomas Hellmann (1998c), "Discussion of 'What Drives Venture Capital Fundraising?' by P. Gompers and J. Lerner," published in M. Bailey, P. Reiss and C. Winston (eds., 1998), *Brookings Papers on Economic Activity: Microeconomics*: 197-203.

consideration of demand side factors reminds us of the trivial but essential fact that in order for the venture capital industry to prosper there must be many venture companies that achieve rapid growth in corporate value and are therefore worth investing in.

Existing demand side theories have been sociological or technological in nature and tried to explain the number of businesses seeking venture capital. Yet, the decision of some entrepreneur to start a business or the availability of a 'critical resource' – for example some new technology – that can constitute the seed of a promising venture are only necessary conditions. The amount of corporate value to be created from this seed depends on the organization of its commercialization. Unfortunately, the focus on 'supply and demand' in the venture capital 'market' systematically neglects the interdependence between venture capital finance and the organization of startup ventures. This is despite of the fact that this interdependence is widely acknowledged. For example, veteran venture capital expert Paul Gompers emphasizes that "it is the nonmonetary aspects of venture capital that are critical to its success" and constitute the competitive advantage of the U.S. venture capital model.[31] Venture capitalists are active investors who identify fledgling companies, invest, help and exercise control to grow the value of the company, before selling their stake to realize their return as capital gain. Venture capital as a source of funds fundamentally influences the organization of the venture startup. In order to understand the rise of venture capitalists we therefore first need to understand the entrepreneurial process in venture capital-backed companies.

By drawing on entrepreneurship theory and modern corporate governance theory, this study analyses the innovative governance system of venture capital-backed startups in Silicon

Valley and Tokyo.[32] Through using a comparative corporate governance framework the study contributes to a better understanding of the conceptual differences between venture capital and venture capital-backed startups in both regions. This takes us beyond arguing about startup ventures in terms of a 'market commodity' and helps us not only to understand differences in the size of national venture capital industries, but also to clarify what kind of contributions venture capital-backed companies make to the national economy.

1. 4. Related Theory

The economic theory of the firm looks at the firm as a going concern and tells us little about the process by which firms are put together. The commendable act of business venturing is attributed to entrepreneurs and with entrepreneurs Joseph Schumpeter comes to mind who most prominently made a case for the essential role of these pioneering leaders in the economy. Yet, Schumpeter did not tell us much about how entrepreneurs go about building firms, either. Moreover, as the stories of Konosuke Matsushita and Jim Clark illustrate forcefully, modern entrepreneurs have found new ways to build great companies that are at odds with traditional concepts of the entrepreneur. Therefore, we need to take a fresh look at what the functions of entrepreneurs really are, and in order to do so we also need to understand the organizational vehicle – the firm – that they use to achieve their purpose.

Modern economic theories of the firm offer various concepts to look at the firm – once it is put in place – for example as a bundle of jointly owned assets (property rights approach), as a nexus of contracts (contractual view of the firm), or in terms of principal-agent

---

[31] Paul A. Gompers (1999), "Resource Allocation, Incentives and Control: The Importance of Venture Capital in Financing Entrepreneurial Firms," Zoltan J Acs, Bo Carlsson, and Charlie Karlsson (eds.), *Entrepreneurship, Small and Medium-Sized Enterprises and the Macroeconomy*, Cambridge: Cambridge University Press: 206-235, p. 231.

[32] In applying corporate governance theory to venture capital, this study closely relates to Sahlman (1990), op. cit.

relationships (agency theory). However, these theories leave the dynamic entrepreneurial process by which numerous people and resources join together to build and grow a new firm very much in the dark.

Corporate governance is the field of theory that is most related to the issue of how different resources, such as finance and human resources, are attracted to the firm. The corporate governance debate was born out of the dissatisfaction of large companies' shareholders with their management and therefore centers on issues related to the large corporation. This study challenges an application of modern corporate governance theory to startup ventures and thereby aims to provide a theoretical understanding of the core question that we need to explain when looking at venture capital-backed startups, namely "how can some of these companies tie together the people and resources to develop from nothing to large and valuable companies in such a short time?"

The identification of this venture governance system represents a contribution to corporate governance theory, extending it to the dynamic context of a startup company. In doing so it sheds light on the process of entrepreneurship in highly developed market economies, and contributes to comparative corporate governance theory. By contrasting venture capital-backed startups with other archetypes of business venturing, the nature of their contribution to innovation in the economy becomes clearer. The study also contributes to the field of comparative institutional analysis and presents a theory-grounded approach to the internationalization of venture capital and the frequently asked question whether the Silicon Valley Model can be applied to Japan.[33]

---

[33] Cf. Katsuhiro Nakagawa (1999), "Japanese Entrepreneurship: Can the Silicon Valley Model Be Applied to Japan?" *Silicon Valley Networks Project*, December 1999, Stanford University.

1. 5. Definition of Key Terms

Following is a brief definition of the key terms and subjects of this study. The terms "venture company," "venture capital," and "governance" are used in very different ways by different authors – depending on the objective of their analysis different definitions are enlisted. In particular, the term "venture" is sometimes used to refer to technology-intensive, or fast growing, or in some other sense risky endeavors. Our approach is to define a venture company by its financing and investment strategy.

Venture Company

In our understanding a "venture" or venture company is a newly established, i.e. startup, company with a business strategy that involves high up-front investments (exceeding $1 million) which exceed the cash flow from operations during the early stages of growth. Since this up-front investment represents sunk costs and the future of the company is uncertain, this company is risky and deserves to be called a venture in the literal sense of the word. Since the founder of the company is cash-constrained, does not want to cover the initial financing deficit with his own funds, or for some other reason prefers to bring in investing partners, he relies on outside equity investment. While this investment could theoretically come from sources such as individual investors, corporate investors, governmental, or institutional investors, this study is concerned with ventures that receive equity investment from professional venture capital firms.

Venture Capital

In correspondence with the above definition of a venture, we use the term "venture capital" for equity capital that is provided by professional venture capital firms to promising newly established companies, with the objective of achieving high returns on investment through capital gains that are realized at the time of sale or initial public offering of the company.

This definition corresponds to what some authors call "classic venture capital."[34] It should be noted that this segment constitutes only a small part of the overall venture capital or private equity market. Venture capital and private equity firms engage in many other types of investments, and statistical data on the industry also usually follows a broader definition of the term.[35]

Governance

The term "governance" in general refers to the exercise of authority, control, and direction.[36] In the context of the firm, "corporate governance" is sometimes understood in a narrow sense as the "ways in which suppliers of finance to corporations assure themselves of getting a return on their investment."[37] We adopt a more inclusive interpretation of the term, broadly regarding corporate governance as being concerned with mechanisms of power that direct the resources that work together in the firm.[38]

---

[34] Cf. William E. Wetzel (1997), "Venture Capital," Bygrave, William D. (ed.), *The Portable MBA in Entrepreneurship*, Second Edition, New York: John Wiley, p. 184.

[35] See Chapter 6. 3. for a discussion of the private equity market.

[36] Luigi Zingales (1997), "Corporate Governance," *Mimeo*, October 31, 1997, Forthcoming in the New Palgrave Dictionary of Economics and the Law, p. 2.

[37] Andrei Shleifer and Robert W. Vishny (1997), "A Survey of Corporate Governance," *Journal of Finance*, 52: 737-783.

[38] The concept is discussed in more detail in Chapter 3.

I. The Governance of Business Venturing

In the following three chapters we develop a corporate governance framework for the comparative analysis of business venturing. Chapter two discusses theoretical concepts of the firm as organizational vehicle that people use in order to engage in business venturing. Chapter three presents the concept of corporate governance as a framework for the analysis of firms and discusses the salient issues in the relationships between the providers of productive and financial assets that constitute the firm. Chapter four reviews findings of the comparative corporate governance analysis of large, publicly traded U.S. and Japanese firms and extends the comparative corporate governance framework by identifying the governance issues peculiar to a startup situation. The chapter concludes in a summary of research issues for the comparative corporate governance analysis of startup ventures that follows.

Chapter 2. Entrepreneurship and Concepts of the Firm

2. 1. The Firm as Entrepreneurial Organization

The discussion of business venturing is frequently focused on individuals – entrepreneurs – rather than firms and follows a strong dichotomy between the large corporation and the individual entrepreneur often drawing on Joseph Schumpeter's descriptions of the heroically pioneering entrepreneur who leads a "process of Creative Destruction"[39] in the economy.[40]

---

[39] Joseph A. Schumpeter (1942), *Capitalism, Socialism and Democracy*, New York: Harper & Row, p. 83. Cf. Joseph A. Schumpeter (1935), "The Analysis of Economic Change," *The Review of Economic Statistics*, Vol. 17, Issue 4, May 1935: 2-10.

[40] Cf. Horst Albach (2002), "Der Unternehmer als schöpferischer Zerstörer – Ein Kolloquium mit Joseph A. Schumpeter," in Schweickart, Nikolaus (ed.), *Unternehmertum am Beginn des 21. Jahrhunderts*, Munich: Piper: 81-96. Horst Albach (1981), "On the Re-Discovery of the Entrepreneur in Economic Policy Discussion," Engels, Wolfram, and Pohl, Hans (eds.), *German Yearbook on Business History 1981*, Berlin: Springer: 11-26. Horst Albach (1984), "Die Rolle des Schumpeter-Unternehmers Heute," Bös, Dieter, and Stolper, Hans-Dieter (eds.). *Schumpeter oder Keynes? Studies in Contemporary Economics*, Vol. 12, Berlin: Springer: 125-146.

The terms 'entrepreneur' and 'entrepreneurship' are frequently used, but hard to define. Broadly speaking, there are four established lines of thought with regard to the entrepreneur, attributing to him the functions of coordination, arbitrage, uncertainty bearing, and innovation. For analytical purposes it is helpful to try and separate the function of the entrepreneur within the firm, and the entrepreneurial function in society.

Schumpeter is concerned with the entrepreneurial function in society.[41] He proposes a broad concept of enterprise, stressing that:[42]

> The defining characteristic is simply the doing of new things or the doing of things that are already being done in a new way (innovation). It is but natural, and in fact it is an advantage, that such a definition does not draw any sharp line between what is and what is not 'enterprise'. For actual life itself knows no such sharp division, though it shows up the type well enough.

"Getting new things done"[43] seems to be an acceptable definition of the entrepreneurial function in society. However, this concept does not clearly define who, as an individual, should be called entrepreneur. The simple reason for this problem lies in the fact that people most commonly choose to work in a group and form organizations – in the business context firms – in order to get (new) things done. Depending on the division of labor within these organizations, it might become hard to single out one person, or there might not even be anybody, who stands out as an entrepreneur. This problem is most apparent in the case of large organizations. As Schumpeter puts it: "In the large-scale corporation of today, the question that is never quite absent arises with a vengeance, namely, who should be

---

[41] Cf. Albach (2002), op. cit. for a discussion of Schumpeter's depiction of the entrepreneur as heroic individual.

[42] Joseph A. Schumpeter (1947), "The Creative Response in Economic History," *Journal of Economic History*, Vol. 7, Issue 2, Nov. 1947: 149-159, p. 151.

[43] Ibid., p. 152.

considered as the entrepreneur."[44] This conceptual question is important as it becomes relevant as soon two people work together.

A review of different authors' views regarding the essential entrepreneurial function in the firm leads to the following spectrum of possible definitions of an entrepreneur:[45]

---

[44] Ibid., p. 154. Cf. Horst Albach (ed., 1989), *Zur Theorie der Unternehmung. Schriften und Reden von Erich Gutenberg. Aus dem Nachlaß*, Berlin: Springer, p. 252, and Thomas Hermann (1994), *Zur Theoriengeschichte des dispositiven Faktors*, Stuttgart: Schäfer-Poeschel, for a discussion of Erich Gutenberg's position.

[45] Cf. Robert F. Hébert and Albert N. Link (1988), *The Entrepreneur: Mainstream Views and Radical Critiques*, Second edition, New York: Praeger, p. 152 for a taxonomy that identifies as many as "twelve distinct themes" relating to the definition of the entrepreneur. Cf. Nicolas Baudeau (1910, first published 1767), *Première introduction à la philosophie économique*, Ed. A. Dubois. Paris: P. Geuthner. Jeremy Bentham (1952), *Jeremy Bentham's economic writings*, Ed. W. Stark. London: Allen & Unwin. John B. Clark (1892), "Insurance and Business Profit," *The Quarterly Journal of Economics*, Vol. 7, Issue 1, Oct. 1892: 40-54. J. M. Clark (1942), "Relations of History and Theory," *Journal of Economic History*, Vol. 2, Issue Supplement: The Tasks of Economic History, Dec. 1942: 132-142. Arthur H. Cole (1942), "Entrepreneurship as an Area of Research," *Journal of Economic History*, Vol. 2, Issue Supplement: The Tasks of Economic History, Dec. 1942: 118-126. Arthur H. Cole (1946), "An Approach to the Study of Entrepreneurship: A Tribute to Edwin F. Gay," *Journal of Economic History*, Vol. 6, Issue Supplement: The Tasks of Economic History, May 1946: 1-15. Herbert Davenport (1913), *Economics of Enterprise,* New York: Macmillan. W.T. Easterbrook (1949), "The Climate of Enterprise," *The American Economic Review*, Vol. 39, Iss. 3, May 1949: 322-335. George Heberton Evans (1949), "The Entrepreneur and Economic Theory: A Historical and Analytical Approach," *The American Economic Review*, Vol. 39, Issue 3, May 1949: 336-348. Herberton G. Evans Jr. (1959), "Business Entrepreneurs, Their Major Functions and Related Tenets," *Journal of Economic History*, Vol. 19, Issue 2, Jun. 1959: 250-270. Gottfried Haberler (1950), "Joseph Alois Schumpeter 1883-1950," *The Quarterly Journal of Economics*, Vol. 64, Issue 3, Aug. 1950: 333-372. Frederick B. Hawley (1893), "The Risk Theory of Profit," *The Quarterly Journal of Economics*, Vol. 7, Issue 4, Jul. 1893: 459-479. Frederick B. Hawley (1900), "Enterprise and Profit," *The Quarterly Journal of Economics*, Vol. 15, Issue 1, Nov. 1900: 75-105. Frederick Barnard Hawley (1927), "The Orientation of Economics on Enterprise," *The American Economic Review*, Vol. 17, Issue 3, Sep. 1927: 409-428. John Haynes (1895), "Risk as an Economic Factor," *The Quarterly Journal of Economics*, Vol. 9, Issue 4, Jul. 1895: 409-449. John Maynard Keynes (1964), *The General Theory of Employment, Interest, and Money*, New York: Harcourt, Brace & World. Israel M. Kirzner (1973), *Competition and Entrepreneurship,* Chicago: University of Chicago Press. Hans von Mangoldt (1855), *Die Lehre vom Unternehmergewinn,* Leipzig. Alfred Marshall (1920), *Principles of Economics,* 8th edition. London: Macmillan. John Stuart Mill (1848), *Principles of Political Economy with Some of Their Applications to Social Philosophy*, London. Ludwig von Mises (1949), *Human Action: A Treatise in Economics,* New Haven: Yale University Press. A. C. Pigou (1929), *Industrial Fluctuations,* 2nd edition. London: Macmillan. F. Rexhausen (1960), *Der Unternehmer und die wirtschaftliche Entwicklung,* Berlin. Claude-Henri Saint-Simon (1977), *Ausgewählte Schriften,* Ed. Lola Zahn. Berlin. Jean Baptiste Say (1840), *Cours complèt d'économie politique pratique*, Second edition. Paris: Guillaumin. G. L. S. Shackle (1966), *The Nature of Economic Thought,* Cambridge: Cambridge University Press. Werner Sombart (1909), "Der kapitalistische Unternehmer," *Archiv für Sozialwissenschaft und Sozialpolitik.* XXIX: 689-758. James H. Stauss (1944), "The Entrepreneur: The Firm," *Journal of Political Economy*, 52, 2: 112-127. Charles A. Tuttle (1927), "The Function of the Entrepreneur," *The American Economic Review*, Vol. 17, Issue 1, Mar. 1927: 13-25. Amasa Walker (1866), *The Science of Wealth,* Boston: Little, Brown. Francis Walker (1887), "The Source of Business Profits," *Quarterly Journal of Economics*, 1: 265-288. Léon Walras (1954), *Elements of Pure Economics,* Translated by W. Jaffé. Homewood: Irwin. Max Weber (1930), *The Protestant Ethic and the Spirit of Capitalism,* Translated by Talcott Parsons. New York: Scribner's. S. Wellisz (1952), "Entrepreneur's Risk, Lender's Risk, and Investment," *The Review of Economic Studies*, Vol. 20, Issue 2, 1952-53: 105-114.

- The act of initiating the business, or the decision that it "shall go"[46] (Lewis, Haynes), where the entrepreneur, if his resources are limited, has to "sell"[47] (Knight) his idea to other stakeholders, could be regarded as the distinctive function defining an entrepreneur
- The entrepreneur could be defined as somebody who identifies a new combination of productive factors in the sense of Schumpeter, or establishes and coordinates relationships in the sense of Clark.
- The fact that an entrepreneur promises other productive factors compensation, while accepting a residual claim (Lewis) for himself could serve as distinction. As an extension thereof, risk-taking in the sense of Hawley and Knight, by backing this promise with his own capital, could be seen as the critical aspect of the entrepreneur.

These various definitions center on the functions of initiation, coordination and uncertainty bearing, respectively. The crux is that these functions are not at all independent of each other. John Bates Clark for whom the entrepreneur is "the man who co-ordinates labor and capital, without in his own proper capacity furnishing either of them"[48] stresses that in reality one has to "take into account the merging of radically unlike functions in the same actual man. In business an entrepreneur usually has to be, to a certain extent, both a capitalist and a worker."[49]

Regardless of which individual is singled out as entrepreneur, the organization that performs the entrepreneurial function of innovation in society needs to integrate the entire spectrum of initiation, coordination, and uncertainty bearing. The spectrum of functions that

---

46 Ben W. Lewis (1937), "The Corporate Entrepreneur," *The Quarterly Journal of Economics*, Vol. 51, Issue 3, May 1937: 535-544, p. 536.
47 Frank H. Knight (1942), "Profit and Entrepreneurial Functions," *Journal of Economic History*, Vol. 2, Issue Supplement: The Tasks of Economic History, Dec. 1942: 126-132, p. 130.
48 Clark (1892), op. cit., p. 46.

any individual member is assuming depends on the organizational mode of business venturing. All functions might be combined in one person, which would make it obvious to qualify him as an entrepreneur. But more likely, various functions are performed by various members and stakeholders of the firm, and the firm as entrepreneurial organization, rather than the individual, should become the level of analysis. To single out one function that clearly defines the entrepreneur as a person appears to be impossible. Actually, as Schumpeter stresses in one of his later writings, the definition needs to be kept elastic in order to accommodate historical changes in industrial organization:

> In some cases, or to some observers, it [entrepreneurship] may be the activity of 'setting up' or 'organizing' that stands out from the others; in other cases, or for other observers, it may be the breaking down of the resistances of the environment; in still other cases, or for still other observers, simply leadership or, again, salesmanship. Thus, it seems to me, there was a type of entrepreneur in early capitalist society that is best described as a 'fixer'. Modern history furnishes many instances of entrepreneurship vested in a company promotor. The typical industrial entrepreneur of the nineteenth century was perhaps the man who put into practice a novel method of production by embodying it in a new firm and who then settled down into a position of owner-manager of a company, if he was successful, or of stockholding president of a company, getting old and conservative in the process.[50]

Consequently, the approach in this study is to make a distinction between the entrepreneurial functions in society and in the firm and identify them as follows:

- We follow Schumpeter in defining the act of innovation or "getting new things done" as the entrepreneurial function in society. In order to stay afloat any corporation – whether new or established – needs to engage in what Schumpeter describes as "The recognition

---

[49] Ibid.

[50] Schumpeter (1947), op. cit., p. 154.

and carrying out of new possibilities in business."[51] These new possibilities can be classified in five categories: [52]

1. New products and product qualities
2. New production methods
3. New forms of industrial organization
4. New sales markets
5. New sources of supply

Our analysis focuses on how the firm as organizational vehicle for entrepreneurship integrates the functions of initiation, coordination, and uncertainty bearing in the entrepreneurial process.

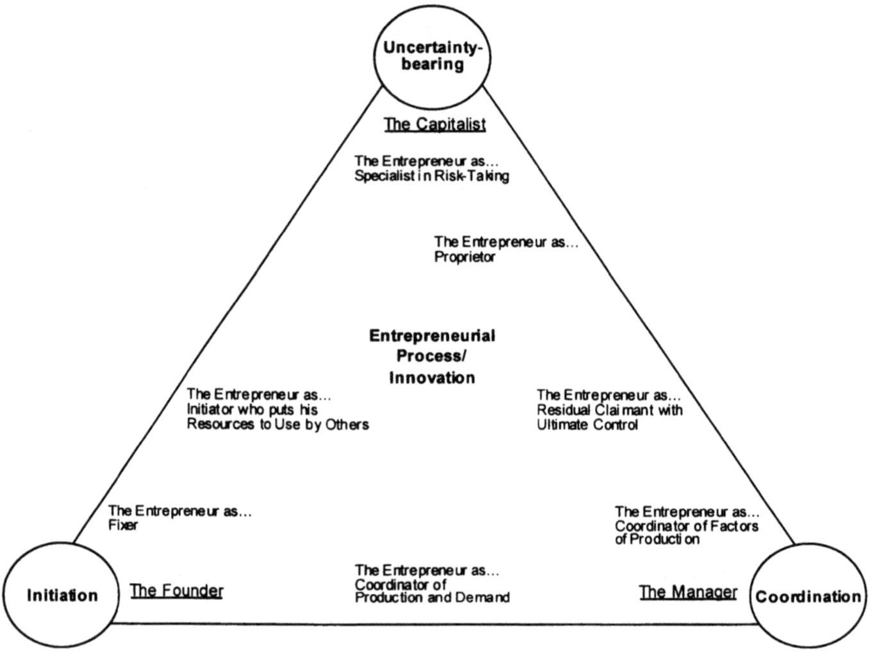

Figure 2: Entrepreneurial Functions and Different Views on the Entrepreneur

---

[51] Joseph A. Schumpeter (1987), *Beiträge zur Sozialökonomik*, Edited and translated by Stephan Böhm, Wien: Böhlau, Article "Unternehmer," pp. 137-157, p. 151.
[52] Ibid.

– We refrain from proposing a way of defining the entrepreneur as individual by his function within the entrepreneurial organization because an unambiguous definition seems neither possible nor desirable.[53] Figure 2 gives an overview of the functions involved in the entrepreneurial process and the variety of views on the entrepreneur. In practice, individuals who are recognized as entrepreneurs appear to perform a more or less broad spectrum of these functions.

2. 2. Types of Assets and Fundamental Governance Mechanisms

The firm, often in the legal form of a corporation, is an organization that engages in some kind of production process that involves the combination of a variety of assets. Following Masahiko Aoki, productive assets assembled in the firm can be typified as follows:[54] Physical assets, such as machines and buildings, can be distinguished from information assets, which in turn can be separated into alienable and inalienable information assets. Examples of alienable information assets are software, inventions, digital content, customer lists, etc. On the other hand, people (human assets) can be regarded as inalienable information assets because they contribute their knowledge and information processing capacity to the productive effort.[55]

---

53 Amar V. Bhidé (2000), *The Origin and Evolution of New Businesses*, Oxford: Oxford University Press, takes the pragmatic approach of defining entrepreneurs as people who start their own company. However, he acknowledges the difficulty of a functional definition (ibid., p. 26): "I refrain from debating which of these roles [risk-taking, innovation, coordination] are truly 'entrepreneurial'." Stevenson/Roberts/Grousbeck/Bhidé (1999) op. cit., argue that the definition of the entrepreneur as a founder is equally untenable (ibid., p. 5): "We believe, however, that neither of these approaches is sound. Consider for example, the degree to which entrepreneurship is synonymous with bearing risk, innovation, or even founding a company. Each of these terms focuses on some aspects of some entrepreneurs. But if one has to be the founder to be an entrepreneur, then neither Thomas Watson of IBM nor Ray Kroc of McDonald's will qualify, yet few would seriously argue that both these individuals were not entrepreneurs."

54 Masahiko Aoki (2001), *Toward a Comparative Institutional Analysis*, Cambridge: MIT Press, p. 118.

55 For the term "inalienable information asset" cf. Erik Brynjolfsson (1993), "An Incomplete Contracts Theory of Information, Technology and Organization," *Mimeo*, revised June 1993.

In general, the term "governance" refers to the exercise of authority, control, and direction.[56] While economic agents in a free-market economy have the autonomy to individually engage in (market) transactions, these dealings between equal partners governed by Adam Smith's invisible hand do not provide a complete picture of the economy. Firms evolve as "system[s] of relationships" which, as Ronald Coase famously formulated, "supersess the price mechanism"[57] and form islands of conscious power[58] in the economy where the entrepreneur and management "take the place of the price mechanism in the direction of resources."[59] Recognizing bounded rationality and opportunism as the salient attributes of human actors, Williamson regards the economies of specialization and governance as the origin of the fundamental regularities of organization and views "specialization, as a means by which to economize on mind as a scarce resource, and governance, as a means by which to induce order, relieve conflict, and realize mutual gains."[60]

Thus, the relationships between the firm and its productive assets can be regarded as the fundamental issue of corporate governance. These relationships can be formalized either by contract or by ownership. Contracts are symmetrical relationships that only come into place when both partners realize gains. Coase emphasizes two channels through which the firm saves on transaction costs compared to market transactions: By eliminating the need to find the relevant prices and by allowing for long-term supply contracts, such as employment contracts in which the employee promises to submit to organizational coordination within certain limits in exchange for a fixed or somehow contingent compensation.[61] Within the

---

56 Zingales (1997), op. cit., p. 2.

57 Ronald H. Coase (1937), "The Nature of the Firm," *Economia*, November 1937, 386-405, p. 389.

58 Ibid., p. 388.

59 Ibid., n. 2. Coase takes a functional approach in defining the entrepreneur as "the person or persons who, in a competitive system, take the place of the price mechanism in the direction of resources." Therefore, it seems to be fair to replace his term "entrepreneur" for our purposes with "entrepreneur and/or management."

60 Oliver E. Williamson (1999), "Human Actors and Economic Organization," *Mimeo*, University of California, Berkeley, February 1999, p. 37.

61 Coase (1937), op. cit., pp. 390-392.

firm, ongoing relationships take the place of one-shot transactions and allow the organizational authority to direct resources within the limits specified by contract. While often legally enforceable, any contract involves the risk that a partner bails on the other. Moreover, contracts cannot completely specify all contingencies; therefore it can be important that they be complemented by trust derived from the observation of past choices in uncontractible events, such as by building an entrepreneurial reputation or corporate culture in the sense of David Kreps.[62]

Ownership is a much stronger formalization of a relationship. The owner of a productive asset, such as a machine for instance, holds both the residual rights of control that allow him to exclude others from its use and the residual cash flow rights to all returns from the asset. He can grant others access to the asset, thereby delegating his control right, however if unspecified circumstances arise, the owner's residual rights of control apply, and he has the final say. While the residual control that comes with ownership is by its nature not divisible, residual rights of income can be split up and contracted out, as in the case of profit sharing.[63]

Contractual relationships and ownership differ in regard to the options of expressing dissatisfaction with the relationship that they grant. Albert Hirschman identified "exit" and "voice" as the two primary mechanisms by which individuals can express their dissatisfaction with organizations.[64] Ownership is an asymmetrical relationship that gives the owner the ability to exercise control (voice) or sell (exit) what he owns. For partners in contractual relationships, exit is often the only possible way to express their dissatisfaction.

---

[62] David Kreps (1984), "Corporate Culture and Economic Theory," *Mimeo*, May 1984.
[63] Cf. Oliver Hart (1995), *Firms, Contracts, and Financial Structure,* Oxford: Clarendon Press, p. 64.
[64] Cf. Albert O. Hirschman (1970), *Exit, Voice and Loyalty*, Cambridge: Harvard University Press.

The three fundamental groups of productive assets (physical assets, alienable information assets, and inalienable information assets) that emerge from the above typology display some fundamental differences relevant to their governance (see Figure 3).

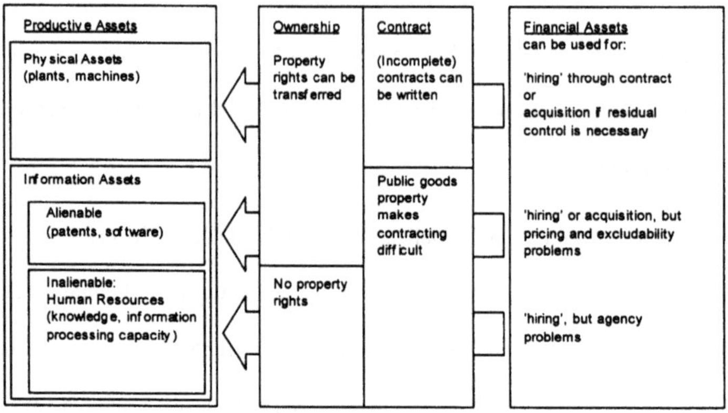

Figure 3: Productive Assets and Governance Properties

While both, physical assets and alienable information assets can be owned, i.e. can be acquired by using financial assets, in the absence of slavery, human (information) assets cannot be owned. Information assets are special in yet another sense. Ownership usually involves control and the right to deny access. However, as information assets display aspects of public goods, owners must make special provisions in order to exclude others from using the asset after having them granted access once. Moreover, the legislator might place limits on the private use of information assets, such as intellectual property rights, for the social good (e.g. by limiting patent life). Different concepts of the firm vary in their description of the relationships between finance and the different kinds of assets involved in the production process.

2. 3. The Vertical Model of the Firm

In the incomplete contract theory model developed by Grossman, Hart, and Moore, property rights and the residual rights of control associated with them, are considered fundamental to the governance system.[65] The organization is internally governed by the integration of hierarchical control and ownership of physical assets. Within functional hierarchies, the distinct operational tasks of employees are specified in contracts. However as these contracts cannot completely specify all details and contingencies, and residual rights of control over human resources cannot be acquired, the employer's power to direct human resources can only be derived from the control over physical assets that the workers need in order to be productive: "authority over [non-human] assets translates into authority over people."[66] The firm is therefore identified with the non-human assets that it possesses.[67]

When this concept of the firm as a bundle of alienable assets is applied to the public corporation, a sharp dichotomy between "owners" of the firm – presumably the shareholders – and other productive assets that are "hired" emerges.[68] Corporate governance issues derive from the emergent chain of vertical relationships. At the top of the corporation, the agency relationship between those who own and those who are hired to make productive use of the firm's assets, i.e. between shareholders and management, is characterized by hidden information, hidden action, and moral hazard. Likewise are the hierarchical relationships on lower levels of the organizational pyramid. These problems of principal-agent relationships

---

65 Cf. Sanford J. Grossman and Oliver Hart (1986), "The Costs and Benefits of Ownership: A Theory of Vertical and Lateral Integration," *Journal of Political Economy*, Vol. 94, Issue 4, Aug. 1986, 691-719. Oliver Hart and John Moore (1990), "Property Rights and the Nature of the Firm," *Journal of Political Economy*, Vol. 98, Issue 6, Dec. 1990, 1119-1158. Hart (1995), op. cit.

66 Hart and Moore (1990), op. cit., p. 1150.

67 "we identify a firm with the assets it possesses and take the position that ownership confers residual rights of control over the firm's assets: the right to decide how these assets are to be used except to the extent that particular usages have been specified in an initial contract." Hart and Moore (1990), op. cit., p. 1120.

are the predominant concern of the investor-oriented approach to corporate governance. We will refer to this concept of the firm as the vertical model.[69]

2. 4. The Horizontal Model of the Firm

An alternative view of the firm stresses the importance of diverse non-tangible assets and cooperative, horizontal interaction in the firm as an organization that can be conceptualized as a form of team production.[70] If production is characterized by horizontal information sharing and cooperation within the framework of a hierarchy, a moral hazard problem arises and team members might be tempted to free ride on others' efforts. In order to save team members from their own opportunistic instincts, and to maximize the common interest of the team, some monitoring function appears to be warranted. However, if denying the dichotomy established in the vertical model of the firm, it is less clear how ownership and control should be allocated to provide for a monitoring function. In a sense, the team could be regarded as principal hiring a monitor in order to prevent shirking by team members.[71]

Aoki proposes a contingent governance structure for team production whereby ex post control of the team output and its continuation shifts between the internal management (as a quasi team member) and the monitoring agent (such as a relational bank) contingent upon the

---

[68] Cf. Eugene F. Fama (1980), "Agency Theory and the Theory of the Firm," *The Journal of Political Economy*, Vol. 88, Issue 2, Apr. 1980: 288-307. Eugene F. Fama and Michael C. Jensen (1983), "Separation of Ownership and Control," *Journal of Law and Economics*, 26 (June): 301-325.

[69] This terminology is not to be confused with Chie Nakane's influential distinction of the vertical and horizontal nature of human relationships in Japanese and Western societies. Cf. Chie Nakane (1967), *Tate Shakai no Ningen Kankei*, Tokyo: Kodansha.

[70] Armen A. Alchian and Harold Demsetz (1972), "Production, information costs, and economic organization," *American Economic Review*, 62: 777-795, 777 define team production as "production in which 1) several types of resources are used [...] 2) the product is not a sum of separable outputs of each cooperating resource [and] 3) not all resources used in team production belong to one person."

[71] Cf. Steven N. S. Cheung (1983), "The Contractual Nature of the Firm," *Journal of Labor and Economics*, 26, 1-24, 8 describes that Chinese laborers who hired themselves out as teams to pull boats up river did hire a third party to whip any member of the team who seemed to be flagging.

output state.[72] Coming from a corporate law perspective, Margaret M. Blair and Lynn A. Stout argue that U.S. corporate law of the public corporation establishes the corporation as a separate legal entity that creates a mediating hierarchy for governing team production. They argue that by forming a corporation, all team members including the suppliers of finance create a new and separate entity that takes on a life of its own and thereby "agree to give up control rights over the output from the enterprise and over their firm specific inputs"[73] to an independent board of "disinterested trustees charged with protecting the interests of all the members of the corporate coalition,"[74] serving them depending on their relative bargaining power. We will refer to this concept of the firm as the horizontal model.

Which of these two concepts of the firm better describes reality, seems to depend on the relative importance of different kinds of assets in the production process. A closely held concern that engages in a production process that heavily depends on a specific tangible asset appears to fit well with the vertical concept of the firm. If, on the other hand, information assets embodied in people are the only critical input in a production process, the horizontal model fits better. Moreover, the horizontal model is more general in the sense that it can incorporate the vertical model as a special case where shareholders have dominant bargaining power.

---

72 Masahiko Aoki (1994), "The Contingent Governance of Teams: An Analysis of Institutional Complementarity," *International Economic Review*, 35, 657-675, 658. Cf. Masahiko Aoki (1984), *The Co-operative Game Theory of the Firm*, Oxford: Clarendon Press.

73 Margaret M. Blair and Lynn A. Stout (1999), "A Team Production Theory of Corporate Law," *Virginia Law Review*, Vol. 85, No. 2, March 1999, 247-328, 277. Cf. Melvin A. Eisenberg (1999), "The Conception that the Corporation is a Nexus of Contracts, and the Dual Nature of the Firm," *Working Paper*, Columbia Law School, May 12, 1999.

74 Ibid., p. 283.

Chapter 3. Problems in Corporate Governance

3. 1. The Corporate Governance Debate

As described, corporate governance in the broadest sense is concerned with the mechanisms of power that direct the resources that work together in the firm. In order to develop a comprehensive theory of corporate governance that can serve as analytical framework, the salient corporate governance problems related to different assets involved in the firm have to be analyzed. The above concepts of the firm can be related to the normative, design-oriented debate on corporate governance between those calling for shareholder value orientation and those calling for the explicit consideration of the interests of other stakeholders, such as employees, suppliers, customers, and the community.

If the firm is regarded as an institution in which different stakeholders jointly generate benefits – or quasi-rents – that would not be feasible through pure market transactions, it seems that in dividing these quasi-rents, not only shareholders' interests, but also the interests of other stakeholders of the firm need to be considered.[75] Along these lines, Jean Tirole defines corporate governance as "the design of institutions that induce or force management to internalize the welfare of stakeholders."[76] Erik Berglof and Ernst-Ludwig von Thadden stress the empirical evidence that "independent of whether a good normative argument could be made for a stakeholder perspective it is a fact that in many, if not most, countries stakeholders do share in rents and take part in the decision-making process."[77] Therefore, they argue, corporate governance cannot be solely focused on the mechanisms that investors use in order to protect their interests. Rather, they define corporate governance "as the

[75] Cf. Zingales (1997), op. cit., p. 4.
[76] Jean Tirole (1999), "Corporate Governance," *Mimeo*, January 5, 1999, p. 4.

mechanisms transmitting signals from product and input markets into corporate behavior"[78] and stress that "the pressure generated by external investors is just one of these mechanisms, others include monitoring by employees, suppliers, competitors, and within corporate networks."[79]

The shareholder perspective that sets suppliers of finance apart from other stakeholders of the firm might be justified by saying that shareholders have to sink their funds in exchange for a "piece of paper"[80] in order to acquire the ownership of the firm, while other agents that supply resources can safeguard their interests through legally enforceable contracts or the threat of hold-up in an ongoing relationship with the firm. Shleifer and Vishny provide an investor-oriented definition of corporate governance as "the ways in which suppliers of finance to corporations assure themselves of getting a return on their investment."[81]

From a pragmatic standpoint and with regard to their prescriptions for corporate behavior, the difference between the two perspectives often seems to be insubstantial. For one, if the firm does not satisfy the interests of the shareholders, it will not be able to survive, and thus stakeholders' interests will be hurt as well.[82] Therefore, if taking a long-term view both perspectives will often lead to the same recommendations. However, Tirole has found that in taking the stakeholder perspective it is more difficult to design focused incentives for managers. He does not quite call for a "hard-line position on shareholder value"[83] since that tends to generate choices that are biased. But for any departure from shareholder value-oriented governance he emphasizes the need to value lessons from the economics of

---

77 Erik Berglof and Ernst-Ludwig von Thadden (1999), "The Changing Corporate Governance Paradigm: Implications for Transition and Developing Countries," Paper prepared for the *Annual World Bank Conference on Development Economics*, Washington, D.C., April 28-30, 1999, p. 18.
78 Ibid., p. 26
79 Ibid.
80 Shleifer and Vishny (1997), op. cit., p. 740.
81 Ibid, p. 737.
82 Cf. Masahiko Aoki (2001), op. cit., p. 279.

incentives and control.[84] Similarly, Michael C. Jensen calls for 'enlightened' stakeholder theory that accepts long-term market value as the scorecard for success or failure of the organization.[85]

As we do not follow a normative or design-oriented objective, but want to develop a framework for empirical comparative analysis, we do not delve any deeper into the normative conflict that might exist between shareholder and stakeholder perspectives. We develop our concept of governance by drawing from both the investor-oriented literature that focuses on ways to reduce the agency costs in organizations where finance and management are separated, and the literature that takes the broader approach of looking at corporate governance as ruling the creation and division of organizational quasi-rents. By examining the firm's relationships between its providers of financial capital and the different productive assets, we identify the governance issues salient for comparative analysis.

3. 2. Finance and Agency

Financing Managers

"Corporate governance" as a term did not exist in the English language until some twenty years ago.[86] It initially gained attention in the context of the large public corporation and

---

83 Tirole (1999), op. cit., p. 44.

84 Ibid.

85 Michael C. Jensen (2000), "Value Maximization, Stakeholder Theory, and the Corporate Objective Function," *Working Paper*, No. 00--58, Harvard Business School, April 2, 2000. John Roberts and Eric Van den Steen (2000), "Shareholder Interests, Human Capital Investment and Corporate Governance," *Mimeo*, April 30, 2000, pp. 23-25 also caution to design stakeholder-oriented incentives for executives. However, for the systemic level, they develop a model that justifies clusters of shareholder dominance and clusters of shared governance: "One cluster involves shareholder dominance, low investments in specific human capital and relatively large changes in strategy. It should be seen when relatively large changes in strategy need to be considered, when workers' outside opportunities are good, when their bargaining power in strikes is weak and when the costs to the firm of a strike are low. The other cluster involves shared governance, labor peace, higher investments in firm-specific human capital, inertia in the face of some opportunities for strategic change and then moderated changes in strategy when they do occur." The relative efficacy of both clusters does depend on the current underlying economic environment.

86 Zingales (1997), op. cit., p. 1.

came to be associated with takeovers, financial restructuring, and investor activism. In this sense, it can be regarded as fallout of the rise of the large corporation that separates finance and management and thereby creates a potential for conflicts between management and shareholders. If suppliers of finance no longer manage the company themselves, they have to find mechanisms of governance that assure that management still acts in their interest. These mechanisms are often regarded as not working very well, so from the investor's perspective, corporate governance is frequently seen as a problem and discussion centers on the question of how to design better mechanisms to control the managers of large corporations.[87]

Financial capital is provided to the firm in the form of debt or equity finance, and used for the compensation or acquisition of productive assets. Financial capital can be exchanged for property rights towards physical productive assets, such as machines. Property rights theory argues that ownership is important because it determines power in situations unspecified by contract and therefore highly complementary assets should be jointly owned.[88]

Debt and equity finance differ in important ways. Providers of debt finance are compensated by a fixed set of repayments with nonpayment triggering default of the firm. In the case of default, claims of debt holders are senior to those of equity shareholders. On the other hand, providers of equity finance receive dividends if the company chooses to pay them, and the value of their stake in the company changes with the overall company value. By electing the board of directors and voting on major decisions, they take part in controlling the corporation.

---

[87] Various large institutional investors have issued corporate governance guidelines to that effect. For example: California Public Employees' Retirement System (1998), *Corporate Governance Core Principles & Guidelines (The United States)*, April 13, 1998, Sacramento: Calpers. OECD (1999), "OECD Principles of Corporate Governance," Ad Hoc Task Force on Corporate Governance, SG/CG(99)5, Paris: OECD. European Association of Securities Dealers (2000), *EASD Corporate Governance Principles and Recommendations*, Brussels: EASD. World Bank (1999), "Corporate Governance: A Framework for Implementation – Overview," Washington D.C.: World Bank.

[88] Hart (1995) op. cit., pp. 5-8.

As future contingencies cannot be specified exactly in the financing contract, the contract remains incomplete and the allocation of residual rights of control, i.e. the rights to make decisions in circumstances that are not specified by the contract, have to be assigned. Since shareholders do not want to manage the company by themselves, they delegate control to the manager who "ends up with substantial control rights and therefore discretion to allocate funds as he chooses."[89] This discretion allows managers to enjoy private benefits, pursue pet projects, or entrench themselves rather than maximize the return on the investor's money, thus corporate governance becomes an issue.

Protecting Shareholders

Shleifer and Vishny present an inclusive survey of corporate governance from the perspective of the suppliers of finance.[90] Their design-oriented approach to the issue of corporate governance asks how different mechanisms can protect the interests of investors in firms where finance and management are separated. For the protection of equity investors, (1) incentive alignment, (2) legal protection, (3) concentrated ownership, and the (4) market for corporate control are discussed.

An obvious and frequently practiced answer to the agency problem is the granting of highly contingent long term incentive contracts that align the incentives of management and investors. These arrangements face the problem of opening up "opportunities for self-dealing for the managers," and may also face political resentments towards extremely high levels of pay.[91] Moreover, as Hart shows, high-powered incentive contracts might induce short-

---

89 Shleifer and Vishny (1997), op. cit., p. 741.
90 Ibid.
91 Ibid., pp. 744-745.

termism.[92] Shleifer and Vishny make a case that incentive contracts do not solve the agency problem entirely, which they support with ample empirical evidence.[93]

Legal protection and large investors are presented as further approaches to corporate governance that help to make corporate securities valuable assets rather than mere pieces of paper.[94] The financing contract between the firm as legal entity and the financiers gives the financiers certain rights vis-à-vis the assets of the firm. Shleifer and Vishny argue that the legal obligations that managers have to the financiers as well as the legal enforcement of these obligations through the courts, account for much of the difference between corporate governance systems.[95] Through control rights, voting rights, and an affirmative duty of loyalty of the managers to shareholders, investors gain legal protection of their claims. Shleifer and Vishny argue that this special duty of loyalty to shareholders over other stakeholders, such as employees, communities, etc. is justified because "investments by shareholders are largely sunk, and further investment in the firm is generally not needed from them. [...] To induce them to invest in the first place, they need stronger protections, such as the duty of loyalty."[96]

However, Shleifer and Vishny argue that in most non-OECD countries, legal protection is not sufficient to secure investors' rights, and even in highly developed countries, the legal system leaves managers with considerable discretion and is no sufficient assurance for investors. Therefore, large investors and concentration of ownership are needed to "leverag[e]

---

92 Hart (1995) op. cit., p. 65. Hart (Ibid., p. 128) stresses that while incentives might work well in motivating managers to exert effort, they are less effective in getting them to cut back on empire-building or to relinquish control. To that purpose, he argues, it might be better to "force" managers by means of a hard budget constraint e.g. through a debt financing contract, rather than to "bribe" them with incentives.

93 Shleifer and Vishny (1997), op. cit., pp. 746-748.

94 They also mention reputation effects and excessive investor optimism as factors that allow companies to issue securities even in the absence of much investor protection. Ibid., pp. 748-750.

95 Ibid., p. 750.

96 Ibid., pp. 751-752.

up legal protection"[97] and address the agency problem. This concentration can take the form of large shareholdings, takeovers, and large creditors.

While relatively uncommon in the United States and the United Kingdom, they conclude, "heavily concentrated share holdings and a predominance of controlling ownership seems to be the rule around the world."[98] Controlling shareholders can make effective use of their control rights (voice) in order to protect their interests, while minor shareholders have a fundamentally different role that Berle and Means have termed "beneficial ownership"[99] in order to stress their lack of influence on the workings of the firm.

Hostile takeovers, on the other hand, are most common in the US and Britain and can be regarded as a "rapid-fire mechanism for ownership concentration" which, as Shleifer and Vishny argue, is "widely interpreted as the critical corporate governance mechanism in the United States, without which managerial discretion cannot be effectively controlled."[100] For minor shareholders, the market for corporate control protects the value of their (exit) option of selling their shares.

Japan is notable for the absence of an active market for corporate control, and while shareholders' rights enjoy strong legal protection, high-powered incentives and concentrated ownership that Shleifer and Vishny count as other important mechanisms to protect shareholders' interests are not strongly developed in Japan either. Product market competition and internal control by the body of employees have been named as mechanisms that provide

---

97 Ibid., p. 753. Cf. Rafael La Porta, Florencio Lopez-de-Silanes, Andrei Shleifer, and Robert W. Vishny (1998), "Law and Finance," *Journal of Political Economy*, Vol. 106, No. 1: 1113-1155. Rafael La Porta, Florencio Lopez-de-Silanes, Andrei Shleifer, and Robert W. Vishny (2000), "Investor Protection and Corporate Governance," *Mimeo.*

98 Ibid., p. 755. Cf. Rafael La Porta, Florencio Lopez-de-Silanes, and Andrei Shleifer (1998), "Corporate Ownership Around the World," *Mimeo*, October 1998. Marco Becht (1999), "European Corporate Governance: Trading Off Liquidity Against Control," *European Economic Review*, June 1999.

99 Adolf A. Berle and Gardiner C. Means (1967), *The Modern Corporation and Private Property*, Revised edition (first edition 1932), New York: Harcourt, Brace & World, p. xv.

100 Shleifer and Vishny (1997), op. cit., p. 756.

checks on managers in Japanese corporations engaging in wasteful or self-serving behavior.[101]

Protecting Creditors

While creditors do not obtain voting rights, significant creditors are also potentially active investors. Their power derives from two sources. First, they obtain control rights in cases of a violation of covenants or in the case of default. Moreover, when they lend short term, borrowers have to come back at regular intervals. In contrast to equity, debt might be a tougher governance mechanism when it is not concentrated, since renegotiation with a large number of creditors is difficult and more likely to force the borrower into bankruptcy.[102] Concentrated equity has to be regarded as more powerful than concentrated debt, because of the voting rights attached. However, large creditors have played a strong governance role in the Japanese main bank system where control in many cases shifted from insiders to a bank-led rescue team, and in many German corporations, where universal banks combine equity ownership with the supply of credit and proxy voting for large blocks of shares not owned by them.[103]

Combined Finance

Whilst the existence of large investors represents an important mechanism to control management, it also creates some costs. First of all, holding large rather than diversified investments per se increases an investor's risk. Moreover, the power that large investors gain

---

[101] Hiroyuki Itami (1994), "The 'Human-Capital-ism' of the Japanese Firm as an Integrated System," Kenichi Imai and Ryutaro Komiya (eds.), *Business Enterprise in Japan: Views of Leading Japanese Economists*, Cambridge: MIT Press: 73-88, p. 81. Ryushi Iwata (1992), "The Japanese Enterprise as a Unified Body of Employees," Shumpei Kumon, and Henry Rosovsky (eds.), *The Political Economy of Japan, Volume 3, Cultural and Social Dynamics*, Stanford: Stanford University Press: 170-197, p. 194.

[102] Berle and Means (1967), op. cit., pp. 762-764.

over other stakeholders allows them to redistribute wealth in both efficient and inefficient ways. Thus, in extreme cases, they can exploit business relationships with the company, or expropriate minority shareholders.[104] These problems become particularity significant when other investors have a different pattern of claims in the company. For example, a powerful equity holder might encourage the firm to take on too much risk, since he shares the upside, while other investors that supply credit bear the costs of failure without having a chance to share in the upside. Conversely, a large creditor might cause the company to forego promising investment projects as he only shares in the risk, but not in the upside. Furthermore, "large investors might have greater incentives to redistribute rents from employees to themselves than the managers do."[105] On the other hand, "large investors, whether shareholders or creditors, may be soft when they themselves are corporations with their own agency problems."[106]

The most pressing corporate governance issue for proponents of the investor-oriented perspective is the reduction of agency costs at the top of the organization. If the firm is regarded as a bundle of tangible productive assets whose control is contractually delegated by shareholders to management, the question becomes, as Rajan and Zingales formulate, how the surplus created can be "prized out from the sticky fingers of top management and given to the rightful owners, the dispersed shareholders."[107]

If, however, the firm is regarded as producing a surplus through the cooperative efforts in a team of diverse productive assets, governance concerns go beyond making sure that top

---

[103] Cf. Masahiko Aoki and Hugh Patrick (eds., 1994), *The Japanese Main Bank System: Its Relevance for Developing and Transforming Economies*, New York: Oxford University Press. OECD (1995), op. cit. Ekkehart Boehmer (1999), "Corporate Governance in Germany: Institutional Background and Empirical Results," *Arbeitspapier*, Nr. 78, Humboldt University Berlin, March 24, 1999.
[104] Shleifer and Vishny (1997), op. cit., pp. 758-759.
[105] Ibid., p. 760.
[106] Ibid., p. 761.

management is replaced if it cannot deliver satisfying financial returns to investors. Conceivably, informed and active investors could contribute better to effective monitoring of the firm's internal control systems, strategy (ex ante), behavior (ad interim), and results (ex post). Blair and Stout argue that "shareholders enjoy special legal rights not because they have some unique claim on directors, but because they often are in the best position to represent the interests of the coalition that comprises the firm."[108]

The above discussion of the nature of the firm's relationship with its investors was assuming the most prominent legal form that a firm can adopt: the corporation. However, firms might be organized as proprietorships or partnerships. A proprietorship does not make a distinction between the owner and its business – agency costs are a non-issue here. In a limited partnership there are two classes of partners. Limited partners have no say in management and their liability is limited to their investment. General partners share equal management rights and unlimited liability for the general partnership's obligation. Profits and losses can be allocated between the limited and general partners in various ways, and the life of the partnership is limited.[109] Partnerships are a widespread legal structure for professional services firms, investment vehicles, and venture capital firms. In contrast to the corporation where the board has to strike a balance and satisfy the minimum demands of all resource providers in order to protect the integrity of the firm, limited partnerships are insider-controlled. Limited partners supply finance without receiving full control rights, therefore other mechanisms, such as the dissolution of the partnership after a specified life time

---

[107] Raghuram G. Rajan and Luigi Zingales (1998a), "The Governance of the New Enterprise," *Mimeo*, University of Chicago, December 8, 1998, p. 2.
[108] Blair and Stout (1999), op. cit., p. 289.
[109] Jacqueline A. Daunt (1997), "Venture Capital: A Strategy for High Technology Companies," Palo Alto, Fenwick & West LLP, pp. 5-6.

combined with the general partner's dependence on its reputation need to give the investor some assurance.[110]

3. 3. Governing Human Assets

Attracting Human Resources

The relationship of human assets and the firm is usually formalized in an employment contract. Accordingly, human assets do not hold residual control rights and usually do not hold residual claims to income either, but are compensated by a more or less predetermined compensation that is periodically adjusted. The productivity of an employee can be expected to increase over time if he invests in general or firm-specific human capital, e.g. through formal training or training on the job. The firm's human resource needs are interdependent with the other productive assets involved in the firm's production and innovation process. Consequently, firms differ with regard to the specificity of the human assets required, and their needs change over time.

The resulting corporate governance issue with regard to human assets is how the firm makes sure to attract human assets. In order to be attracted, human resources need to expect something in exchange for their services and the investments they make in their own human capital. To the degree that employees have outside options in the labor market, they can threaten to end the employment relationship and join another firm. This reservation wage

---

[110] Meir Kohn (1999), "The Capital Market Before 1600," *Working Paper*, No. 99-06, Department of Economics, Dartmouth College, explains that when joint stock companies were first set up to finance (trading) ventures, limited life and periodic liquidation to determine and distribute profits was the norm. Although transferable, shares remained personal in nature and shareholders had to involve themselves in the affairs of the company to protect their interests.

gives them bargaining power in the relationship with the firm. Competitive labor markets can make sure that employees receive a fair compensation for their skills if they are portable.[111]

Inducing Specific Investments

The relationship becomes more complicated if the nature of the firm's production process requires the employees to make investments in firm-specific human capital (skills) that has no outside value. How can the employee be sure to reap the rewards for this investment? Firm and employee might face a prisoner's dilemma situation and end up in a sub optimal equilibrium where no firm-specific investments are made. In order to resolve this dilemma a reputation mechanism is required that allows the employee to trust in being compensated for his firm-specific human capital.[112] Therefore, firms that do not behave myopically build a reputation for fair compensation and promotion policies. Moreover, firms have developed different kinds of incentive schemes to discourage shirking, encourage investment in human capital and promote long-term attachment to the firm.

For example, the compensation of core employees in large Japanese firms is characterized by standardized assessment procedures through the personnel department, a ranking hierarchy detached from the functional hierarchy, in which 'high flyers' rise considerably faster than plodders, and a one-time separation payment at retirement. The resulting steep tenure-earnings profile does not only reflect the employee's growing human capital. It involves elements of a performance bond and combined with the firm's commitment to long-term employment, this system creates incentives for firm-specific investments.[113] By earning less than their productivity would warrant in their young years, employees acquire a bond

---

[111] Cf. Gary Becker (1962), "Investment in Human Capital: A Theoretical Analysis," *Journal of Political Economy*, LXX: 9-49.

[112] Cf. Kreps (1984), op. cit.

that they later recover in the form of seniority wages and separation payment.[114] Recently, bonding mechanisms seem to figure prominently in the United States as well, both in the form of employee share ownership plans and stock options or in the ranking hierarchies of the many human capital-intensive firms that are organized as partnerships. Even in firms that are organized as public corporations, employee ownership is on the rise, which is at least in part attributable to the firm's intention to align incentives, tie employees to the firm, and reduce attrition.[115]

Protecting the Integrity of the Firm

Rajan and Zingales claim that, due to an increased importance of human capital in many modern production processes, the question of how to provide incentives to human assets should in fact become the central issue of corporate governance. They argue that in the past highly specialized inanimate assets (such as plants or brands) that were hard to replicate were primarily what made the firm unique and "ownership of unique assets was the primary source of power" [116] and rents in the corporation. However, as the importance of unique alienable assets declines, ownership becomes less helpful in gaining power over human capital-

---

113 Cf. Edward Lazear (1979), "Why is there Mandatory Retirement?" *Journal of Political Economy*, 89, 841-864. Edward P. Lazear and Robert L. Moore (1984), "Incentives, Productivity, and Labor Contracts," *Quarterly Journal of Economics*, 99, 275-295.

114 The central importance of this aspect of the Japanese firm is widely acknowledged. Cf. Masahiko Aoki (1988), *Information, Incentives & Bargaining in the Japanese Economy*, Cambridge: Cambridge University Press, chapter 3. Hideshi Itoh (1994), "Japanese Human Resource Management from the Viewpoint of Incentive Theory," Masahiko Aoki and Ronald Dore (eds.), *The Japanese Firm: The Sources of Competitive Strengths*, New York, Oxford University Press: 233-284; Kotaro Tsuru (1995), *The Japanese Market*, Tokyo: LTCB International Library Foundation, p. 56; Tadao Kagono and Takao Kobayashi (1994), "The Provision of Resources and Barriers to Exit," Kenichi Imai and Ryutaro Komiya (eds.). *Business Enterprise in Japan: Views of Leading Japanese Economists*, Cambridge: MIT Press: 89-104.

115 Margaret M. Blair and Douglas L. Kruse (2000), "Worker Capitalists?" *Leading Companies*, Online Magazine of the Foundation for Enterprise Development, available at: http://www.fed.org/onlinemag/Mar00/trends.htm, Reprinted from *Brookings Review*, Fall 1999 present a number of other factors that contribute to this trend. Cf.Brian J. Hall and Jeffrey B. Liebman (1997), "Are CEOs Really Paid Like Bureaucrats?" *NBER Working Paper*, No. W6213. Horst Albach (2000), "Globalisierung und Organisationsstruktur mittelständischer Unternehmen: Eine Analyse aus europäischer Sicht," Schneider, Uwe H, Hommelhoff, Peter, and Schmidt, Karsten (eds.), *Deutsches und europäisches Gesellschafts-, Konzern- und Kapitalmarktrecht - Festschrift für Marcus Lutter zum 70. Geburtstag*, Köln: Verlag Dr. Otto Schmidt.

intensive organizations and the firm's command and control system are weakened. Therefore, it is argued, "the focus of corporate governance must shift to studying mechanisms that give the firm the power to provide incentives to human capital."[117]

An illustrative example of a firm's loss of control over human assets is the case of the defection of Salomon Brother's bond trading group in the early 1990s. When John Meriwether, the head of the group, was fired after being made responsible for an enormous loss through a misguided deal, most of his team followed suite and joined him in a new – now famous – venture called Long Term Capital Management. The group of people who left had made up for 87 percent of Salomon's profits between 1990 and 1993. While Salomon's CEO, Derek Maugham, had assumed that "those guys are all tied to Salomon,"[118] the bonds of human capital apparently proved much stronger than the bonds of ownership.[119] This illustrates that Salomon had very little power over these people. In fact, as Rajan and Zingales put it, the group "merely rented space, Salomon's name, and capital and turned over some share of its profits as rents."[120] There are plenty of similar cases in the financial services industry, as well as in other very human capital-intensive industries. Another famous case is that of the advertising agency Saatchi and Saatchi. After major shareholders opposed the award of a generous option package to chairman Maurice Saatchi, he together with some key executives left to form a rival agency (M&C Saatchi) that quickly captured some of the major accounts of the original Saatchi & Saatchi.[121] Apparently, the shareholders' ownership of these companies gave them not enough power over the specialized human assets to preserve the integrity of their firm.

---

[116] Rajan and Zingales (1998a), op. cit., p. 2.
[117] Ibid., p.4.
[118] Quoted from ibid., p. 17, n. 20.
[119] Ibid., p. 17.
[120] Ibid.
[121] Ibid., p. 30.

These cases point to at least three aspects of the human capital-intensive firm. First, attachment of human assets to each other may prove stronger than attachment to the firm with almost inseparable groupings emerging. Second, ex post performance monitoring of key human assets might leave the firm with a very costly exit option as the only governance mechanism. Therefore, firms can be held hostage by key employees. Third, in determining an employee's bargaining power, the firm needs to closely examine which relationships he or she can control as an individual independently from the firm.

The Firm as a Nexus of Complementarities

The recognition of the human capital-intensive firm calls for a fundamental rethinking of questions such as: what is the entity being governed, how does the governance system obtain power over it, what determines relative power, and what is the objective of governance?[122]

Rajan and Zingales propose to regard the firm as "a nexus of specific investments: a combination of mutually specialized assets and people [...] that cannot be replicated by the market."[123] In contrast to the contractual view of the firm as a nexus of contracts, this definition stresses the fact that a firm as a combination of mutually specialized assets cannot be instantaneously replicated.[124] In contrast to the property rights view, which defines the firm by its legal boundaries as a collection of jointly owned assets, Rajan and Zingales regard

---

[122] Ibid., p. 3.

[123] Zingales (1997), op. cit., p. 5; Cf. Raghuram G. Rajan and Luigi Zingales (1998b), "Power in a Theory of the Firm," *Mimeo*, University of Chicago, forthcoming in the Quarterly Journal of Economics. Raghuram G. Rajan and Luigi Zingales (2000), "The Firm as a Dedicated Hierarchy: A Theory of the Origin and Growth of Firms," *Mimeo*, University of Chicago, May 5, 2000. Cf. Allan R. Cohen and David L. Bradford (1989), "Influence Without Authority: The Use of Alliances, Reciprocity, and Exchange to Accomplish Work," *Organizational Dynamics*, 17: 4-17. Richard M. Emerson (1962), "Power-Dependence Relations," *American Sociological Review*, Volume 27, Issue 1, Feb. 1962: 31-41.

[124] Cf. for the contractual view of the firm Alchian and Demsetz (1972), op. cit. According to this view, the firm "is just a legal fiction which serves as a focus for the complex process in which the conflicting interests of individuals [...] are brought in equilibrium within a framework of contractual relationships." Michael C. Jensen and William H. Meckling (1976), "Theory of the Firm: Managerial Behavior, Agency Costs and Capital Structure," *Journal of Financial Economics*, 3, 305-360, p. 312.

all parties that are mutually specialized as belonging to the firm, accepting that this definition sometimes might not coincide with the legal boundaries of the firm.

Based on this concept of the firm, they point to corporate governance issues that are being neglected by the agency cost-dominated discussion along the lines of the vertical model of the firm. Building on Williamson's general concept of governance,[125] Zingales defines corporate governance as "the complex set of constraints that shape the ex-post bargaining over the quasi-rents generated by a firm,"[126] with a special focus put on the "link between the way quasi-rents are distributed and the way they are generated."[127] He argues that this link between the ex-ante need to sink specific investments and the ex-post division of quasi-rents works through the three channels incentives, bargaining, and risk distribution. The resulting objectives of a corporate governance system are: 1) to maximize the incentives for value enhancing investments while minimizing inefficient power seeking through "influence activities;"[128] 2) to minimize inefficiency in ex-post bargaining; 3) to minimize any "governance risk" created by the governance system and allocate the residual risk to the least risk-averse parties.[129]

In order to take account of the inalienability of human capital in the firm, Rajan and Zingales develop a theory of power in the firm that is based on access as a way to allocate power. They define access as "the ability to use, or work with, a critical resource."[130] The critical resource that composes the core of the firm may be a machine, an idea, or human assets. They argue that "the essence of internal coordination [...] is the differential access

---

125 Oliver E. Williamson (1985), *The Economic Institutions of Capitalism*, New York: Free Press. Oliver E. Williamson (1975), *Markets and Hierarchies*, New York: The Free Press.

126 Zingales (1997), op. cit., p. 4.

127 Ibid.

128 Cf. Paul R. Milgrom (1988), "Employment Contracts, Influence Activities, and Efficient Organization Design," *The Journal of Political Economy*, Vol. 96, Issue 1, Feb. 1988, 42-60, p. 43.

129 Zingales (1997), op. cit., p. 4.

130 Rajan and Zingales (1998b), op. cit., p. 1.

agents within the firm have to the unique physical and human assets that compose the core of the firm."[131] In the human capital-intensive firm, which Rajan and Zingales term "new enterprise" (in contrast to Berle and Means' "modern business enterprise"), power derives not so much from granting access to physical assets, as from "building links that cause the person or unit to be better off voluntarily following the firm's commands rather than going their own way."[132] Such a link is characterized by the economic concept of 'complementarity'. It exists when the unit and the firm can together create more value than they can create going their own separate ways. Rajan and Zingales maintain, "while ownership legally links an inanimate asset to a firm, complementarities link some person or unit that cannot be owned to the firm."[133]

Gaining Power over Specialized Human Assets

Firms must encourage employees to build complementarities by making investments in technical or firm-specific specialization. However, they cannot rely on employees' technical specialization to acquire power over them. In order to tie them to the firm, they need to give them incentives to make firm-specific investments that are more valuable within the firm than outside and compensate them with a share of the resulting quasi-rents. The mechanism that the firm can use in order to convince employees to specialize is to offer "controlled access"[134] to key resources of the firm for the employees to build complementary specializations. As examples of such a process, Rajan and Zingales name brokerage firms that give newcomers controlled access to customer leads. This practice has parallels to customer-supplier relationships. For instance, carmaker Toyota grants preferential access to only two suppliers for each component, which motivates them to make specialized investments in the

---

[131] Ibid., p. 4.
[132] Rajan and Zingales (1998a), op. cit., p. 21.
[133] Ibid.

relationship.[135] The critical resources that make access valuable can be very different in nature. It can be inanimate assets such as physical assets or reputation. However, it can also be the web of past specific investments in specialization by a group of people, as for example in the case of the Salomon group of bond traders.[136]

Rajan and Zingales argue that since being defined by complementarities rather than ownership, the economic boundaries of the "new enterprise" are less clear-cut than their legal boundaries. Moreover, "since the enterprise gets power over a unit only because it commits to share surplus with the unit, the surplus is shared much more evenly through the enterprise. This democratization of rents expands the job of governance beyond simply watching the top managers."[137]

While Rajan and Zingales develop their theory as an extension of the property rights approach, the results resemble the stakeholder perspective and endorse a horizontal model of the firm. Yet, while the latter one is often based on a normative argument, their results are derived from the – technologically determined – increased criticality of human assets in the firm. The feasibility of their incentive scheme of 'controlled access' and 'democratization of rents' requires further substantiation. Traditionally, the stylized Japanese firm has been effective in inducing employees' firm-specific investments, albeit within a system of strong insider control and implicit rent sharing.[138] Apart from these narrow economic arguments, it

---

134 Ibid., p. 22.

135 Cf. Yannis Bakos and Erik Brynjolfsson (1997), "Organizational Partnerships and the Virtual Organization," C. Kemerer (ed.), *The Future of Markets and Organizations: How IT Shapes Competition*, Kluwer Acacemic Press, argue that even if coordination costs are reduced firms limit the number of their business partners in order to give them stronger ex post bargaining power over rents which allows them to make specific investments.

136 Rajan and Zingales (1998a), op. cit., pp. 23-26.

137 Ibid., p. 27.

138 Cf. Paul Sheard (1994), "Interlocking Shareholdings and Corporate Governance," Masahiko Aoki and Ronald Dore (eds.), *The Japanese Firm: The Sources of Competitive Strengths*, New York: Oxford University Press: 310-349.

also has to be considered that non-monetary factors play a large role in employee attachment and motivation in the firm as a social organization.

The critical role of human assets in many contemporary organizations also seems to warrant reassessment of the merits of insider versus outsider monitoring. Ad interim monitoring of behavior performed by insiders appears to be critical in the human capital-intensive firm. Such processes illustrate this as the 'election' of partners in professional service firms.

3. 4. Governing Information Assets

The Firm as an Information System

Friedrich August von Hayek identifies the "utilization of knowledge not given to anyone in its totality"[139] as the fundamental economic problem of society. He stresses that knowledge is dispersed, and important but unorganized knowledge – "the knowledge of the particular circumstances of time and place"[140] – gives practically every individual some informational advantage over all others. Decisions depending on this type of information need to be left to the "man on the spot."[141] Yet, how can these decentralized decision-makers be supplied with the necessary information to fit their decisions into the "whole pattern of changes of the larger economic system?"[142] Hayek stresses the "marvel"[143] of the "price system as such a mechanism for communicating information"[144] and thereby enabling decentralized decision-making.

---

[139] Friedrich August von Hayek (1945), "The Use of Knowledge in Society," *American Economic Review*, Vol. 35, Issue 4, Sep. 1945: 519-530, p. 520.
[140] Ibid., p. 521.
[141] Ibid., p. 524.
[142] Ibid., p. 525.
[143] Ibid., p. 527.
[144] Ibid., p. 526.

However, as Coase argues, firms do evolve as alternative systems in situations where conscious organizational coordination within the firm is superior to market coordination with prices as signals. Aoki shows that firms establish different kinds of internal information and coordination systems and "within the general framework of a hierarchy, different kinds of information can flow vertically, upward and downward, as well as horizontally, within individual firms."[145]

The Production of Information Assets

Lately, the development of information processing and communications technology has increased the information-intensity of modern production processes to a degree that the OECD regards us as being on the way to an "information society – a society where a majority of workers will soon be producing, handling and distributing information or codified knowledge."[146] Underlying this development is the fact that technology has increased the possibility of codifying knowledge and thereby moved the border between tacit and codified knowledge. As a consequence, information assets frequently represent intermediate products or even the output of production processes.

Obviously, these technological developments do have some impact on the organization of the firm as an information-processing entity. One result is that digitized information can be easily made accessible to large groups of people, which can impact the relative merit of centralized versus decentralized information processing. Erik Brynjolfsson et al. show that firms that make heavy use of information technology (computers) have distinctly different organizational characteristics, which involve teams, broader jobs, and greater decentralization

---

145 Aoki (2001), op. cit., p. 96.

146 OECD (1996c), "The Knowledge-based Economy," OCDE/GD(96)102, Paris: OECD, p. 13. Cf. on the economic impact of information and communication technology OECD (2000), "Is There a New Economy? First Report on the OECD Growth Project," Paris: OECD. Department of Commerce (1998), *The Emerging Digital Economy,* Washington D.C.: Department of Commerce.

of decision-making.[147] On the other hand, technology also enables owners of digitizable information assets to realize additional incomes by distributing their information widely at low marginal cost.

However, two characteristics of information assets might limit the opportunities arising from the possibilities of transferring information assets. First, much information is still tacit and embodied in humans, thus inalienable. Moreover, pricing and contracting of information is difficult due to what Kenneth Arrow termed the "fundamental paradox" of information: "its value for the purchaser is not known until he has the information, but then he has in effect acquired it without cost."[148] Therefore, oftentimes information cannot be sold, but only shared.[149] Brynjolfsson argues that because complementary human assets cannot be centralized under the ownership of a single agent, "incentive problems will be particularly severe in large, knowledge-intensive enterprises,"[150] while incentives are best in small firms and proprietorships. He argues that this might lead to more small firms and a decline in vertical integration. However there are countervailing arguments, such as informational economies of scale and central monitoring. Williamson stresses the importance of specialization and the "division of cognitive labor"[151] in any organization that is to exceed the ability of its individual members. In order to realize division of labor in the production of information assets, human assets need to be granted access to valuable information assets. If these valuable information assets are inalienable, which is to say embodied in other human assets and no centralized control through ownership is possible, the above issue of how to

---

[147] Erik Brynjolfsson, Lorin M. Hitt, and Shinkyu Yann (2000), "Intangible Assets: How the Interaction of Computers and Organizational Structure Affects Stock Market Valuations," *MIT Working Paper*, July 2000.

[148] Kenneth J. Arrow (1971), *Essays in the Theory of Risk Bearing*, Chicago: Markham, p. 152. Cf. Kenneth J. Arrow (1962), "Economic Welfare and the Allocation of Resources for Invention," Richard R. Nelson (ed.), *The Rate and Direction of Inventive Activity*, Princeton: Princeton University Press.

[149] For a critique of technocentric arguments regarding the impact of information technology on organizations cf. John S. Brown and Paul Duguit (2000a), *The Social Life of Information*, Harvard: Harvard Business School Press, chapter two.

[150] Brynjolfsson (1993), op. cit., p. 20.

motivate human assets to make specific investments pertains. However, even if the valuable information asset is alienable, the human assets – inside or outside the firm – that are being granted access to and work with it might gain partial ownership of the valuable information merely through having access to it.

Consequently, the rising importance of information assets in modern production processes aggravates the above mentioned human resource-related governance issues. Moreover, the corporate governance problem with regard to information assets in general is how organizations can control the production process of information assets in light of their pricing and excludability problems.[152]

Chapter 4. A Framework for Comparative Venture Governance

4. 1. Comparative Corporate Governance

Internal and External Complementarities

The above analysis of the relationships that tie investors and different productive assets to the firm suggests that these relationships are strongly interdependent. For instance, the mechanisms that investors use to protect their interests are related to the ways in which the firm can attract human resources and motivate their investments in specific skills. This in turn is related to how the firm processes information and allocates decision-making and thereby determines what kind of production process and market strategy it can engage in.

---

[151] Williamson (1999), op. cit., p. 7.

[152] For a discussion of the 'digital dilemma' that politics face in designing appropriate protection of intellectual property rights amid the technological advances in information processing cf. Paul A. David (2000), "The Digital Technology Boomerang: New Intellectual Property Rights Threaten Global 'Open Science'," *Working Paper*, Stanford University, October 2000.

Interestingly, the empirically observed differences in corporate organizational structures appear to be stronger between countries than between industries within one country. Even though it should be expected that corporate structure depends on the production process as the organizational task, which would speak towards industry-specific heterogeneity and international homogeneity of organization. The observation that differences between countries are more pronounced suggests that the local national economy as the environment of the firm plays an important role.[153] In particular, the ups and downs in relative competitiveness of U.S., Japanese, and German companies during the latter half of the twentieth century have sparked interest in these differences and their impact on national competitiveness.[154]

A-Firm versus J-Firm

An especially strong contrast has been observed between the organization of large American and Japanese manufacturing firms of the 1960s to 1980s. The stylized features of the American firm (A-firm) and the Japanese firm (J-firm) that emerge from these studies are summarized in Table 1.

---

[153] Aoki (1994), op. cit., p. 34. Masahiko Aoki (1990), "Toward an Economic Model of the Japanese Firm," *Journal of Economic Literature*, Vol. XXVIII, March 1990: 1-27, p. 23.

[154] Yoshimori (1995), op. cit. Tadao Kagono, Yujiro Nonaka, Kiyonori Sakakibara, and Akihiro Okumura (1985). *Strategic vs. Evolutionary Management: A US-Japan Comparison of Strategy and Organization.* New York: North-Holland. Hideki Kanda (1998), "Comparative Corporate Governance Country Report: Japan," Klaus J Hopt, Hideki Kanda, Mark J. Roe, Eddy Wymeersch, and Stefan Prigge (eds.), *Comparative Corporate Governance: The State of the Art and Emerging Research*, Oxford: Clarendon Press. Steven N. Kaplan (1998), "Top Executive Incentives in Germany, Japan and the U.S.: A Comparison," *Mimeo*, February 1998, University of Chicago.

	J-Firm	A-Firm
Human Resources	Recruiting directly from school, no mid-career hiring, long-term employment guarantee	Job-specific hiring from internal and external labor market
	Broadly defined positions, job rotation, general training, enterprise-based unions	Narrow job specifications, professional training, job-based unionism
	Ranking hierarchy administered by central personnel department, seniority and skill-based pay, steep tenure earnings profile, bonding through separation payment and non-portable pensions	Job-based pay, promotion in functional hierarchy, performance-based incentives
Labor Market	Little mid-career hiring for long-term positions, transition costly due to loss in rank	Competitive job market
Internal Coordination/ Information Structure	Contextual skills, horizontal information sharing	Individuated skills, vertical information flow in functional hierarchies
	Incremental decentralized innovation based on stock of knowledge	Centralized innovation by specialists
Financial Capital	Main bank-monitored contingent governance, financial control by bank cum stockholders only exercised in business crisis, stable (cross-) shareholding	Stockholder-control through the delegation of control rights combined with market-oriented incentives and the threat of takeover, dispersed shareholding
	Insider-dominated board, ad interim monitoring by body of permanent employees, decisions subject to dual control of owners and employees	Board as independent supervisor
Financial Markets	Regulated markets, relational banks, size-based competition of financial institutions	Competitive equity markets, market for corporate control, specialized monitoring institutions
Business Strategy	Growth bias, limited vertical integration, quality-based competition,	Vertical integration of complementary assets, oligopolistic competition
	Tendency to spin off new businesses	
Inter-firm Relationships	Keiretsu networks, long-term supply relationships, organized competition between limited number of suppliers	Competitive, active M&A market

Table 1: Stylized Features of J-Firm and A-Firm[155]

[155] Cf. Aoki (1988), op. cit. Aoki (1990), op. cit. Masahiko Aoki (1995), "An Evolving Diversity of Organizational Mode and Its Implications for Transitional Economies," *Journal of the Japanese and International Economies*, 9: 330-353. Paul Milgrom and John Roberts (1994), "Complementarities and Systems: Understanding Japanese Economic Organization," *Estudios Económicos*, Vol. 9, No. 1, 1994: 3-42. Paul R. Milgrom and John Roberts (1990), "The Economics of Modern Manufacturing: Technology, Strategy, and Organization," *American Economic Review*, Volume 80, Issue 3: 511-528. Sheard (1994), op. cit. Itoh (1994), op. cit. Nicholas Kaldor (1975), "What is Wrong With Economic Theory," *Quarterly Journal of Economics*, Vol. 89, Issue 3: 347-357.

Aoki describes how different attributes of the Japanese firm's organization are interconnected and mutually sustain each other.[156] Milgrom and Roberts advance the concept of feature complementarity to describe Japanese economic organization as a coherent system that cannot be changed or copied in a piecemeal fashion. They regard features as being complementary if "doing (more of) one increases the return to doing (more of) the other."[157]

One such complementary interconnectedness can be identified between the centralized administration of the ranking hierarchy-based incentive mechanism administered through the personnel department and the horizontal information sharing and decentralized decision-making in the J-firm.[158] If evaluation were to occur decentralized tied to a narrowly defined operating task, cooperative attitudes could suffer, therefore the decentralized horizontal coordination system and the centralized hierarchical incentive system can be regarded as complements. On a more general level, insider-control and limited power of financial investors during the normal state of business performance makes the permanent employment and seniority wage promise credible, and the absence of an active labor market makes the ranking hierarchy an effective incentive mechanism to encourage both general and specific human capital investments and continuous innovation.[159]

In the stylized depiction of the American firm, competitive labor and financial markets represent indispensable complementary institutions. Narrow job specifications allow employees to build portable skills that are valued in the labor market. Shareholder control combined with markets for corporate control and fluid labor markets allows shareholders to maximize the residual after meeting contractual obligations to employees and management that include incentive components.

---

156 Aoki (1994), op. cit.
157 Milgrom and Roberts (1994), op. cit., p. 18.
158 Aoki (1990), op. cit., p. 14.

Obviously, these descriptions of A-firm and J-firm are dated simplifications and history has moved on. The stylized A-firm was challenged by Japanese and European manufacturing firms in the 1980s, as well as by newly established firms and rapid technological change. Financial markets have reacted to poor returns on capital by exercising shareholder control more actively. During the 1980s, LBOs and hostile takeovers fundamentally transformed corporate governance. Their legacy of cost of capital orientation, high-powered incentives, and small, active, and independent boards persists. Steven N. Kaplan even argues, "today's institutional shareholders are the raiders and LBO sponsors of the 1990s." [160] Large institutional investors, such as pension funds often hold considerable stakes in firms, which increases their relative value of exercising voice versus exit. They have also contributed to the rising number of truly independent directors on corporate boards.[161] After the burst of the equity market bubble in 2001 and a wave of corporate scandals and bankruptcies, excessive executive salaries and excessive incentive compensation have become the target of public criticism.

The stylized J-firm on the other hand, was left in a governance vacuum after piecemeal financial deregulation increased the independence of successful firms from banks and diminished the power of main banks in the 1980s. The burst of the asset inflation bubble at the beginning of the 1990s led into a prolonged deflationary recession with a severe credit

---

[159] Milgrom and Roberts (1994), op. cit., p. 28.

[160] Steven N. Kaplan (1997), "The Evolution of U.S. Corporate Governance: We Are All Henry Kravis Now," *Mimeo*, November 1997, University of Chicago, p. 12. Cf. Ronald J. Gilson (2000), "Globalizing Corporate Governance: Convergence of Form or Function," *Working Paper*, No. 192, Stanford Law School, John M. Olin Program in Law and Economics. Michael C. Jensen (1993), "The Modern Industrial Revolution, Exit, and the Failure of Internal Control Systems," *Journal of Finance*, Vol. XLVIII, No. 3: 831-879. Shivaram Rajgopal and Mohan Venkatachalam (1998), "The Role of Institutional Investors in Corporate Governance: An Empirical Investigation," *Mimeo*, October 1998.

[161] Cf. California Public Employees' Retirement System (1998), op. cit. for their influence on corporate governance.

crunch pressure to restructure. However, with the governance function of stakeholders such as main banks, labor unions, and the bureaucracy having vanished, the insider-dominated governance structure of Japanese firms was left without any mechanism to make top management accountable for corporate performance. Board membership or corporate auditor positions form the pinnacle of the 'salary man' career, and all corporate organs are de-facto presided by the company's President. In many instances top management did prove to be ineffective and should have been sanctioned, however, even managers who had to step down because they got entangled in scandals still had enough power to name their successors.

Comparative Institutional Analysis

While inevitably stylized in nature, the approach of looking at complementarities between 1) features of the relationships among productive assets and financial capital that define the firm's internal workings and 2) these relationships and the larger economic environment is indispensable for the comparative analysis of corporate governance structures. The evolving field of comparative institutional analysis takes on these issues and inquires into the "reasons for, and possible benefits from, diverse institutional arrangements across economies and over time."[162]

For the purpose of comparative analysis, and adopting a game-theoretic framework, Aoki defines corporate governance as a "set of self-enforceable rules (formal or informal) that regulates the contingent action choices of the stakeholders (investors, workers, and managers) in the corporate organizational domain."[163] In accordance with this conceptual framework, the empirical analysis in this study attempts to explore the rules, convention, and expectations that constrain and guide different stakeholders in their relationship with the firm.

---

[162] Aoki (2001), op. cit., p. 33. Cf. Avner Greif (1997), "Economic History and Game Theory: A Survey." *Mimeo*, Draft June 25, 1997.

4. 2. Governance Issues in the Startup Venture

Applicability of Corporate Governance Framework

Corporate governance has traditionally been discussed for large corporations and was less of an issue in the context of startup companies. If approaching the typical startup company from an investor-oriented approach the lacking interest in corporate governance is not surprising since agency costs and the conflicts between finance and management do not occur in the typical newly established company where the entrepreneur integrates many functions that are performed by separate agents in the case of the large corporation.

However, the separation of finance and management is exactly what characterizes the venture capital-backed startup. In this type of startup company corporate governance – even in the narrowly defined investor-oriented sense – becomes an issue. Questions such as how do investors "make sure that managers do not steal the capital they supply or invest it in bad projects?"[164] which Shleifer and Vishny are trying to answer on behalf of the stockholders in large corporations, are equally relevant for the venture capital investors in privately held startups. Yet the mechanisms to protect investors' interests can hardly be the same as in the large public corporation.[165]

If adopting a broader concept of corporate governance, including the firm's relationships with various productive assets, it becomes applicable to any business organization, even a founder-owned startup. Comparative analysis along these lines calls for an integrative perspective that takes account of the interrelated nature of the relationships between resources that work together in the firm. Yet some issues peculiar to the situation of a startup firm need to be added to the ones identified in the general corporate governance debate.

---

[163] Ibid., p. 281.
[164] Shleifer and Vishny (1997), op. cit., p 737.

Business venturing, described above as the entrepreneurial function in society, occurs in a variety of different types of economic organizations. While organizational diversity prevails, economic history is also the history of the rise and decline of certain institutionalized types of business venturing organizations. Probably the most noted historical development of this kind is the rise of the large stock corporation that began in the second half of the nineteenth century.

This development heavily influenced Schumpeter's writings, in which he draws the distinction between the individual entrepreneur and the large corporation as the two basic organizational archetypes of business venturing. Schumpeter is most noted for his description of the heroically pioneering individual entrepreneur. He pictures these individuals as leading the process of renewing the economic structure through creative destruction, and is alarmed about their looming extinction through the rising preeminence of large corporations.[166]

Schumpeter's pioneering entrepreneur takes the initiative and leads others. Therefore, the entrepreneurial function of initiating an innovation and the managerial function are integrated in the person of the entrepreneur: "there is first the 'entrepreneurial' function as distinct from the mere 'managerial' function – although they may, and mostly must, meet one another in the same individual – the nature of which only shows up within the process of innovation."[167]

The large corporation was born when family- and financier-controlled enterprises grew in size and had to hire layers of professional managers, and the founders or financiers gradually withdrew from operations, becoming part-time board members, similar to "ordinary

---

[165] Cf. Sahlman (1990), op. cit.

[166] Joseph A. Schumpeter (1928), "The Instability of Capitalism," *The Economic Journal*, Vol. 38, Issue 151, Sep. 1928: 361-386, pp. 385-386.

[167] Ibid., p. 380.

stockholders."[168] Like new businesses, established large companies must continue to be innovators in the Schumpeterian sense, developing new products, new markets, and new processes in order to stay afloat.[169] However, the entrepreneurial functions of initiation, coordination, and uncertainty-bearing are not anymore integrated in one person who could be called an entrepreneur.

Chandler gives credit to the salaried manager – "this new subspecies of economic man"[170] – for being able to cope with the complexities of new technologies and growing markets that create a need for administrative coordination in a forward-looking way: "Where the new enterprises were able to coordinate current flows of materials profitably, their managers [those of multiunit business enterprises] also allocated resources for future production and distribution."[171] Inspite of the apparent advantages of professionalization, the rise of the corporation that separates ownership and management created a new set of problems. Namely, the challenges for owners to have the corporation run in their interest without actually managing it themselves. To Schumpeter, this was not merely an issue of finding effective economic arrangements; he was concerned about this development's impact on the structure of society and the type of leadership that the corporation helps to breed.

> Progress becomes 'automatised', increasingly impersonal and decreasingly a matter of leadership and individual initiative. This amounts to a fundamental change in many respects, some of which reach far beyond the sphere of things economic. It means the passing out of existence of a system of

---

168 Alfred Dupont Chandler (1977), *The Visible Hand*, Cambridge, Mass.: The Belknap Press, p. 10.

169 A distinction between adaptation and innovation is not fruitful. Nathan Rosenberg (1976), *Perspectives on Technology*, Cambridge: Cambridge University Press. argues that Schumpeter's sharp conceptual disjunction of innovation from other economic activities led us to "focus disproportionately upon discontinuities and neglect continuities in the innovative process" (p.77). As an example of the continuous nature of innovations and their diffusion, he states, "it is economically absurd to consider the innovation of the automobile as having been accomplished when there were a few buffs riding around the countryside terrifying horses [...] an innovation acquires economic significance only through an extensive process of redesign, modification, and a thousand small improvements" (p. 75). Knight (1942) op. cit. comes to the same conclusion and says, "adaptation is different from innovations in degree and in detail rather than in principle. Adaptive change is to be added to innovation as a second function of the entrepreneur" (p. 129).

170 Chandler (1977), op. cit., p. 484.

171 Ibid.

> selection of leaders which had the unique characteristic that success in *rising* to a position and success in *filling* it were essentially the same thing – as were success of the firm and success of the man in charge – and its being replaced by another more akin to the principles of appointment or election, which characteristically divorce success of the concern from success of the man, and call, just as political elections do, for aptitudes in a candidate for, say, the presidency of a combine, which have little to do with the aptitudes of a good president.[172]

Schumpeter's historical prediction of the unfortunate but inevitable and increasing dominance of the large corporation over the individual entrepreneur requires reassessment in light of the historical developments of the last few decades. While the revenues of Fortune 500 companies as share of U.S. GNP increased during most of the twentieth century, this trend has changed since the 1980s, and the importance of startup companies is resurgent again.[173]

The question then is how we can explain the continuing diversity of organizational archetypes of business venturing. Moreover, it is interesting to examine whether modern startup companies fit the Schumpeterian concept of the individual entrepreneur.

Amar V. Bhidé presents an empirically motivated typology of modern venturing initiatives and categorizes initiatives according to their investment strategy and uncertainty-profit profile. Along these lines, we can distinguish (see Figure 4):

- Promising startups, exemplified by Inc. 500 companies.
- Corporate initiatives, undertaken by large public companies.
- Marginal startups, i.e. small proprietorships that have little prospect of attaining significant size or profitability.
- VC-backed startups with funding from professional venture capitalists.
- Revolutionary ventures that incorporate a significant large-scale innovation.

[172] Schumpeter (1928), op. cit., p. 385.

[173] Cf. Jerry Useem (1999), "Entrepreneur of the Century," *Inc.*, Twentieth Anniversary Issue, pp. 159-174. OECD (1998), op. cit., p. 5. The rising contribution of young high-growth firms to economic growth and employment is not limited to the U.S. but can be observed throughout the group of OECD countries.

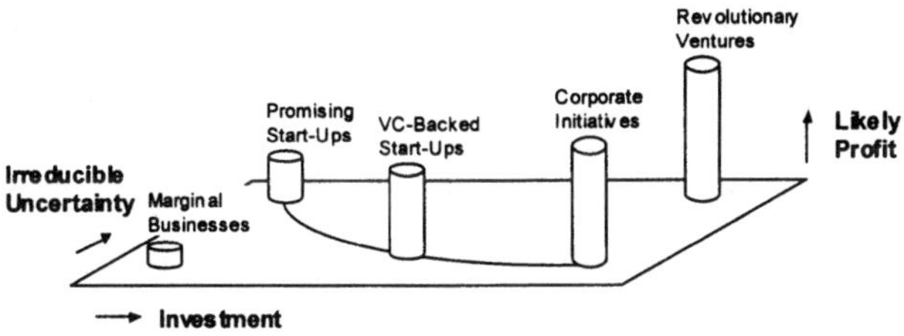

Figure 4: Modern Archetypes of Business Venturing[174]

As Bhidé states, in many ways, "VC-backed startups represent an intriguing combination of individual enterprise and professional management,"[175] that allows the pursuit of initiatives that are larger than the typical promising venture and is able to operate in areas with higher uncertainty than corporate initiatives. Therefore, venture capital-backed startups represent an innovative modern archetype of business venturing that is different from the typical startup. The explanation of its remarkable features requires a closer look at the relationships between the participants in venture capital-backed startup firms.

Startup versus Going Concern

Two features characterize the venture companies that are subject of this study. First, they are newly established, that is, startup companies. Second, they adopt a business strategy that involves high up-front investments that exceed the cash flow from operations during the early stages of growth. Both characteristics of the venture company set it apart from an established company – a going concern.

In order to point out some fundamental differences between a venture startup and a going concern it is useful to adopt a framework of looking at the firm as a nexus of relationships between financial capital, productive assets, suppliers, and customers. Along these lines, a

[174] Bhidé (2000), op. cit, p. 26.

going concern can be characterized as an independently viable entity with established relationships to providers of finance (financial capital) and productive assets (human capital, suppliers) that constitute the input to its production process, and to customers that buy its output. These relationships are embedded in the financial markets, product markets, and labor markets that constitute the economic environment of the firm (see Figure 5)

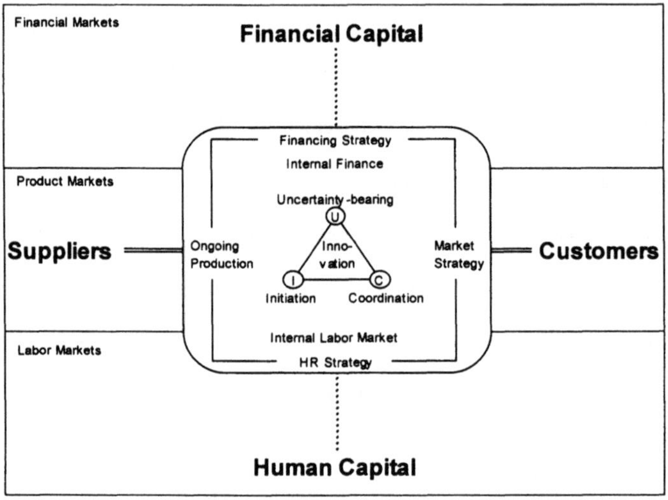

Figure 5: Governance Framework of a Going Concern

A going concern does not require continuous gathering of additional financial or human resources. The different tasks of the ongoing production process and the entrepreneurial process of innovation are allocated to members of the organization. The firm can draw on accumulated financial resources and operating cash flow before relying on external finance.[176] Likewise, the firm can internally reallocate human resources instead of turning to

---

175 Ibid., pp. xiv-xv.

176 Cf. Martin Hellwig (1998), "On the Economics and Politics of Corporate Finance and Corporate Control," *Mimeo*, University of Mannheim, p. 7 on the governance implications of the 'pecking order' of internal finance and loans over new share issues.

the labor market for additional hiring. These internal financial and human resources, and the web of mutually specialized assets and people allow the firm to pursue an investment and market strategy of 'organic' growth and innovation.

Moreover, the established links to suppliers and customers in the product market provide an important governance mechanism.[177] Only if ongoing production, innovation and market strategy are such to maintain working relationships with suppliers and customers, the firm can preserve its independence. Furthermore, the firm's performance in product markets allows financial markets as well as suppliers, customers, and employees to assess the firm based on its results as expressed in sales and profit figures.

In contrast to the going concern, a startup venture has yet to build relationships to productive assets, providers of financial capital, suppliers, and customers. It is not yet a viable business and has yet to gather external resources and build additional relationships in order to become a going concern. As there is no established ongoing business process, product markets cannot provide the firm with much sense of direction. Moreover, there is no track record that potential providers of resources could turn to in order to assess reputation, performance and prospects of the venture. At the very beginning, there is merely the initiator and a technology or business idea, or some other critical resource that makes the venture a promising project to pursue. In contrast to a going concern, the situation of a venture startup can be depicted as in Figure 6. The initiator faces the task to decide on financing, human resource and market strategies, which are obviously interconnected.

---

[177] Cf. Armen A. Alchian (1950), "Uncertainty, Evolution, and Economic Theory," *Journal of Political Economy*, 58: 211-221; Oliver Hart (1983), "The Market Mechanism as Incentive Scheme," *Bell Journal of Economics*, 14: 366-382.

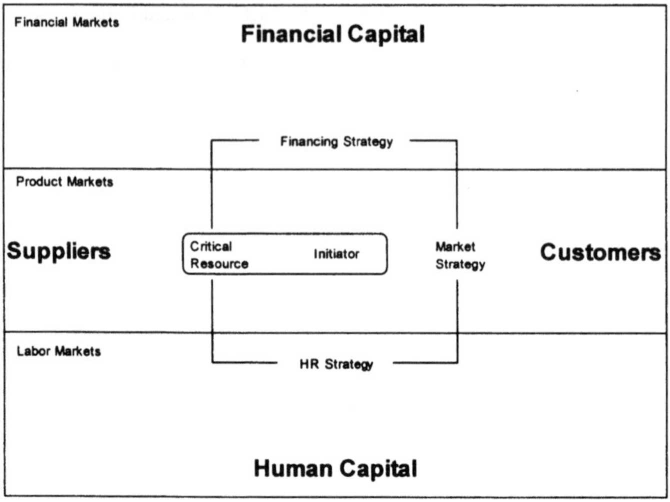

Figure 6: Governance Framework of a Startup Venture

Sequential Gathering of Resource Commitments

These peculiarities of the startup venture call for a focus on its process of building relationships and gathering resource commitments. In this process, the initiator of a startup venture often faces unwieldy interdependencies since different resource providers rely on each other for external validation in their decision whether to commit or not. Customers, employees, suppliers and investors all face more risk if they commit first, thus they often try to hold off their commitment until others have signed on.

Stevenson et al. argue that gathering resources usually takes the form of a "ham and egging" process of "ask[ing] for a small increment of commitment from a participant, parlay that commitment into another increment of commitment from the next participant, and repeat[ing] the cycle for as many times as is necessary."[178] While they claim that getting

[178] Stevenson/Roberts/Grousbeck/Bhidé (1999), op. cit., p. 166.

everybody on board simultaneously was the "the ultimate ham and egging solution," Hellmann develops a formal model for the gathering of resource commitments that emphasizes the importance of sequencing. In this game theoretic model an entrepreneur (or initiator) sequentially gathers commitments from partners who need to evaluate the opportunity and then bargain on the division of the surplus generated by the relationship.[179] He points to the fact that the sequencing of resource commitments plays a critical role. Ideally, the initiator sequentially gathers commitments that are conditional on all other partners also committing. However, if partners are unwilling to commit, the entrepreneur might shuttle between different parties for a long time, fail to gather any commitments or choose partners that do not provide the highest value. Hellmann's model also suggests that the initiator's credibility, wealth, and private benefit in pursuing the venture affect the optimal sequence of gathering resource commitments. If the initiator has no credible outside option when negotiating with the first partner, he will approach the highest value partner first in order to maximize his bargaining position in the next stage. However, if the initiator does have credibility or has gained external validation by having gathered the commitment of one partner, he will approach partners in increasing order of value in order to retain a larger fraction of the rents. This points to a trade-off between efficiency and bargaining power that can lead the initiator to choose a partner that does not maximize the total value of the opportunity but allows him to retain a larger share of the rent. Moreover, inefficient partners may be chosen for their willingness to commit first, thus there is a second trade-off between efficiency and urgency.[180]

The take away for empirical analysis is that the sequencing of resource commitments, rather than that of resource deployments is the strategically relevant item of analysis and that

---

[179] Thomas Hellmann (2000), "Entrepreneurship and the Process of Obtaining Resource Commitments," *Mimeo*, February 2000.

the initiator faces trade-offs in designing the optimal sequence. To decide on the sequence of approaching potential resource providers is the imminent strategic task of the initiator.

Protecting the Critical Resource

Even before the initiator sets out to gather finance and productive resources, he must possess some sort of critical resource that promises to generate economic surplus and makes him an attractive partner for other resource providers. This resource can be a technology, industry expertise, good customer or supplier relationships, superior management skills, or just a business idea. The firm as productive organization comes into place when the initiator gathers the commitment of other resource providers to work with the critical resource and jointly produce a surplus. Rajan and Zingales point to the danger of expropriation that the initiator faces in this situation. Providing access to the critical resource is the means by which the initiator enlists other stakeholders, however, at the same time it makes him vulnerable to expropriation: "Managers may steal the business idea, walk away with clients, or mimic the leadership or organizational style, and start up a rival concern."[181] The initiator can reduce this danger by designing the organization in such a way that no individual manager has full access to the critical resource. However, this comes at the cost of inhibiting the manager's ability to specialize.[182] Apart from managers, investors, suppliers, and customers can pose a threat of expropriation. This problem is particularly severe at the very early stages of the firm, when other assets do not yet complement the critical resource. If the critical resource is some piece of information that needs to be shared to attract potential resource providers, the non-excludability feature of information assets aggravates the problem, because the solicited partners will not 'forget' the shared information even if they decide not to commit to the

---

180 Ibid., p. 4.
181 Rajan/Zingales (2000), op. cit., p. 1.
182 Ibid., p. 31.

venture. Thus they represent potential competitors who may even be in a better situation to execute the concept than the initiator is. Therefore, the need to protect the critical resource is another governance issue that poses a peculiar challenge to the startup venture.

4. 3. Research Questions

Based on the corporate governance problems discussed in Chapter 3. as well as the issues peculiar to startup ventures, the following research questions can be identified for comparative analysis. These questions guide the empirical analysis of corporate governance in venture capital-backed startup ventures in Silicon Valley and Tokyo. Throughout, the study attempts to answer these questions by exploring the rules, convention, and expectations that constrain and guide different stakeholders in their relationship with the firm.

Initiation

(1) What is the initiator's motivation for starting the venture?

(2) What is the critical resource that the venture is based on, and what is its relationship to the initiator?

(3) How does the initiator envision complementing and capturing the value of the critical resource?

Resource Gathering

(4) How are relationships to potential resource providers established?

(5) What rationale (increase overall value of the project/retain large share/avoid stand-still) does the sequencing of gathering resource commitments follow?

(6) What are the arrangements between the firm and its providers of finance/venture capital? How are investors attracted to the firm, how are control and cash flow rights allocated?

(7) What are the arrangements between the firm and its employees? How are human resources attracted to the firm, how are effort and firm-specific investments induced?

Market Strategy

(8) What are the product and market strategies, how are they adjusted over time?

(9) In which way does the startup venture evolve into a going concern?

Professionalization

(10) How are the entrepreneurial functions of initiation, coordination, and uncertainty bearing allocated to different members of the firm? How does this allocation change with the growth of the firm?

II. The Silicon Valley Model

Based on the theoretical framework and research questions identified in Part I, Part II develops a detailed analysis of the governance of venture capital-backed startups in Silicon Valley, placing them within what came to be called the 'Silicon Valley Model'.

The organization of startup companies, venture capital, and related topics, are household issues in Silicon Valley. How to start a high-tech venture is the subject of undergraduate courses at local colleges, and there is a lot of shared knowledge and established conventions on these issues. Moreover, there is a large body of academic research, case studies, panel studies, 'how-to' manuals, and a lot of reporting in the popular press. Existing studies shed light on specific aspects of companies in Silicon Valley, venture capital, and the region as such. However, there has been no study yet that takes the single company as unit of analysis and constructs a comprehensive picture of its corporate governance system. Thus, the approach of this study is to construct the stylized governance system of a typical venture capital-backed startup in Silicon Valley by examining the research questions identified in the previous chapter through drawing on existing accounts of specific governance issues, such as financing arrangements, human resource policies, market strategies, and so on.

The analysis of Silicon Valley venture startups proceeds as follows. Chapter five outlines some historical developments and current facts that explain why this region is widely regarded as a special environment for the formation of startup ventures. In chapter six, the development of the Silicon Valley venture capital industry and the functioning of venture capital firms are analyzed. The structure of chapter seven follows the research issues identified above and presents stylized facts of the organization of startup ventures established in this region and funded by professional venture capital, leading to a depiction of their distinctive corporate governance system.

Chapter 5. Silicon Valley's Regional Economy

5. 1. From the Valley of Heart's Delight

Defining Silicon Valley

Geographically, Silicon Valley refers to California's Santa Clara Valley, centering on Santa Clara and San Mateo Counties with the cities of Palo Alto, Menlo Park, and Mountain View. Nowadays, Silicon Valley has grown to cover much of the area south of San Francisco down to San Jose and beyond.[183] Like Manchester and Birmingham, England during the First Industrial Revolution, Silicon Valley has been mythologized as the birthplace of the semiconductor and other high-technology industries of the Information Age. Its regional economic system has gained fame for being conducive to the commercialization of technological innovations, and for giving birth to entire new industries producing rapid economic growth.

The Silicon Valley clustering is widely regarded as a supportive environment for entrepreneurial firms, with the term "entrepreneurial" loosely referring to their technologically innovative character, or their young age. Silicon Valley is also the world's premier cluster of venture capital activity. Many of the most successful companies in Silicon Valley are funded by venture capital, and venture capitalists are regarded as a key element of the regional economic system.

The Birthplace of Modern Electronics

The history of Silicon Valley is usually being told along the lines of the founding of well-known companies or important technical inventions that led to the birth of new industries.

Asked for the beginning of Silicon Valley, Hewlett-Packard co-founder William Hewlett named the invention of the vacuum tube in 1906, which made Palo Alto the birthplace of modern electronics and opened the door for the development of radio, television, radar, tape recorders, and computers.[184] Its inventor, Lee de Forest, worked at the Federal Telegraph Company (FTC), an early electronics firm in the Palo Alto area. He also had contacts to Stanford University and in 1909 Stanford President David Starr Jordan helped to bankroll his development of the audion tube with $500. FTC also cooperated closely with Stanford University's High Voltage Laboratory.[185] During World War I, FTC was a leading supplier of advanced military communications equipment and was known as the "navy's darling."[186] The company generated some significant spin-offs, such as Magnavox (1910), Litton Industries (1932), Fisher Research Laboratories (1936), and some other innovative electronics companies were located in the area.[187]

However, compared to industrial centers on the east coast, Santa Clara Valley was in these days still a remote and economically insignificant place that was known for its success in agriculture but without much industry. It was characterized by its benign climate and idyllic scenery of abundant fruit orchards that earned the region the name "Valley of Heart's Delight." Only in the 1960s did easterners who traveled to the semiconductor firms by then clustered in the area come up with the term "Silicon Valley." Journalist Don Hoefler picked

---

[183] For a detailed geographic description, see Joint Venture (2000), *Joint Venture's 2000 Index of Silicon Valley*, San Jose: Joint Venture: Silicon Valley Network, p. 36.

[184] Carolyn Tajnai (1995), "Links Between Stanford University and Industry," *Computer Forum*, Stanford University, available at URL: http://www.internetvalley.com/archives/mirrors/tajnai-links.html, retrieved: November 14, 2000. Department of Special Collections (1989), "Frederick Emmons Terman Biography," *Frederick Emmons Terman Papers*, SC160, Stanford University Archives: Stanford, available at URL: http://www.oac.cdlib.org/dynaweb/ead/stanford/sc0160, retrieved: November 20, 2000.

[185] Timothy J. Sturgeon (2000), "How Silicon Valley Came to Be," Martin Kenney (ed.), *Understanding Silicon Valley*, Stanford: Stanford University Press: 15-47, p. 21. Jim McCormick (1998), "Silicon Valley History," *Silicon Valley Online*, available at URL: http://www.silvalonline.clever.net/history.html, retrieved November 22, 2000.

[186] Sturgeon (2000), op. cit., p. 21.

[187] Cf. for pre-war electronics industry in the region Sturgeon (2000), op. cit.

up on this when he wrote a series of articles, "Silicon Valley USA," for Electronic News in 1971 that popularized the name.[188]

Stanford University and the Father of Silicon Valley

It is essential to note that in contrast to many present day initiatives to copy it, Silicon Valley developed not as the result of conscious (political) planning, but through an evolutionary process in which formal organizations and policies do not play a decisive role. Nevertheless, some individuals and institutions stand out for making major contributions to its development. First of all, Stanford Professor Frederick Emmons Terman – who is sometimes called the Father of Silicon Valley – was instrumental in shaping the rise of Stanford University into a leading U.S. research university and its contribution to the regional economic system. He also assisted directly in the initiation of some important early Silicon Valley firms.[189]

The son of a Stanford professor, Terman grew up and studied at Stanford – including a short internship at FTC – before heading east to get his Ph.D. from Massachusetts Institute of Technology (MIT) under Professor Vannevar Bush. Upon completion of his degree in 1924, Terman returned to his hometown Stanford for the summer, planning to accept a professorship at MIT in fall. However, he contracted serious tuberculosis and was forced to spend the next year in bed. While still convalescing, he accepted a part time teaching job at Stanford in 1925. His health gradually improved but he stayed in the area and by 1937 he became chair of Stanford's Electrical Engineering Department.

---

[188] Carolyn Tajnai (1985), "Fred Terman, The Father of Silicon Valley," *Computer Forum*, Stanford University, May 1985, available at URL: http://forum.stanford.edu/About/History/terman.html, retrieved: March 7, 1998.

[189] Ibid.

With the Great Depression in the 1930s and little local industry, Stanford faculty was concerned by the lack of local opportunities for its graduates. Terman was particularly bothered by the fact that his best graduates had to move three thousand miles east in order to find employment in his field of expertise, radio engineering. In this situation, he encouraged some of his promising students to start companies in the area, commercializing technology developed at Stanford. Two early examples of such companies are Hewlett-Packard and Varian Associates. In 1939, his former students William Hewlett and David Packard established their company in a garage shop in Palo Alto and began producing the audio oscillator and other electronic instruments. Terman's encouragement and his assistance in getting a $1000 grant from Sperry Gyroscope helped to start operations. Since then, Hewlett-Packard has developed into one of the world's largest computer and electronic equipment companies, employing thousands of people in Silicon Valley and all around the world. In 1937, William Hansen, an assistant professor in physics, teamed with Sigurd and Russel Varian, and was later joined by Ed Ginzton, a Ph.D. student under Terman, in the research on the klystron tube that was a milestone for radar and microwave technology. Stanford allowed them to use the laboratory space for free and paid $100 a year for materials and supply. After World War II, the Varians, Hanson and Ginzton started Varian Associates, which also developed into a billion dollar company.[190] During the war years, Terman headed a defense research project at Harvard University developing radar countermeasures. When he returned to Stanford in 1946 as Dean of Engineering, he had learned a lot about Harvard's successful administrative structure and policies, and made contacts that helped him to obtain federal government contracts for Stanford. In order to strengthen Stanford he focused on three things: the use of government research contracts, development of a symbiotic relationship with local

---

[190] Tajnai (1995), op. cit.

industry, and the distribution of funds for maximum academic benefit.[191] He encouraged faculty members to build contacts with engineers in industry and Terman himself acted as a board member of newly established companies and was a frequent speaker at industry meetings. He describes his approach as follows: "I encouraged our new, young faculty members to get out and get acquainted with local industry and with the people in it who where doing interesting and creative things. Likewise, I encouraged industry to know their university by getting acquainted with what was going on at Stanford as it related to their own technical interests, and to make the acquaintance of those university people who had similar interests."[192]

At the beginning of the 1950s, Varian Associates, a firm that was largely made up of current or former Stanford faculty, expressed the desire to relocate their facilities from Santa Clara closer to Stanford campus and approached the university with a proposal for leasing land from it.[193] Being endowed with abundant land but in need of cash to finance its post-war growth, President Wallace Sterling, David Packard and Terman developed the idea to lease part of the Stanford land to industry, forming what was termed the Stanford Industrial Park (later renamed Stanford Research Park). Terman regarded this park as the university's "secret weapon"[194] and suggested that leases be limited to high technology companies that might be beneficial to Stanford. Varian was the first company to settle there in 1953, and Eastman Kodak, General Electric, Preformed Line Products, Admiral Corporation, Lockheed, and Hewlett-Packard followed soon. Around the same time, Terman also brought in some key personnel in the chemistry department and encouraged biomedically or chemically oriented

---

[191] Department of Special Collections (1989), op. cit.
[192] Tajnai (1985), op. cit.

enterprises to settle in Stanford Research Park. The early post-war period also saw the founding of defense company Watkins-Johnson by electrical engineering professor Dean Watkins, and the establishment of a number of companies in biology and medicine, such as Syva, Zoecon, and Alza. The character of the area as a agglomeration of high technology and electronics companies took hold during that period. Large established firms like Sylvania, Westinghouse Electric, Ford Philco, and IBM all established facilities in Palo Alto and neighboring cities, even as far south as San Jose where IBM built a large research center.[195]

On the initiative of local management Stanford also made it possible for local employees to continue their university education. Since the 1950s, various options exist to take classes and pursue degrees on a part-time basis. Moreover, in 1967 the Stanford Instructional Television Network began to broadcast classes by television to affiliate companies, giving viewers the option to call in and participate in class discussion.[196]

The Silicon in Silicon Valley

In 1947, another major invention in electronics occurred when AT&T Bell Laboratory engineers in New Jersey demonstrated amplifying an electrical current using a solid semiconducting material, thus paving the way to the transistor that was to replace vacuum tubes and give birth to the semiconductor industry based on silicon as raw material. Co-inventor William Shockley decided to start a firm to exploit the transistor technology. After failing to obtain corporate or venture capital funding at the East Coast he was funded by

---

[193] Valerie Smith (1997), "Varian - An Early History," *Varian Associates,* Corporate Information, available at URL: http://www.varian.com, retrieved March 7, 1998. Carolyn Tajnai (1996), "From the Valley of Heart's Delight to the Silicon Valley: A Study of Stanford University's Role in the Transformation," *Computer Forum,* Stanford University, December 1996, available at URL: http://www-forum.stanford.edu/About/History/valley_of _hearts.html, retrieved: March 7, 1998.

[194] Tajnai (1985), op. cit.

[195] McCormick (1998), op. cit.

[196] Tajnai (1995), op. cit.

Beckman Instruments from Los Angeles and therefore returned to the West Coast.[197] Encouraged by Terman, he chose to locate in his hometown Palo Alto because, as he explains, he liked the fact that there are more trees in the area than there are in Southern California, and because of Stanford.[198] The Shockley Transistor Laboratory of Beckman Instruments was established in 1955 and Shockley was joined by a number of young electronics specialists gathered from various research laboratories. While Shockley's company fell gradually apart due to his erratic and unpopular management style, it is the origin of an astounding genealogy of companies. In 1957, the 'Traitorous Eight' group of young engineers left Shockley to form Fairchild Semiconductors in Palo Alto which flourished for over a decade, pioneering the first silicon transistor produced in the batch process, integrated circuits, the microprocessor, and other major product and process breakthroughs. Fairchild really became the seedbed of the semiconductor industry, directly spawning more than 30 new companies, including Intel (1968), National Semiconductor (1967), and Advanced Micro Devices (1969), and indirectly leading to more than 120 offsprings.[199]

Beyond Silicon

By the late 1960s, the area had earned its name Silicon Valley and had developed an infrastructure that made it comparatively easy for new technology-based companies to get started and financed. For a long time, the Silicon Valley remained geographically bounded, with mountains in the west, the bay to the east and vast farmlands in the south. Throughout

---

[197] Martin Kenney and Urs von Burg (1999), "Technology, Entrepreneurship and Path Dependence: Industrial Clustering in Silicon Valley and Route 128," *Industrial and Corporate Change*, Vol. 8, No. 1: 67-103, p. 81. Annalee Saxenian (1999a), "Comment on Kenney and von Burg, 'Technology, Entrepreneurship and Path Dependence: Industrial Clustering in Silicon Valley and Route 128'," *Industrial and Corporate Change*, Vol. 8, No. 1: 105-110.

[198] Tajnai (1985), op. cit.

the 1970s, the expansion north was limited by the fact that San Francisco and Oakland were highly unionized and regarded as 'industrial' cities. Therefore, for a long time, Silicon Valley remained contained within an area of about fifty square miles.[200]

Semiconductors as fundamental components were the base for the computer, communications, software, and Internet industries that presented ample business opportunities. While during the 1960s not many of these startups originated at Stanford, between 1971 and 1993, members of the university community founded more than 300 new companies, many in professional software, computers, communications, and networking. The commercial development of the Internet in the second half of the 1990s led to even busier activity and brought along the strongest boom that the region had experienced yet. Some outstanding cases of successful Stanford related startup ventures are 3Com, Logitech, Sun Microsystems, Silicon Graphics, Netscape, Healtheon, Cisco, Excite, and Yahoo.[201] Thus, Stanford University, and its post-war development into a leading research university contributed to and benefited from the area's transformation from an agricultural paradise into the world's most famous cluster of high technology firms.

However, Silicon Valley is not the only cluster of its kind. There are other prominent clusters of technology-intensive firms located near corporate research laboratories and leading research universities which benefited heavily from government funding during the Cold War. It was only in the 1980s that Silicon Valley's success clearly outpaced that of the previously leading and longer established Route 128 area around MIT. Both regions had experienced problems in the mid-1980s due to cut backs in defense spending and Japanese

---

[199] Gordon E. Moore (1995), "Interview with Gordon E. Moore," *Silicon Valley Project*, Stanford University Libraries, available at URL: http;//www-sul.Stanford.edu/depts./hasrg/histsci/silicon genesis/moore-ntb.html, retrieved: November 20, 2000. Kenney and von Burg (1999), op. cit., p. 83.

[200] Regis McKenna (1995), "Interview with Regis McKenna," *Silicon Valley Project*, Stanford University Libraries, Available at URL: http;//www-sul.Stanford.edu/depts./hasrg/histsci/silicon genesis/regis-ntb.html, retrieved: November 20, 2000.

competition in electronics, but Silicon Valley was faster to recover and displayed an ability for rapid industrial change and the creation of new industries that led to its extraordinary performance in the 1990s.[202] With the Internet boom in the second half of the 1990s other clusters with catchy names emerged in various places, such as San Francisco's Multimedia Gulch, Los Angeles' Silicon Coast, Seattle's Silicon Forest, Washington, D.C.'s Silicon Dominion, Austin's Silicon Hills, and New York's Silicon Alley. At the same time, Silicon Valley continued to build out its exceptional character having long moved beyond the silicon-based semiconductor industry into new high-tech industries.[203]

5. 2. Silicon Valley Industry Clusters

Diverse Knowledge-based Industries

At the turn of the century, the Silicon Valley area is characterized by a diverse population of about 2.5 million of which 49% are White, 24% Hispanic, 23% Asian/Pacific Islander, 4% African American, and 32% are foreign born. There are 1.3 million jobs in the area and the average wage of $53,700 is 59% above the national average ($33,700). During the 1990s, per capita income in the area increased by 32% versus 13% for the nation. This increase was driven by the incomes of skilled labor, while the income of a representative household of the lowest 20th percentile of the income distribution remained slightly lower than at the beginning of the 1990s. With the economic downturn since 2000, in 2001 the area lost jobs for the first time since 1992.[204] The share of workforce being employed in R&D related jobs is above

---

[201] Tajnai (1996), op. cit.
[202] Kenney and von Burg (1999), op. cit., p. 68.
[203] Joint Venture (1999), Joint Venture's Internet Cluster Analysis, San Jose: Joint Venture: Silicon Valley Network, pp. 6-7.
[204] Joint Venture (2002), *Joint Venture's 2002 Index of Silicon Valley*. San Jose: Joint Venture: Silicon Valley Network, p. 4.

10%, more than twice the national figure of 4%. Currently, the following industrial clusters drive economic growth in the region and make up for 40% of jobs:

- Computers/communications
- Semiconductors/semiconductor equipment
- Software
- Bioscience
- Defense/space
- Innovation services
- Professional services

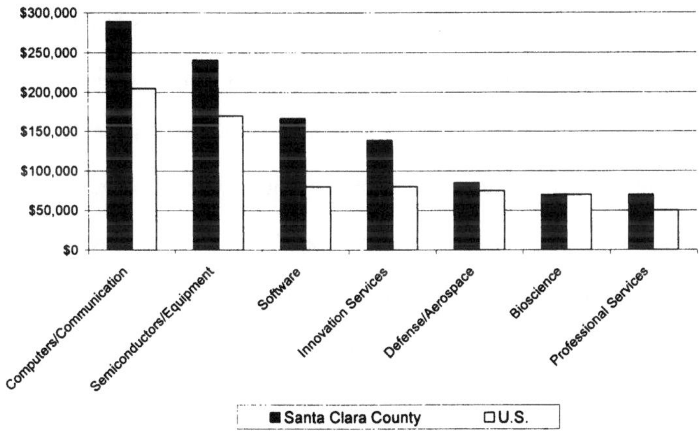

Figure 7: Value Added per Employee by Silicon Valley Industry Cluster[205]

While the industry classification system does not allow for its identification, in recent years an Internet cluster has emerged that is comprised of companies from established industry clusters such as computers/communications, software, financial services and retail, as well as companies from the new "dot com" sector.[206] The economic value created by companies in these clusters is illustrated by their high and rising value-added per employee that is well above the national average (see Figure 7). Average wages are highest in the software cluster

[205] Source: Joint Venture (2000), op. cit., p. 17

with $95,800 per year in comparison to the area's largest employing sector, local and visitor services with $22,900.[207]

Growth Companies

These industry clusters are dynamic in nature, which is illustrated by the fact that between the second quarters of 1998 and 1999, software, innovation services, and professional services showed net job gains of more than 20,000, while semiconductors, defense/aerospace and bioscience showed net job losses of approximately the same magnitude. Silicon Valley is home to a disproportionate share of the fastest growing companies in the United States. In 1999, 61 of the 500 fastest growing U.S. high technology companies, including three of the top five, were located there. Moreover, 86 Silicon Valley companies, that is 20% of the area's public companies, are so-called gazelle companies (public firms that grow revenues by more than 20% for four years starting with at least $1million). This remarkable economic performance suggests the question of what it is that makes this region such a fertile ground for rapid technological innovation and fast growing companies.[208]

5. 3. An Entrepreneurial Habitat

Specialized Creation Economy

Silicon Valley's capacity for rapid industrial change shows that since the 1960s, the area has evolved into more than a clustering of companies in a specific industry. It has turned into a business environment or, as Stanford professor William F. Miller calls it, a 'habitat'

---

[206] Joint Venture (1999), op. cit.
[207] Joint Venture (2000), op. cit., pp. 2, 4, 15-17, 36.
[208] Joint Venture (2000), op. cit. As a result of the economic cool down since spring 2000, the number of fast growing companies in 2000 was somewhat lower than in 1999 (gazelle companies down to 66 from 86; fastest growing companies down to 48 from 61). Cf. Joint Venture (2001), *Joint Venture's 2001 Index of Silicon Valley*. San Jose: Joint Venture: Silicon Valley Network, pp. 4, 13.

conducive to high-technology entrepreneurship.[209] Concentration and diversity characterize the area and make it a center for the creation of new companies and industries.[210]

Everything that is necessary to quickly start and build a new company is available. Companies working on cutting-edge technology in new industries spawn many business opportunities in the development of new products and processes. There are many 'high net worth' individuals with either a technical or a management background who act as angel investors. Moreover, Silicon Valley features the largest concentration of professional venture capital. Apart from funding, newly established firms rely on a number of services in order to realize fast growth. In Silicon Valley, many business and professional services firms exist that are specialized to the needs of high technology startups. Law firms specializing in high technology and venture capital problems, such as Wilson, Sonsini, Goodrich & Rosati, the Venture Law Group, Drobeck, Phleger & Harrison and others have grown large Silicon Valley offices and specialize in corporate, securities, and intellectual property law, making use of their structurally central position in the business community to play a role that goes beyond pure legal services.[211] Large accounting firms maintain specialized practice groups in the area that assume a similar position. Moreover, some boutique investment banks developed special skills in analyzing high-technology companies and managing their public offerings. The firms of Hambrecht & Quist, Robertson Stephens, and Montgomery Securities were started with that mission, which led major Wall Street firms to acquire them or establish their own offices in the region. Other professional services include executive search firms that are sometimes highly specialized on filling specific types of positions, as well as public

---

209 William F. Miller (2000), "The 'Habitat' for Entrepreneurship," *Silicon Valley Networks Project*, July 2000, Stanford University.

210 McKenna (1995), op. cit.

211 Mark C. Suchman (2000), "Dealmakers and Counselors: Law Firms as Intermediaries in the Development of Silicon Valley," Martin Kenney (ed.), *Understanding Silicon Valley*, Stanford: Stanford University Press: 71-97.

relations, and marketing specialists, such as the McKenna Group.[212] These firms are accessible for startups because they sometimes offer free initial advice, defer compensation or take equity en lieu of cash.[213] Contract manufacturing, equipment leasing, support services for print and graphics, engineering design, land and building development are other services that cater to the needs of startup companies and allow them to quickly grow their business. At the same time, due to the experimental nature of many Silicon Valley startups, failure is frequent and in absolute numbers more startups are failing than ever before. In this situation, turnaround and work-out experts, 'remarketer' investment bankers trying to sell off a firm for the value of its assets or its engineering team. Headhunters, and finally specialized liquidators for both real assets and intellectual property come in and try to put the oftentimes mostly intangible assets of the failing firm to good new use.[214]

Knowledge-intensive Network Structure

Silicon Valley is not all made up of startups but there are many large established companies that are thriving in this environment as well. These going concerns are sometimes referred to as 'pillar' companies. They have more staying power than the fledgling startups around them and interact in various ways with them.[215] In fact, the interaction and interrelatedness of the various elements of the Silicon Valley business environment is widely regarded as its distinctive characteristic.[216] As sociologist Annalee Saxenian finds, "relationships are what

---

212 Alex Gove (1999b), "Head's Up," *Red Herring*, July 14, 1999, available at URL: http://www.redherring.com, retrieved: July 20, 1999.

213 McKenna (1995), op. cit. Kenney and von Burg (1999), op. cit., p. 74. Ben Templin (1999), "Creative Financing," *Red Herring*, Supplement Guide to Professional Services 1999, available at URL: http://www.redherring.com, retrieved: July 20, 1999.

214 Tia O'Brien (1998), "Feasting on Failure," *Upside*, June 29, 1998, available at URL: http://www.upside.com, retrieved July 13, 1998.

215 Joint Venture (1999), op. cit.

216 Cf. Annalee Saxenian (1994), *Regional Advantage: Culture and Competition in Silicon Valley and Route 128*, Cambridge, Mass.: Harvard University Press. Kenney and von Burg (1999), op. cit. Miller (2000), op. cit.

matters"[217] in Silicon Valley. Venture capitalist John Doerr stresses that the area's structure is "a network as opposed to a hierarchy,"[218] and Miller argues that the value of networks and the value that its linkages create are the key to understanding Silicon Valley.[219]

Other clusters, such as Boston's Route 128 have also been described as networks.[220] However, Saxenian's comparative study of both regions found some remarkable structural differences. She describes Silicon Valley as a regional network-based economy, and puts it in stark contrast to the Route 128 region that she found to be organized around a structure of independent, vertically integrated firms. She characterizes Silicon Valley as follows:[221]

> Silicon Valley has a regional network-based industrial system that promotes collective learning and flexible adjustment among specialist producers of a complex of related technologies. [...] The functional boundaries within firms are porous in a network system, as are the boundaries between firms themselves and between firms and local institutions such as trade associations and universities.

The network-like property of Silicon Valley expresses itself in a stunning density of social networks, as documented by Emilio Castilla et. al, and points to some aspects of product and labor markets in Silicon Valley.[222] Firms are often connected through hybrid relationships, such as alliances and partnerships. However, these are neither based on trust derived from social capital as for example ascribed to the business networks of familial communities in

---

217 Stanford News Service (1996), "Networking Lessons from Silicon Valley," available at URL: http://www.stanford.edu/dept/news/pr/96/960923siliconval.html, retrieved: August 19, 1999.

218 Joan O' C. Hamilton and Linda Himelstein (1997), "A Wellspring Called Stanford," *Business Week*, August 25 1997.

219 William F. Miller (1998), "Stanford's Role in Silicon Valley," Presented at the Conference "What We Can Learn from Silicon Valley" June 9, 1998 at the U.S. Embassy in Stockholm, available at URL: http://www.usemb.se/Silicon, retrieved November 20, 2000.

220 Cf. Nitin Nohria (1988), *Creating New Business Ventures: Network Organization in Market and Corporate Contexts*, *Ph.D. dissertation*, Massachusetts Institute of Technology. Bharat N. Anand and Mikolaj Jan Piskorski (2000), "(Why) Are Networks Important?" *Working Paper*, Harvard University.

221 Saxenian (1994), op. cit., pp. 2-3.

Northern Italy or the Overseas Chinese, nor on long-term relationships as in the case of Japanese Keiretsu. John Seely Brown and Paul Duguit argue that supplier relationships in Silicon Valley are based on what Meyerson, Weiss, and Kramer call 'swift trust' that can develop over short intense periods of interaction and reciprocity, and on communities of practice formed by industry professionals.[223] This type of relationship is not easily replaced but rather reinforced by communication technology. In Silicon Valley, producers are typically focused on cutting-edge technology and not vertically integrated. This makes it easy for new companies with unique technology to find customers. On the other hand, there are integrated pillar companies with global reach that connect the area with world markets. Labor markets are fluid and California Law does not permit covenants not to compete.[224] The region features an exceptional pool of talent, there is a steady inflow of immigrants, and universities in the area are producing a large number of engineering graduates.[225] Figure 8 summarizes some characteristics of the regional economic system.

---

[222] Emilio J. Castilla, Hokyu Hwang, Ellen Granovetter, and Mark Granovetter (2000), "Social Networks in Silicon Valley," Lee, Chong-Moon, Miller, William F., Gong Hancock, Marguerite, and Rowen, Henry S. (eds.), *The Silicon Valley Edge*, Stanford: Stanford University Press. Cf. Mark S. Granovetter (1985), "Economic Action and Social Structure: The Problem of Embeddedness," *American Journal of Sociology*, 91 (3): 481-510. David Krackhardt (1992), "The Strength of Strong Ties," Nitin Nohria and Robert G. Eccles (eds.), *Networks and Organizations: Structure, Form, and Action*, Boston: Harvard Business School Press: 220-239.

[223] John Seely Brown and Paul Duguit (2000b), "Mysteries of the Region: Knowledge Dynamics in Silicon Valley," available at URL: http://www.slofi.com/mysteries.htm, retrieved: November 20, 2000. Debra Meyerson, Karl A. Weick, and Roderick M. Kramer (1996), "Swift Trust and Temporary Groups," Kramer, R. M., and Tyler, T. (eds.), *Trust in Organizations: Frontiers of Theory and Research*, Tousand Oaks: Sage: 166-195.

[224] Ronald J. Gilson (1999), "Silicon Valley's Idiosyncratic Legal Infrastructure," presented at the Conference "Silicon Valley: Center of Innovation" June 3, 1999 at Stanford University, available at URL: http://aparc.stanford.edu/events/june1999/index.html, retrieved November 22, 1999.

[225] Cf. for the role of immigrants Annalee Saxenian (1999b), *Silicon Valley's New Immigrant Entrepreneurs*, San Francisco: Public Policy Institute of California.

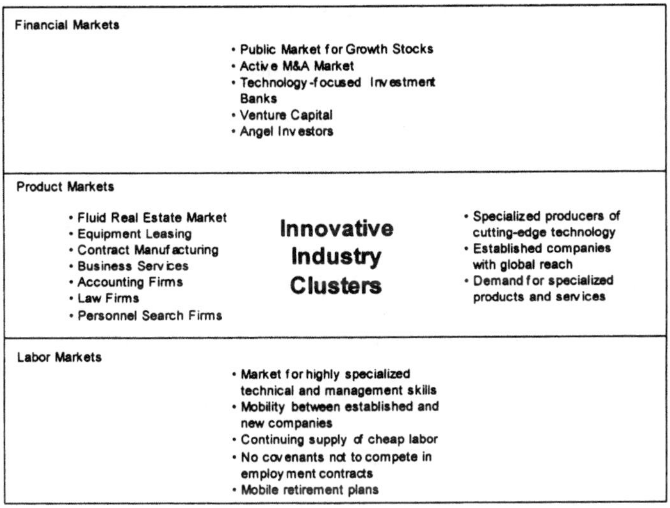

Figure 8: The Silicon Valley Regional Economic System

Miller stresses the special importance of "interaction between the creation of knowledge and its entrepreneurial exploitation"[226] that contributes to the high knowledge intensity in the region. The interplay of these various elements, including the research universities Stanford and Berkeley, leads to mutual cross-fertilization, and using Regis McKenna's metaphor "they're all sitting in the same petri dish called Silicon Valley [and] the fertilizer for that petri dish, you might call, is the venture capitalist."[227]

Chapter 6. Classic Venture Capital

Many of the most successful Silicon Valley companies, such as Intel, Apple, Sun Microsystems, Cisco, Yahoo to name only a few, began as venture capital-backed startups. Classic venture capital is a segment of the private equity market and can be defined as equity

---

[226] Miller (2000) op. cit., p. 7.
[227] McKenna (1995), op. cit.

capital invested by professional venture capital firms in newly established privately held companies that are characterized by a high growth orientation and high business risk. Venture capital firms are active investors and provide funding, other assistance, and active monitoring to fledgling companies with the aim of selling their stake and realizing capital gains after a holding period of five to seven years. Thus venture capital investments are characterized by a) a risk of loss of all or part of the investment, b) a high rate of return in the event of success, c) lack of instant liquidity, d) the aim of realizing capital gains by selling the investment.[228]

Since World War II, organized private equity and venture capital in the United States experienced several waves of phenomenal growth. More than a third of all companies that embarked on an IPO during the 1990s were backed by venture capital and in 2000 venture capital firms invested a record volume of more than $100 billion.[229] Classic venture capital represents a variable share of usually less than one fifth of the private equity volume, but with the growth of the overall market the number of venture capital-funded startups in Silicon Valley also increased substantially. Venture capitalists hold a central position in the Silicon Valley network economy and assume a key enabling function for startup ventures that drive innovation in the region. In order to examine the peculiar corporate governance system that these startup ventures are operating in, this chapter first analyses the development and workings of the firms providing classic venture capital in Silicon Valley.

---

228 Liles (1977), op. cit., p. 5.

229 Venture Economics. Cf. also Price Waterhouse Coopers (2000b), "Global Private Equity 2000," available at URL: http://www.pwcmoneytree.com, retrieved: November 20, 2000.

6. 1. Historical Development

The Ancestors of Venture Capital

Venture capital in the United States traces its roots to the late 19th century, when investments by wealthy families in promising undertakings helped in the establishment of some prominent companies. The 1874 investment of Boston attorney Gardiner Green Hubbard and Salem leather merchant Thomas Sanders in Scot Alexander Graham Bell's experiments on the telephone, and the subsequent establishment of the Bell Telephone Company, is an early account of this. In the early 20th century, potent industrialist families like the Rockefeller, the Bessemer and the Whitney hired professional managers to manage their investments in promising young companies.[230] Companies drawing on such private venture capital sources included Eastern Airlines, Xerox, Polaroid and Raytheon. [231] This direct, non-intermediated, reallocation of industrial fortunes to innovation embodied in new firms, conforms to Schumpeter's concept of 'the entrepreneur financing new entrepreneurs'.[232] Prior to World War II, merchant banks and personal investments by wealthy individuals represented the only sources of finance for high-risk situations that were not suited for traditional bank lending or institutional portfolios. Nowadays referred to as Angel Finance, these investments by individuals are still the largest source of startup financing. The venture capital firm as a specialized financial intermediary emerged only after World War II.

---

[230] Paul A. Gompers (1994), "The Rise and Fall of Venture Capital," *Business and Economic History*, Vol. 23, No. 2, Winter 1994: 1-26, 5.

[231] Bygrave/Timmons (1992), op. cit., p. 16. Saxenian (1994), op. cit., p. 13.

After World War II, the formalization of venture capital finance proceeded along two lines. First, wealthy individuals and families continued to professionalise their investment activities and, second, venture capital firms were established as financial intermediaries dedicated to the commercialization of science and technology. Around World War II, some wealthy individual investors organized small staffs of professional managers and began to regularly identify, evaluate, consummate and monitor venture investments.[233] Typically, investments were focused on areas of particular interest to these individuals who both, supplied the funds and participated in the investment process. J. H. Whitney, Inc., Rockefeller Brothers, Inc., and Payson and Trask, are examples of such concerns.[234] These firms were and are typically not limited to classic venture capital but engage in various kinds of investments.

In a separate development, the organized venture capital industry came into being, when on June 6, 1946 American Research and Development (ARD) was established under Massachusetts law. It was the first firm to raise funds in the public market and the first professionally managed firm dedicated solely to enterprise venture investing.[235] The birth of ARD has to be placed within the ideological debate at the time which was characterized by a confluence of anti big government and anti big business sentiments, with some people – such as Schumpeter – fearing the destruction of the free enterprise system as a prelude to the loss

---

[232] In Schumpeter's theory, the entrepreneur has the remarkable ability to have other people supply financial and other resources for a fixed, or at least limited, compensation, while still securing a residual claim. The credit necessary for the entrepreneurial process is drawn from the industrial fortunes created by earlier entrepreneurs: "it is this entrepreneurs' profit which is the primary source of industrial fortunes, the history of every one of which consists of, or leads back to, successful acts of innovation. [...] This process of innovation in industry by the agency of entrepreneurs supplies the key to all the phenomena of capital and credit. [...] As, however, innovation, being discontinuous and involving considerable change and being, in competitive capitalism, typically embodied in new firms, requires large expenditure previous to the emergence of any revenue, credit becomes an essential element of the process." Schumpeter (1928), op. cit., pp. 380-381.

[233] Jack S. Levin (1998), *Structuring Venture Capital, Private Equity, and Entrepreneurial Transactions*, 1999 Edition, Gaithersburg: Aspen Publishers, p. 1-14.

[234] Liles (1977), op. cit., p. 3.

of democracy in the nation.[236] In particular, financial institutions, such as investment trusts and managed funds were criticized at the time for failing to meet the risk capital needs of the economy. Moreover, personal income tax was blamed for discouraging investments by individuals.[237]

The initiative for the establishment of ARD is attributed to Ralph E. Flanders, then president of the Federal Reserve Bank of Boston who was concerned about the lack of new company formation and the inability to tap institutional capital. In an address to the National Association of Security Dealers in 1945, Flanders argued against the restrictive requirements of the Investment Act of 1940, and proposed to enable fiduciary funds to invest up to 5% of their assets in the equity of new enterprises. As he stated:[238]

> American business, American employment and the prosperity of the citizens of the country as a whole cannot be indefinitely assured under free enterprise unless there is a continuous birth of healthy infants in our business structure. We cannot depend safely for an indefinite time on the expansion of our old big industries alone. We need new strength, energy, and ability from below. We need to marry some small part of our enormous fiduciary resources to the new ideas which are seeking support.

Flander's views were shared by Harvard Business School professor General George F. Doriot, MIT president Karl Compton and various MIT faculty, local entrepreneurs, financiers, and other civic leaders. They all shared the belief that risk capital was lacking and that a lot of the technology developed at MIT and elsewhere during World War II had the potential of commercial application. ARD's mission was to build new enterprises by supplying equity financing and making available the technical and administrative experience of its management and advisors. It was independent from government support and operated for

---

[235] Liles (1977), op. cit., p. 9, Bygrave/Timmons (1992), op. cit., p. 17.
[236] Cf. Berle/Means (1967), op. cit. Adolf A. Berle and Gardiner C. Means (1930), "Corporations and the Public Investor," *The American Economic Review*, Vol. 20, Issue 1, Mar. 1930: 54-71. Hayek's Road to Serfdom (Friedrich A. Hayek (1944), *Road to Serfdom*, Chicago: University of Chicago Press) and Schumpeter's writing provided some underpinning for these views.
[237] Liles (1977), op. cit., pp. 22, 27.
[238] Bygrave/Timmons (1992), op. cit., p. 17.

profit, however its goals were semi-philanthropic and it intended to serve as a role model by demonstrating that a venture capital company of its kind could be profitable.[239]

Only amid enormous difficulties, ARD succeeded in raising $3.5 million of its $5 million target by issuing shares. By the end of 1947, insurance companies, investment companies, and universities (MIT, the University of Pennsylvania, and the University of Rochester) owned roughly half of ARD while the company's directors and officers owned the other half.[240] One of ARD's first investments was $200,000 in High Voltage Engineering Corporation (HVEC), which was founded by five physicists and engineers from MIT to develop X-ray technology in the treatment of cancer.[241] HVEC became one of the first venture-capital backed high-technology firms listed at the New York Stock Exchange. Continued investing, negative cash flows and lack of capital gains early on, led to both profitability and liquidity problems, and made Doriot and his colleagues become increasingly involved with their portfolio companies. ARD's philosophy was to provide industry and management expertise in order to increase the funded companies' chances of success. Therefore, ARD management or advisors joined the board of invested companies and ARD assured itself control rights, which were sometimes used to replace the incumbent management.[242] Doriot described ARD's role as "to watch, push, worry, and spread hope."[243] After the first years of operation, ARD's performance appeared less than appealing from a purely financial perspective. Net asset value per share had declined, the operating deficit continued to build up, and most portfolio companies were operating at a loss. Basically, the money for investment and expenses did not have counterbalancing cash inflows. Judging from its initial financial performance, its aura of mission, and array of prestigious people who

---

239 Liles (1977), op. cit., pp. 32-33.
240 Bygrave/Timmons (1992), op. cit., p. 18.
241 Gompers (1994), op. cit., p. 5.
242 Liles (1977), op. cit., pp. 40, 69.

were not working full time for the firm, ARD looked like a philanthropic nonprofit endeavor. ARD had to raise capital again in spring 1949, however no underwriter could be found, and by the end of the year 74% of the $4 million offering remained unsold. ARD began to charge its portfolio companies consulting fees and structured investments as convertible bonds in order to realize interest incomes and make its financials look better. It also experimented with various ways of performance reporting. For most of the years it reported net asset value based on management's estimation of the fair value of the investments. However, auditors were not willing to certify these valuations as part of ARD's financial statements. Later, the firm supplemented its financials with qualitative reviews of portfolio companies. However, this practice was terminated because portfolio companies found the public presentation of their problems and business outlook to be harmful for business.[244]

By the end of 1951, ten of ARD's 26 portfolio companies came to operate at a profit, and further investments became possible. However, looking back after five years of operation, initial investors who had purchased the stock at $25 per share in 1946 were down 24%, while the Dow Jones Industrial Averages had increased by over 50% during the same period.[245] ARD's share price continued to falter and in 1953 the firm decided to start paying dividends in order to give investors some kind of return. ARD's management spent an increasing portion of its time troubleshooting for portfolio companies. This active management approach kept its write-offs low, but it also tied up management time and capital in holdings that achieved only small returns.[246] ARD did not pay its employees high salaries, and because it was regulated by the Investment Act of 1940 it could not offer stock options to its employees. Most of its long-term members were connected to the firm through a close association with

---

243 Bygrave/Timmons (1992), op. cit., p. 19.
244 Liles (1997), op. cit., pp. 43, 49-50, 52-54.
245 Ibid., p. 58.
246 Ibid., p. 72.

one of the ARD directors. During the late 1950s ARD's performance eventually improved and it became possible to raise additional funds in 1959 and 1960.

ARD's decisive investment was the $70,000 it invested in 1957 for a 77% stake in Digital Equipment Corporation (DEC), a company founded by four MIT graduate students. In the following 14 years, the value of this investment increased to $355 million, and the investment in DEC made up for almost half of all the money earned by ARD in its 26-year life. At the end of the 1960s, DEC dominated the ARD portfolio, 97,6% of portfolio holdings were in publicly quoted companies, but ARD shares were trading at almost 30% discount from net asset value. This made the company an attractive take-over target for investors interested in liquidation or in taking control of DEC. In 1972, ARD announced that Textron, Inc., a diversified group, agreed to acquire all ARD assets after distribution of DEC shares to ARD stockholders. When ARD was sold to Textron, it had since its inception achieved a 14.7% compounded annual rate of return, which without DEC would have been only 7.4%, and is compares to 12.8% that the Dow Jones Industrial Averages achieved over the same period.[247]

It is instructive to keep the issues and problems that ARD has faced as a pioneer in organized venture capital in mind when looking at the further development of the industry. ARD's success proved the potential payoff of providing private venture capital in the form of equity and active management assistance and control. However, its experiences also illustrated some inherent challenges of venture capital investing. Namely, the need to live with negative cash flows for a number of years, the need to exercise control to limit losses, and the dependence on a few superstar investments for total portfolio return. ARD's experience put in doubt whether the continuous scrutiny of public markets was conducive to this kind of business and if a public corporation was the best legal structure.

---

[247] Ibid., p. 83.

After ARD had pioneered organized venture capital, Small Business Investment Companies (SBICs) and private limited partnerships emerged as two competing alternative organizational structures for venture capital. Inspired by ARD's and other private venture capital firms' activities, the government began to take an active role in the mobilization of risk capital. [248] In 1958, the Small Business Administration (SBA) was given the authority to charter Small Business Investment Companies to provide early stage financing for new firms. SBIC shares were in high demand during the unprecedented boom in over-the-counter stocks at the beginning of the 1960s.[249] Many banks set up SBIC subsidiaries and in the 1960s and 1970s this form of government-supported venture capital was to play a major role, although its functioning was totally different from that of private venture capital firms. The privately-managed and SBA licensed SBICs were able to leverage their own funds by three times as much in government-guaranteed loans and faced favorable tax treatment.[250] To cover their interest obligations, they in turn chose to finance firms largely by loans rather than by equity. Since debt financing is more suitable to stable industries and companies with a lower risk-return profile, the SBICs typically focused on those and provided little support beyond finance. By the mid-1960s, 700 SBICs controlled the majority of venture capital investments, and in the bullish IPO market of the late 1960s, many SBIC-funded companies did very well. However, due to moral hazard problems associated with the government guarantees, individual SBICs had incentives to gamble and investment monitoring was weak. The recession of the early 1970s hit the highly leveraged SBIC system hard and many SBICs were liquidated. ARD's Doriot criticized these developments and complained in 1972 "venture capital seems to have shifted from a constructive, difficult task to a new method of

---

[248] Bygrave/Timmons (1992), op. cit., p. 22.
[249] Liles (1977), op. cit., p. 100.

speculation."[251] Nowadays, two-thirds of SBICs' capital is supplied by banks and their role as venture capitalists has sharply diminished to a very minor one.[252]

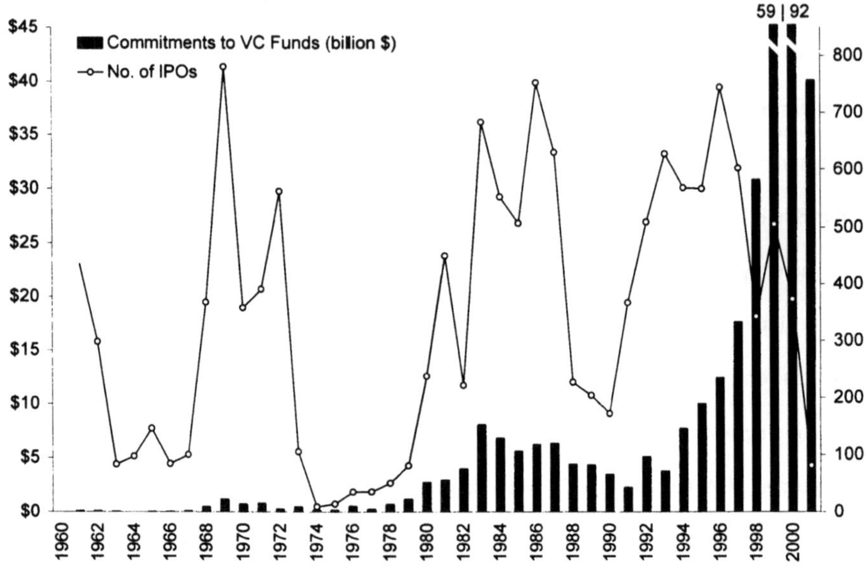

Figure 9: Commitments to VC Funds and No. of IPOs (1961-2001)[253]

The end of the 1968-69 IPO boom and the recession in the early 1970s not only hit the SBICs hard, but also caused problems for the private venture capital firms. Capital commitments kept shrinking through 1977 and the first-best way of exiting an investment – the IPO market – was in a depressed state (see Figure 9). Therefore, investors looked for alternative

250 OECD (1996a), op. cit., p. 18.

251 Liles (1977), op. cit., p. 81.

252 Gompers (1994), op. cit., p. 8; Levin (1998), op. cit., p. 1-14.

253 Includes only limited partnerships, no SBICs or closed-end public funds. Venture capital commitments for 1961 to 1991 are in 1994 $, based on Venture Economics data in Gompers/Lerner (1998), op. cit. Commitments calculated as product of average fund size and number of funds raised. 1992 to 2001 data is not adjusted for inflation and based on VC commitments as reported by Venture Economics.

investment opportunities in expansion financing and leveraged buy-outs. Startup and early-stage investing were "nearly non-existent through the mid-1970s."[254]

At the time, not only SBICs but also the viability of ARD-style publicly owned entities making long-term investments in young companies was called into question, and an impetus was given to create a structure less dependent on short-term evaluation. This led to the increasing adoption of the 10-year private limited partnership structure.[255] The firm that adopted this structure first and at the same time represents one of the first initiatives for organized venture capital on the west coast is Draper, Gaither, Anderson, which was formed in 1958 in San Francisco. Three senior officers of ARD who left the firm during 1966 and 1972 to form their own venture capital firms also chose this structure, which indicates that it solves some of the problems encountered by ARD.[256] In the limited partnership arrangement, the venture capitalist as general partner manages a fund, limited partners supply funds, do not take active part in the investment decision, receive no current income, and cannot withdraw their investments before the statutory end of the partnership's life after seven or ten years. This illiquidity matches the requirements of venture investing. The general partners enjoy a so-called carried interest that entitles them to a disproportionate share of the partnerships profits and aligns their incentives with the interests of the limited partners. Since the mid-1970s, this structure has evolved to dominate the industry. It is sometimes referred to as the Greylock model in reference to the firm Greylock & Co. that was founded by ex-ARD manager William Elfers.[257]

---

[254] Bygrave/Timmons (1992), op. cit., p.23.
[255] Ibid.
[256] William Elfers, Henry W. Hoagland, and William H. Congleton left ARD to start the venture capital firms Greylock & Co., Fidelity Ventures Limited, and the Palmer Organization. Liles (1977), op. cit., p. 148.
[257] Bartlett (1999), op. cit., p. 6.

Transformation of the Industry in the 1980s

The 1980s brought about a new stage in the development of the venture capital industry. Prior to 1979, the annual flow of money into new venture capital funds was never more than some hundred million dollars. However, in the 1980s commitments reached the level of several billion dollars.[258] This dramatic change is attributable to a number of regulatory changes that were implemented in order to revive the industry.[259]

- In 1978 the Revenue Act reduced the capital gains tax rate from 49.5% to 28%, and thereby increased the attractiveness of long-term equity investments.
- In 1979 the Employee Retirement Income Security Act's 'prudent man' rule was revised and clarified to explicitly allow pension funds to invest in higher-risk investments such as venture capital. Prior to that, the Employee Retirement Income Security Act (ERISA) of 1974 prohibited pension funds from investing in high-risk assets such as venture capital funds. This clarification also inspired the increasing formation of focused early stage funds.[260] While stocks performed poorly in the 1970s, venture capital was earning in excess of 25% p.a. in this period, so pension fund managers made use of their new opportunities and poured money into new funds at rapid pace.[261]
- In 1980 the Small Business Investment Incentive Act redefined venture capital firms as business development companies. Previously, they had to register as investment advisers with the Securities and Exchange Commission (SEC). Thereby, the reporting

---

258 It would be illusive to quote more concrete numbers since there is no comprehensive data on the volume of venture capital funds. The most comprehensive source is Venture Economics, but in particular data prior to the 1980s understates the true volume somewhat, as many funds did not report their size and many venture capital investment firms were not structured as limited partnerships.

259 Bygrave/Timmons (1992), op. cit., pp. 24-27.

260 Gompers/Lerner (1998a), op. cit., p. 32.

261 Gompers (1994), op. cit., p. 13.

requirements were reduced and the risk of violating investment adviser regulations eliminated.

- The 1980 ERISA 'safe harbor' regulation made clear that venture capital fund managers would not be considered fiduciaries of pension fund assets invested in the funds under their management. This removed a serious risk exposure in accepting pension funds as limited partners.
- The 1981 Economic Recovery Act further lowered the capital gains tax from 28% to 20%

The enormous inflow of capital led to a transformation of the industry in the 1980s. Swamped with money, investors turned to larger and later-stage non-venture private equity investments. However, these fell out of favor after changes in U.S. income tax law and banking regulations in 1986.[262] Industry returns fell and new commitments bottomed out in 1991 and 1992 at below $2 billion. At the beginning of the 1990s, one venture capitalist alleged that the venture capital industry had been "restructuring itself in a way that is eroding its historic role"[263] and many shared this pessimism.

Differentiation and Internet Boom in the 1990s

What many saw as the end of classic venture capital proved to be a mere cyclical downturn. After 1993, the venture capital industry again experienced spectacular growth. Helped by a decade of spectacular economic growth and booming equity markets, in particular for Internet and technology stocks, venture capital investments reached new record levels, funds posted three-digit internal rates of return, and the industry boomed throughout the 1990s with only a short rupture due to the financial market crisis of 1998. Like in the 1980s, the size of the industry again increased by an order of magnitude. In the 1980s, annual commitments were in the order of several billion dollars, and funds with volumes of some fifty to hundred million dollars were regarded large funds. Yet during the second half of the 1990s, commitments increased to the order of several tens of billions and peaked at around $100 billion in 2000. At the same, time startup valuations and the average investment size increased considerably (see Figure 10).

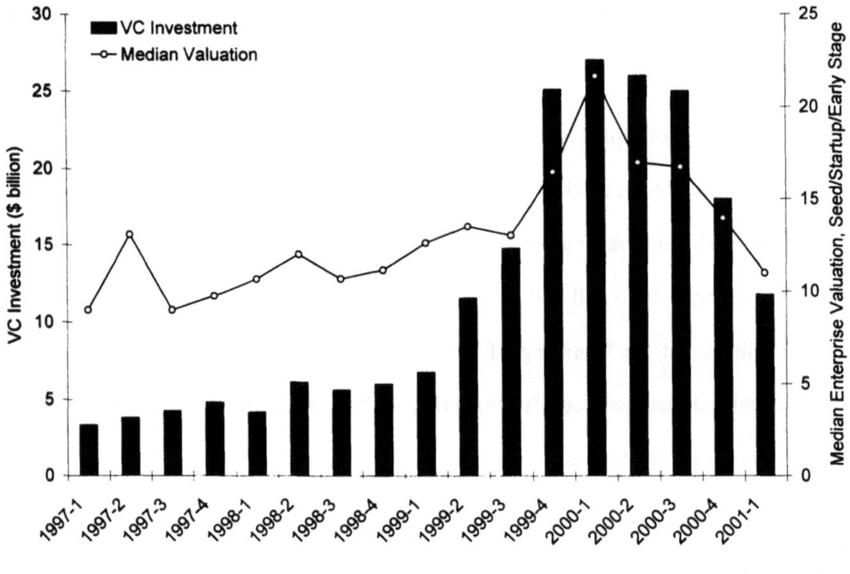

Figure 10: Venture Capital Investment and Valuation Bubble (1997-2001)[264]

Many new firms entered the market and established firms raised larger and larger funds. The number of billion-dollar funds increased, with 19 such funds being raised in the year 2000. The structure of the private equity industry has, since the shake-out of the late 1980s/early

---

[262] David Brophy (1996), "United States Venture Capital Markets: Changes and Challenges," OECD, *Venture Capital and Innovation*, OCDE/GD(96)168, Paris: OECD, p. 46

[263] Bygrave/Timmons (1992), op. cit., p. 28.

[264] Source: Venture Economics.

1990s, become much more heterogeneous, and many firms decided to raise funds that are specialized on a certain industry or a certain investment stage.[265] The boom of the late 1990s also attracted capital from sources such as corporations, banks, late-stage private equity firms, professional service firms, and others to startup venture capital investments.

When the stock market bubble finally began to burst in the spring of 2000, venture capital veterans pointed their fingers at "bankers, consultants, and techies" as inexperienced investors of startup and 'incubator' funds, blaming them for the failure of many venture capital-funded startups to raise a next round of financing or to develop into viable businesses.[266] However, while inexperienced entrepreneurs and investors had their share in feeding the booming equity markets, even those who early recognized and criticized the excesses of the time could not afford not to ride the wave. Venture capital activity has since slowed down considerably, exit prospects are dim and a large share of venture capital investments made prior to the end of the boom has turned sour. As Silicon Valley investment banker, William R. Hambrecht summarizes, "It was the biggest bubble I've ever seen in my 40 years of business and the biggest meltdown, I think it's difficult to underestimate the damage to the market."[267]

Emerging West Coast Dominance

Silicon Valley is by far the dominant cluster of venture capital activity in the United States and worldwide. However, this was not always the case. The industry was initially centered on the east coast, in particular in New York and Massachusetts. West coast venture capital traces its origins to the late 1950s. In 1958, Draper, Gaither & Anderson was established in Palo

---

[265] Sahlman (1990), op. cit., p. 489. George W. Fenn, Nellie Liang, and Stephen Prowse (1996), "The Economics of the Private Equity Market," Extended version of a staff study published in the Federal Reserve Bulletin, January 1996: 26-27, Available at URL: http://www.imdr.com/venture/preqmkt.htm, retrieved: February 9, 1998.

[266] Jonathan Shieber (2000), "Europe Sets the Table for the Future of VC," *Venturewire*, Friday, December 15, 2000.

Alto raising money from the Rockefeller group. In 1959, Frank Chambers who was a student of Doriot at Harvard raised $5.5 million for his Continental Capital Corporation. Two years later, Arthur Rock who previously was an investment banker at Wall Street firm Hayden Stone and had arranged funding for the 'Traitorous Eight' to form Fairchild Semiconductors, set up a venture capital partnership with Thomas Davis. If Doriot was the "father of venture capital"[268] on the east coast, then Arthur Rock can claim this title for the west coast. His investment of $257,000 in Scientific Data Systems turned into $100 million after its sale to Xerox in 1969 and was a landmark achievement at the time that helped to pave the way for dozens of new firms to be formed in the 1970s.[269]

In the early days, West coast venture capital was an illustrious group of investors, called the 'Boys Club' or the 'Silicon Valley Mafia' that gathered in the Western Association of Venture Capitalists and frequently got together to exchange ideas, hear entrepreneurs' pitches, and exchange gossip. In the 1970s, that group moved down to Sand Hill Road in Menlo Park, adjacent to the Stanford Campus. After stagnating for most of the 1960s, the number of venture capital partnerships grew through spin-offs from existing firms and by new people entering the industry. Fairchild Semiconductors was an important nucleus to the process. Four of its founders had invested in Arthur Rock's partnership with Thomas Davis that lasted until 1968 when Davis set up the Mayfield fund. In 1972, Donald Valentine, former head of Marketing at Fairchild, formed Capital Management services, which later became the venerable Sequoia Capital. In the same year, Thomas Perkins – also a student of Doriot – and Eugene Kleiner, one of the 'Traitorous Eight', set up shop at 3000 Sand Hill Road. This unpresuming office complex was soon to become synonymous with venture capital and

---

[267] Margaret Young (2001), "Business School students get gloomy view of prospects for venture capital funding," *Stanford Report*, February 28, 2001.
[268] Gompers (1994), op. cit., p. 5.
[269] David Toll (2000), "Private Equity Primer," *Mimeo*, Asset Alternatives.

constituted the center of the West coast venture capital industry that grew from some 20 firms at the end of the 1960s to more than 60 firms within a decade.[270] As a result, the Silicon Valley area became one of the largest centers for venture capital in the late 1960s and early 1970s when the IPO market for high-tech stock was hot and venture capital experienced its first boom.

Figure 11 illustrates the importance of spin-offs in the evolution of Silicon Valley venture capital. Points (nodes) represent a firm, and the presence of a line (tie) indicates that they share at least one founder. The graph shows that only a small number of firms was established by new entrants to the industry.

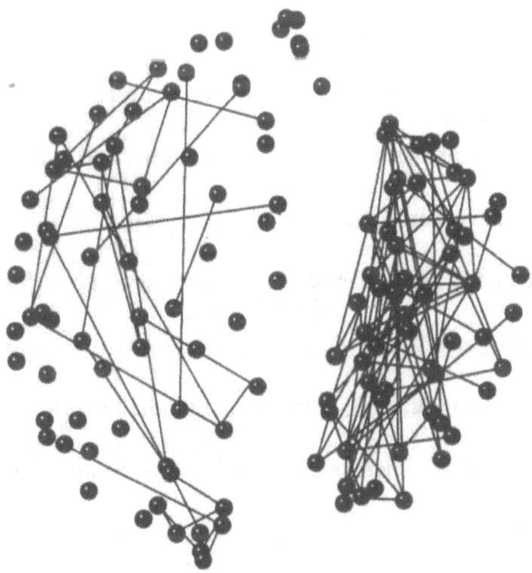

Figure 11: Connections Among Early Silicon Valley Venture Capital Firms[271]

---

[270] Castilla/Hwang/Granovetter/Granovetter (2000), op. cit., pp. 234-237.

[271] Ibid., p. 240. Based on the genealogy chart 'West Coast Venture Capital – 25 years' created by the Asset Management Company in 1984, covering 129 firms established during 1958 and 1983.

Most firms had at least one experienced venture capitalist as founder; however, these people were often joined by engineers and high-tech executives, and by the early 1980s Silicon Valley venture capital was dominated by people who had migrated from industry rather than from backgrounds in finance. As Wilson summarizes:[272]

> Born in New York, nurtured in Boston, and almost smothered in Washington, venture capital did not really come of age until it moved to California and joined forces with the brash young technologists who were using bits of silicon to create an information revolution as profound as the industrial revolution a century earlier.

Ever since, Silicon Valley venture capital has maintained its character of being particularly 'technology savvy' and the region has emerged as the dominant cluster of venture capital activity. Out of the more than 103 billion dollars of venture capital invested in 2000, Companies based in Northern California received by far the most investments: $33 billion. The Greater New York area was a distant second with $12 billion and companies in the New England received $10 billion in investment. Seed, Startup, and Early Stage venture capital accounts for roughly 25% of the venture capital volume, and a disproportionate share of the several hundred startup ventures that receive early stage venture capital each year in the United States are located in Silicon Valley. In contrast to New York and Chicago, venture capital in Boston and Silicon Valley evolved in tandem with technology entrepreneurship.[273] The mix of funds in Silicon Valley includes many smaller funds that are focused on early stage technology investments, whereas on the East coast balanced and later stage funds make up for a larger share.[274]

---

[272] John W. Wilson (1985), *The New Venturers: Inside the High-Stakes World of Venture Capital*, Menlo Park: Addison-Wesley, pp 31, 50-51.

[273] Martin Kenney and Richard Florida (2000), "Venture Capital in Silicon Valley: Fueling New Firm Formation," Kenney, Martin (ed.), *Understanding Silicon Valley*, Stanford: Stanford University Press: 89-123., p. 98.

[274] Gompers/Lerner (1998a), op. cit., p. 31.

6. 2. Organization of Professional Venture Capital

Legal Structure of a Venture Capital Fund

The most common legal structure for venture capital firms in the United States is the limited partnership. While in the 1960s and 1970s, SBICs and publicly traded closed-end funds were chosen as organizational structures, in the last two decades the limited partnership has evolved to become the markedly dominant organizational form.[275] More than four hundred such firms have joined together in the National Venture Capital Association, and the total number of firms is estimated at around nine hundred.[276]

In the limited partnership the senior managers of a partnership management firm (venture capital firm) act as general partners and outside investors that supply the capital act as limited partners. The lifetime of the partnership/fund is pre-determined to usually ten years. The structure of these partnership agreements is remarkably consistent across the industry and over time.[277] Typically, limited partners contribute 99% of the funds, while – for tax reasons – general partners supply 1% often in the form of a promissory note. Limited partners usually invest a large share of their capital commitment at the close of the fund, and phase in the remainder over time. Transfer of limited partnership units is restricted, and withdrawal from the partnership is prohibited. Severe penalties are imposed on limited partners reneging on a funding commitment. Thus in contrast to equity investments in the public market, investors accept a low degree of liquidity and are not able to easily exit their investment by selling their stake in the fund. Although a secondary market for limited partnership interests has

---

[275] Ibid., p. 5.
[276] Toll (2000), op., cit.
[277] Sahlman (1990), op. cit., p. 491.

developed, it is only with considerable loss and through complex transactions that private equity investors can achieve liquidity.[278]

The management of the fund lies with the general partners and limited partners must not become involved in day-to-day management of the fund in order to maintain their limited liability status. Thus the suppliers of capital do not enjoy control rights with regard to the use of their funds beyond what is stated in the partnership agreement. In other words they give up both 'exit' and 'voice' – mechanisms that they would enjoy as shareholders in a publicly traded corporation. While general partners bear unlimited liability, this is inconsequential since they only supply a nominal share of the capital and venture capital partnerships usually do not borrow and therefore are not exposed to liabilities in excess of assets.[279]

General partners (venture capitalists) receive two sources of compensation for the management of the fund. First, limited partners pay them an annual management fee of 2-3 % of committed capital. Second, general partners are entitled to a 'carried interest' of typically 20 % of the realized gains on the fund. In effect, suppliers of finance to venture capital funds surrender their control rights, but give high-powered incentives to venture capitalists. Speaking in Hart's terms, they 'bribe' their managers (the venture capitalists) to act on their behalf, rather than trying to 'force' them to do so.[280] (See Figure 12.)

This peculiar organizational structure is better suited to enable the high-risk business of venture capital investing than the standard corporate structure that ARD had experimented with.[281] It shows interesting parallels to the medieval predecessors of the modern stock

---

[278] Cf. Private Equity Investors (2001), "Brief History of Secondary Purchases," *Private Equity Investors*, available at URL: http://www.pei.com, retrieved February 20, 2001.
[279] Sahlman (1990), op. cit., p. 490.
[280] Cf. Hart (1995), op. cit., p. 128
[281] Cf. Liles (1977), op. cit., pp. 147-148.

corporation that were also organized as limited life entities with periodic liquidation and distribution of profits.[282]

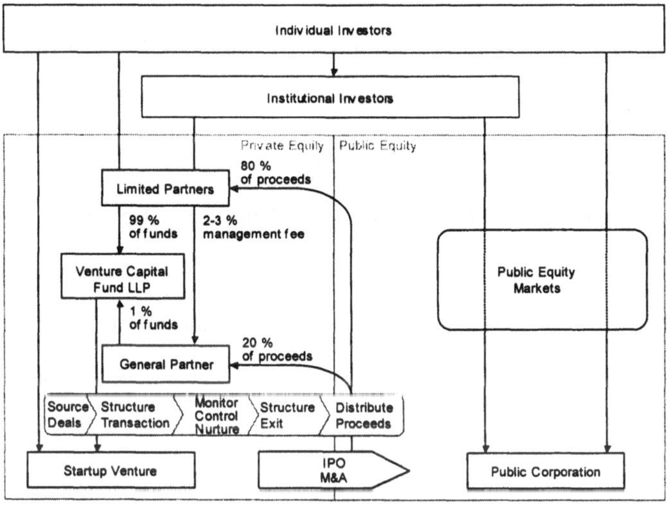

Figure 12: Venture Capital Fund Structure and Business Process

Venture Capital Business Process

Venture capitalists usually invest in preferred stock issued by privately held companies; contribute as active investors to increase the firm's value; and realize capital gains by selling their stake after portfolio companies are acquired or go public. Investment proceeds are distributed to limited and general partners. At the end of a fund's legal existence a final accounting is rendered and all remaining cash and securities are distributed.

While venture capital funds/partnerships are limited life organizations, the life of the management firm that acts as general partner usually extends beyond the life of one fund and venture capital (management) firms raise a series of subsequent funds. In order to

[282] Cf. Kohn (1999), op. cit.

continuously maintain their ability to invest, venture capital firms raise their next fund while the current fund is still not fully invested and not nearly fully distributed, i.e. the lifetime of funds is overlapping. Investment and distribution periods of any particular fund are overlapping as well, however investment activity is typically concentrated in the first five years, so that liquidity can be attained within the remaining lifetime of the fund.

The business process of a venture capital firm can therefore be broadly divided into the periodic task of raising a venture capital fund and the continuing management of funds. Venture capitalists are isolated from investors' interference in their investment process and are thus enabled to make long-term investments within the lifetime of the fund. However, in order to stay in business and remain able to raise subsequent funds, venture capital firms need to build a track record and reputation of successful investing. When raising a new fund from previous or new limited partners, they are judged by the rates of return of their previous funds. Therefore, venture capital firms can be regarded as competing in a reputation contest based on past performance and in this sense their investment activity is subject to ex-post monitoring by investors.

The ongoing process of managing the venture fund involves the following distinct business activities (see Figure 12):

1. Deal sourcing and screening
2. Deal structuring and investment in several stages
3. Monitoring and control of the portfolio company in order to increase its value
4. Planning of liquidity event and structuring of exit
5. Distribution of proceeds as liquid stock or cash

Deal Sourcing and Screening

After having raised a fund, the venture capital firm has to find promising investments and create a deal flow. Screening for investments is done by the venture capitalists, as well as by independent agents who locate candidate firms. While venture capitalists receive many unsolicited investment proposals, most deals come through personal contacts or introductions by trusted sources. As a rule of thumb, in the US, about 1 % of all investment proposals receive funding. This was true for ARD, the first venture capital firm, and it is said to be still the right order of magnitude.[283] This low ratio has to be seen before the background of the high expected rate of return (hurdle rate) that venture capitalist require for their projects and the fact that deals are usually shopped around to many potential investors. Venture capitalists have to at least triple the assets of the fund over its lifetime. Since many projects will perform poorly or turn into total write-offs, only projects that offer the logical possibility of returning five to ten times the amount invested within the lifetime of the fund will get funded. At the same time, depending on the fund's size and the number of professionals, the number of projects is limited and there are certain lower and upper boundaries for the investment volume per deal. Therefore, both expected rate of return and absolute investment volume are criteria in the selection of deals.

Deal Structuring and Investment

The development of a startup venture from its initiation to becoming a going-concern can be regarded as a process of stepwise risk reduction. Consequently, the expected rate of return, or hurdle rate, that the venture capitalist applies depends on the venture's stage of development. However, venture capitalists do not take risks as given, rather they structure deals in such a way as to be able to actively reduce risks and they isolate different kinds of risk by investing in stages. In order to reduce risks, investment contracts give substantial control rights to the investor. These arrangements will be described in detail below. Another mechanism that venture capitalists frequently apply to reduce risk, is to co-invest with other venture capital

---

[283] Cf. Fenn/Liang/Prowse (1996), op. cit.

funds in one financing round with one of the firms assuming the function of a lead investor. Stage financing and syndication of investments are important ways for venture capitalists to reduce their risks through diversification.

Monitoring and Nurturing Growth

Venture capitalists are active investors that try to prevent failure and contribute to the success of all their portfolio companies.[284] They are in close contact with management, often as board members, and provide contacts and advice. While they usually do not take majority stakes in their portfolio companies, they ensure themselves substantial rights of control with regard to the management of the company. The explicit rights that are included in the financing contract, as well as the implicit threat of abandonment that comes with stage financing put the venture capitalists in a powerful position enabling them to actively reduce risks and increase the value of the company.[285]

Planning and Structuring of Exit

The goal of the venture capital firm is to sell (exit) the investment within the lifetime of the fund. The success of an investment depends upon the stock appreciation (capital gain) and the length of the holding period from investment to exit. Exit can take the form of an initial public offering or an M&A transaction. Since venture capitalists usually hold registration rights for their preferred stock they exert strong influence in the decision on the timing and structuring of a liquidity event. In the case of a public offering, venture capitalists are subject to a lock-up period of six month before their stock becomes liquid. If the company is acquired by or merged with another – often public – company, the venture capitalist can

---

[284] Cf. Gompers (1994), op. cit., p. 3.
[285] These contractual arrangements are discussed in section 7. 2.

attain immediate liquidity by exchanging his stock for liquid stock or cash. The median age of venture-backed companies doing IPOs in the US is around six years.[286]

The overall performance of a venture capital fund usually strongly depends on one or two most successful investments. As it was the case with ARD's investment in DEC, venture capitalists still rely on 'homerun' investments in order to achieve outstanding returns. Traditionally, an IPO was regarded as the most attractive exit channel for venture capital investments offering the highest step-up in company valuation. However, during the late 1990s valuations in M&A transactions have often been as attractive as IPO valuations and oftentimes an acquisition was preferred to an IPO, for its instant liquidity and less uncertain long-term prospects for the firm.

Distribution of Proceeds

Provisions with regard to distribution of fund proceeds vary between partnership agreements. Distribution can take place annually or on the discretion of general partners. Proceeds can be distributed as stock or cash. Many partnership agreements include a 'full payout' provision that entitles limited partners to receive an amount equal to their capital contribution before general partners receive their carried interest. The overall performance of a venture capital fund can only be determined after it is liquidated and a final accounting is rendered. However, funds begin to track their ratio of distributed value over paid-in capital and the implied rates of return as soon as they begin to distribute proceeds.

---

[286] Venture Economics.

6. 3. Venture Capital Within the Financial System

The Private Equity Market

Venture capital firms are financial intermediaries, so their business and the money flowing in and out of the industry have to be seen within the context of the industry's positions in the financial system.

The term venture capital is frequently used interchangeably with 'private equity' that can be defined as the market for unregistered securities. The phrase 'private equity' gained widespread use in the late 1980s, when leveraged buyout firms that suffered from a bad public standing due to their infamous history of 'buy and bust' strategies, settled on this innocuous term as a new name for their business.[287] However, private equity is really a broader concept than either venture capital or buyouts. It includes investors that engage in a broad variety of investments, including start-ups, growth equity investments, leveraged and management buyouts, leveraged recapitalizations, carve-outs, industry consolidations, troubled company turn-arounds, and others.[288] In analyzing the structure of the private equity market either a functional or an institutional perspective can be adopted. The functional perspective would distinguish different asset classes or issuers of securities that receive investment capital. Alternatively, the institutional perspective would draw the lines according to institutional characteristics of the investor or intermediary that makes the investment. Adopting these criteria, it becomes apparent that the private equity market consists of numerous specialized sub segments. Following George Fenn et. al., the private equity market in the US can be split into five major segments: the organized private equity market that can be divided in a (1) non-venture and a (2) venture segment, and the three segments of non-

---

[287] Toll (2000), op. cit.
[288] Cf. Levin (1998), op. cit., p. 1-2.

organized private equity: the (3) market for angel capital, the (4) informal private equity market, and the (5) Rule 144A private equity market (see Table 2).[289]

	Investor	Agent/Adviser	Intermediary	Issuer
Non-organized private equity				
SEC Rule 144	Institutional investors		Underwriter	Public firms that want to issue quickly by avoiding registered offering
Informal private equity	Institutional investors Accredited individuals	Agent playing role similar to an underwriter		Similar to public small-cap stocks but unregistered
Angel capital	Wealthy individuals	Informal matchmakers, such as lawyers or accountants	Sometimes semi-formal angel syndicates	Small, closely held companies Start-ups with growth potential and limited capital needs
Organized private equity				
Venture	Institutional investors Pension funds Endowments and foundations Bank holding companies Wealthy individuals Non-financial corporations	Sometimes agent/match-maker	Venture capital firms organized as limited partnerships Publicly traded investment companies Small business investment companies Corporate venture capital firms	Young firms with innovative technology and/or high projected growth Later-stage firms that want to finance rapid growth
Non-venture	Institutional investors	Sometimes agent/match-maker	Buyout firms Mezzanine equity/debt Etc.	Established companies financing expansion (capital expenditure or acquisition) Change in capital structure Change in ownership Public companies issuing a combination of debt and private equity to finance MBO/LBO

Table 2: Segments of the U.S. Private Equity Market

The Rule 144A market is used by public firms for underwritten private equity offerings that are placed with institutional investors. In the informal private equity market, unregistered

[289] Cf. Fenn/Liang/Prowse (1996), op. cit.

securities are sold to institutional and accredited individual investors. However, investors do not acquire controlling stakes, therefore this market segment operates more like the public market for small-cap stocks. The term angel capital (or angel finance) refers to capital that is provided by wealthy individuals who take ownership stakes in small closely held companies, and who may also be active in advising the company. The organized private equity market comprises equity investments by specialized professional intermediaries in the unregistered securities of private and public companies. This segment is estimated to be only a fraction the size of the aforementioned segments of the non-organized private equity market. Organized private equity can be divided into a venture segment that includes classic venture capital investments in young firms and a non-venture segment, which includes investments in special situations, such as buyouts, mezzanine financings, and others. Private equity investors are active investors who seek to regularly achieve higher returns for their investors than the public markets are offering. Table 3 gives an overview of the performance of different private equity segments.

Fund Type	1 Yr	3 Yr	5 Yr	10 Yr	20 Yr
Early/Seed Stage	-35.0	80.0	50.7	33.4	22.0
Balanced Venture	-23.5	44.3	33.2	23.0	15.7
Later Stage Venture	-20.5	22	20.7	23.6	16.6
All Venture	-27.6	49.2	35.9	26.4	17.7
All Buyouts	-14.1	0.7	5.1	10.9	14.5
Mezzanine	-3.1	10.1	10.9	12.4	11.6
All Private Equity	-18.3	13.4	14.9	17.3	16.2

Table 3: U.S. Private Equity Performance Benchmarks, as of 12/31/2001 (IRR % p.a.)[290]

Private equity funds have been showing 20-year annualized rates of return of around 20-25 percent leading to a strong inflow of funds and phenomenal long-term growth of the asset class. On the other hand returns have been cyclical and volatile. Before the mid-Nineties, the buyout segment was much larger and offered higher returns than venture capital. However, during the period from 1995 to 2000, and in particular in 1999, the stock market boom and the Internet Bubble have offered 'once in a lifetime' returns to venture capital investors. Whereas buyouts are expected to pay three to four times the investment in five years, venture capitalists at the time made 10 to hundred times their money in two or three years. One private equity investor summarizing the sentiment at the time stated, "1999 was the year when normal private equity was boring and hard, when private equity investors became second-class citizens and the venture capitalists became the stars."[291] As a result, many buyout experts shifted to venture capital investing and commitments to venture capital funds literally exploded from $8 billion in 1995 to $92 billion in 2000 (see Figure 13).

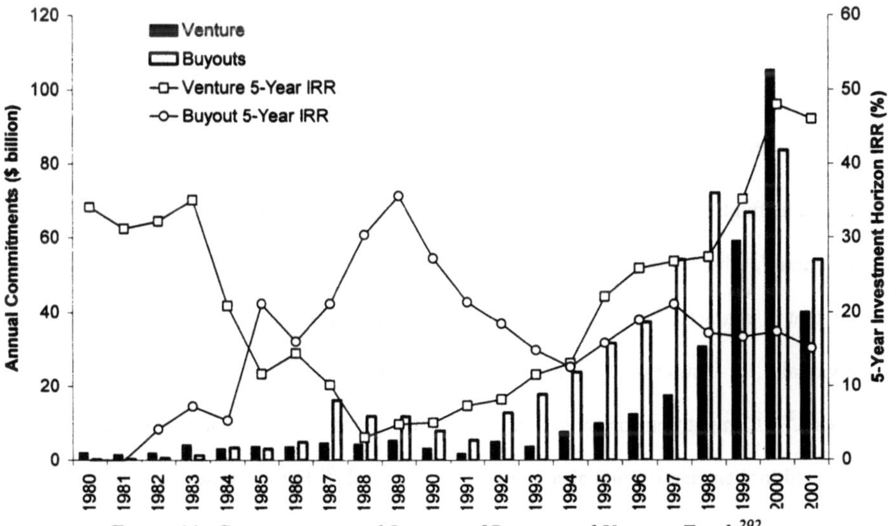

Figure 13: Commitments and Returns of Buyout and Venture Funds[292]

---

[290] Venture Economics data, tracking the performance of over 1200 US venture capital and buyout funds formed 1969-2001, Investment horizon returns as of 12/31/2001, net to investors after fees and carried interest.

[291] David Carey (1999), "The Year in Deals: Buyout Firms Take to Venture Capital," *The Daily Deal*, December 29, 1999, available at URL: http://www.thedailydeal.com, retrieved February 21, 2000.

[292] Venture Economics.

Yet, since the burst of the bubble that started in spring 2000, returns began to fall very sharply (see Table 3), and given that venture capitalists invested about ten times more in 2000 than in 1995, long-term investor expectations cannot be fulfilled. Since the fourth quarter of 2000 the favor has turned to buyout funds again. Venture capital slowed down to $18.4 billion, which was topped by the $20.5 billion committed to buyout funds.[293]

Sources of Funds

When the industry was born, individuals, family and university endowments, and financial institutions were the most important providers of funds dedicated to venture capital investing. However, after regulatory changes in the late 1970s, pension funds have evolved as the most important source of capital commitments. To avoid double taxation for non-tax-exempt partners, the limited partnership is tax transparent, i.e. does not have to pay capital gains taxes, tax only has to be paid by the investors. This makes it particularly attractive for tax-exempt institutional investors, such as pension funds.[294] At the end of the 1990s, corporate sources of capital have grown in importance. (See Figure 14.)

Pension funds typically allocate a single-percentage share of their funds to 'alternative investments', which includes venture, buyout, and hedge funds. Venture capital is an asset class that is characterized by a large spread in performance between funds. The shift from individuals to institutional sources has contributed to professionalize the allocation process.[295] Competition between venture capital firms is based on their reputation as expressed in their relative and absolute IRR track record.[296] For example, the California State

---

[293] Venture Economics.
[294] Cf. Bygrave/Timmons (1992), op. cit. p. 11.
[295] Cf. Mark Van Osnabrugge and Robert J. Robinson (1999c), "The Influence of a Venture Capitalist's Source of Funds," *Working Paper*, Harvard Business School, March 1999.
[296] Gompers (1999), op. cit., p. 209.

Teachers' Retirement System (CalSTRS) wants its funds to beat the median IRR for each vintage year, and beat the Russell 3000 index by 5%.[297]

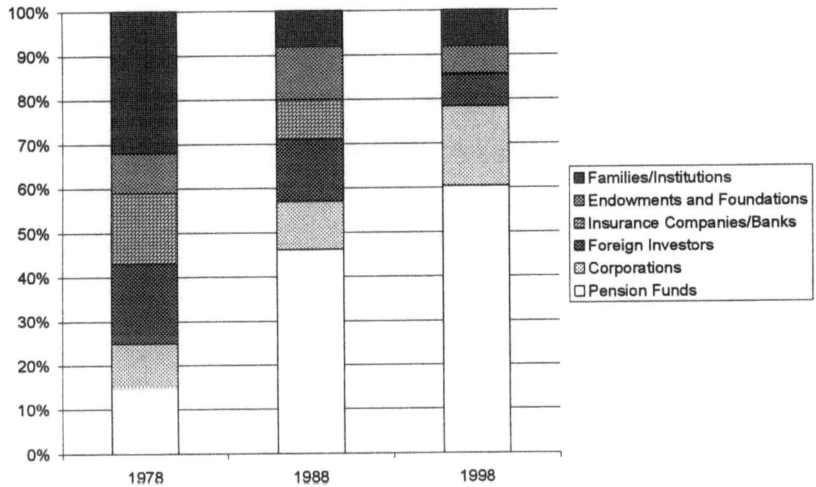

Figure 14: Sources of Commitments to VC Funds[298]

As a result of this kind of allocation criteria, most money goes to partnerships with a long track record and experienced general partners who, as a result, are able to raise larger and larger funds. Venture capitalists also prefer to establish a stable relationship with limited partners that have a long-term commitment to the asset class and understand that ups and downs are an inevitable element of the industry. Successful firms have little room to admit new limited partners, for example, the partnership Kleiner Perkins Caufield & Byers has not admitted a new limited partner in 18 years. Terms of investment are relatively stable, but there are always a few and recently more top firms who take 25 or even 30 percent carried

[297] Shawn Neidorf (1999b), "L.P.s Weigh the Pros and Cons of Venture Capital Investing," *Venture Capital Journal*, July 1, 1999.
[298] Venture Economics.

interest. On the other hand, as fund volumes grow, some firms reduce the management fee to below 2% while others invest part of their management fee in the fund.[299]

On the industry level, fund raising is characterized by a long-term growth trend that is related to regulatory changes, but also by a strong volatility that is related to the market for initial public offerings.[300] On the firm level, the existence of 'homerun IPOs', as expressed in the value of equity in firms taken public the year before, can serve as an indicator of fund size.[301]

Exit Channels

In order to realize returns and give money back to limited partners, venture capitalists have to achieve liquidity of their investment within the lifetime of the fund. The two exit channels that venture capitalists can use to do so are Mergers and Acquisitions, and Initial Public Offerings.

The volatility of the M&A and IPO markets is the chief cause for the swings in venture capital activity. The time from first funding to IPO used to be at least five years, however, during the boom of the late 1990s, many companies managed to go public after less than one and a half years.[302] More than 50% of all IPOs in 2000 were by companies that had previously received venture capital. As a result of the corporate rush to go public and the markets willingness to supply 'public venture capital', venture capitalists were able to realize triple-digit returns.[303]

---

299 Shawn Neidorf (1999a), "Terms Tango," *Venture Capital Journal*, June 1, 1999. Allistair Christopher (2000), "Piecing Together Limited Partner and General Partner Relations," *Venture Capital Journal*, August 1, 2000.

300 Gompers/Lerner (1998a), op. cit., p. 18.

301 Ibid., p. 28.

302 Dado P. Banatao and Kevin A. Fong (2000), "The Valley of Deals," Lee, Chong-Moon, Miller, William F., Gong Hancock, Marguerite, and Rowen, Henry S. (eds.). *The Silicon Valley Edge*. Stanford: Stanford University Press, p. 307.

303 Michael Gannon (1999b), "M&A Deals Gain Cachet," *Venture Capital Journal*, October 1, 1999.

However, the volatility of the public markets represents a lot of risk for the venture capitalists, since they face a lock up period of at least six months before being able to sell their shares. Therefore, if they can achieve a good valuation in an M&A situation and sell their stake for cash or liquid shares, this is a quick and profitable exit channel. During the technology boom, many large companies, such as Microsoft or Cisco, were moving fast to secure new technology and products lines, and therefore often bought up companies before they went public at similar valuations. However, since the middle of 2000, both, the M&A and the public equity market have cooled down drastically, leading to very dim exit prospects for venture capitalists. (See Figure 15.)

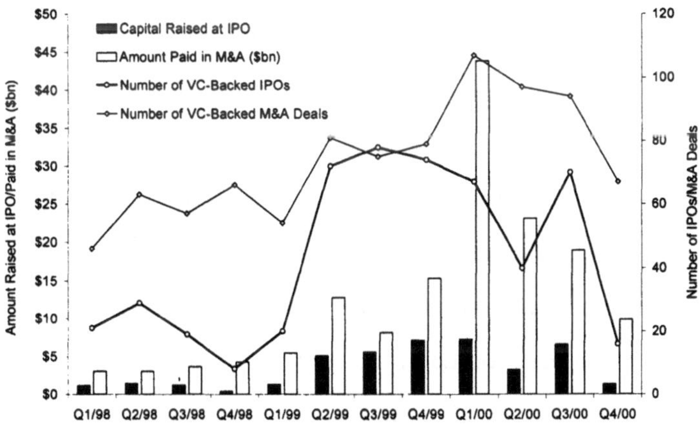

Figure 15: Exit Channels for Venture Capital Investments[304]

Alternative Providers of Classic Venture Capital

The most important providers of finance that can be referred to as classic venture capital in the functional sense are professional venture capital firms organized as limited partnerships as described above. However, professional venture capitalists are not the only source of funds for startup ventures. Individual 'angel' investors, SBICs, publicly traded investment companies, and corporate venture capital programs are important alternative sources of funds. Among these, angel finance and corporate venture capital initiatives play the most prominent role in Silicon Valley and provide large amounts of capital to startups. In spite of this, neither of them can be regarded as institutional alternative to professional venture capital firms, rather these three types of investors coexist in a partly complementary, partly competing, and partly unrelated fashion.

Angel Capital

Angel capital derives from the term 'business angel' that has arguably been coined around 1980 by the Center for Venture Research at the University of New Hampshire.[305] Angel capital refers to finance provided by individuals who might act for a variety of reasons, such as some personal affiliation with the founder of a startup, professional interest, or pure financial motives. There are no precise figures available, but according to estimates by the Small Business Administration the volume of angel capital could be as much as eight times the volume of professional venture capital. Estimates regarding the number of angel investors lie anywhere between three hundred thousand and three million people.[306] Of course such numbers are hard to interpret because it is difficult to draw a line between sophisticated angel investors who provide 'smart money' to promising ventures and are valuable for reasons other than the pure supply of funds, and the founder's father's investment in the new lawn care venture of his son. While part of the angel capital segment represents risk finance, the probably larger part is personal finance of a low risk type that is closer in nature to a bank

---

[304] VentureOne.

[305] Michael Gannon (1999a), "Financing in Purgatory," *Venture Capital Journal*, May 1, 1999.

[306] Daniel T. Kingsley (1999), "The State of the Venture Capital Industry and its Impact on the U.S. Economy," *Mimeo*, Speech before the Conference on Corporate Governance and Equity Offerings, February 24, 1999. Mary B. Grover (1998), "Starting a Company is like going to War," Forbes, November 2, 1998: 184-193. Andrew Moore (2001), "Angel Investing Is Up According to Survey," *Angel Society*, available at URL://www.angelsociety.com, retrieved January 8, 2001.

loan than to venture capital.[307] Nevertheless, there are clear indications that there is a growing group of sophisticated angel investors that is relevant to the business of professional venture capitalists.[308]

Accordingly, individual angel investors appear to serve a variety of functions in the economy that need to be analyzed separately. First, they are the most important source of funding for the overwhelming majority of startup companies (in Bhidé's terms both marginal and promising ventures) that are just not suited for professional venture capitalists because they offer too low returns or are too risky and hard to evaluate. This is certainly the area where individual investors make their biggest contribution, and we have to keep in mind that while there are more than half a million businesses established in the U.S. each year, only several hundred startups are financed by professional venture capitalists. In contrast to this function, a growing segment of sophisticated angel investors supplies early stage funds for promising venture startups whose financing needs are too small to attract the interest of professional venture capitalists or to such startups that prefer to raise their first round of financing from angel investors rather than from professional venture capitalists. These sophisticated angel investors act with the objective to 'prepare' their investment for a subsequent fundraising round led by professional venture capitalists. In this sense, the first-named angel capital segment is mostly unrelated to professional venture capital, while angel investors of the second type may sometimes compete with venture capitalists, but more often are in a complementary relationship with them because they help to build a deal flow.[309]

---

307 Cf. Brophy (1996), op. cit., p. 46.

308 Kingsley (1999), op. cit.

309 Gannon (1999a), op. cit. Cf. also Brophy (1996), op., cit., p. 46. Oliver Pfirrmann, Udo Wupperfeld, and Joshua Lerner (1997), *Venture Capital and New Technology Based Firms: An US-German Comparison.* Heidelberg: Physica-Verlag, p. 58. Milford B. Green (ed., 1991), *Venture Capital: International Comparisons*, London: Routledge.

This type of angel investor plays an important role in the financing of Silicon Valley startups. The typical profile of a Silicon Valley angel investor is that of a previous or current high-tech industry executive who combines personal wealth with valuable industry knowledge and contacts. As Silicon Valley veteran Regis McKenna stresses, "most of the people who have made money in Silicon Valley who are not professional venture capitalists are also investors."[310] These people frequently look at angel investing as a way to make use of their know-how and as a 'fun way to remain involved'. They typically invest amounts of less than $1 million as the first outside investors in seed or very early stage situations. Their due diligence is less intensive than that of venture capitalists. Angel investors usually buy common stock and do not expect to participate in subsequent financing rounds. Therefore they do not aim to exercise control.[311] They expect to make their investments ready for a round of professional venture capital within one to two years, and aim for a return of ten times in 5 years. That is to say that these investors look for investments with a higher risk-return profile and smaller volume than venture capitalists. Angel investors act as individuals, however co-investing is very common and in recent years semi-formal dinner club-style associations of private investors, such as the Band of Angels, Angel Capital Network, or Net Angels have been formed. Some semi-professional angel investors are granted preferential terms for investing in venture capital funds, and have established working relationships with professional venture capitalists.[312] Apparently, the described form of angel investing is highly complementary with professional venture capital. Angel investors – sometimes by investing a

---

310 McKenna (1995), op. cit.

311 Wetzel (1997), op. cit., pp. 194, 205. For a theory of angel investing, cf. Mark Van Osnabrugge and Robert J. Robinson (1999b), "A Comparison of Business Angel and Venture Capitalist Investment Procedures: An Agency Theory-Based Analysis," *Working Paper*, Harvard Business School, March 1999.

312 Alex Gove (1999a), "Those Pesky Entrepreneurs," *Red Herring*, July 10, 1999, available at URL: http://www.redherring.com, retrieved: July 12, 1999.

lot of their time – help to achieve a first step-down in the startup's risk profile and thereby make it ready for a step-up in valuation and funding by professional venture capitalists.[313]

During the equity market boom of the late Nineties, angel investing received a big boost by new investors who were eager to get into early private financing rounds of firms that could possibly become the next Cisco. As venture capitalist Jim Breyer describes the situation at the time, "there's an influx of angels, grandmothers, everyone wanting to get in on deals."[314] However, there are also several long-standing fundamental factors that point towards a continuing rise in the importance of angel capital. First, as venture capital funds grow in size, small investments become less attractive for them, giving angel investors the chance to fill this gap. Second, according to estimates there are more than seven million Americans with investable assets of $1 million or more, and in a decade this number will quadruple to over 25 million.[315] Moreover, angel investors have long been deemed worthy of political support.[316] They have in the past benefited from reductions in capital gains taxes and received an important stimulus by the 1997 decision of Congress to make profits from financing new companies tax-deferred so long as they are rolled into new startup investments within 60 days.[317]

Corporate VC

Corporate venture capital refers to investments by industrial corporations in startup companies. These investments can take the form of direct investment or investment via a limited partnership vehicle that mimics the structure of independent venture capital firms.

---

313 Ibid. Cf. Gompers (1999), op. cit.

314 Georgie Raik-Allen (1999), "Venture Capitalists Feel the Heat," *Red Herring*, May 21, 1999, available at URL: http://www.redherring.com, retrieved: July 12, 1999.

315 Moore (2001), op. cit.

316 Cf. Liles (1977), op. cit., p. 14, Miller (2000), op. cit., Grover (1998), op. cit.

The history of corporate venture capital is characterized by strong ups-and-downs that have followed the overall venture capital industry in an exaggerated manner.[318] Corporate venture capital initiatives usually combine financial and strategic motives that are often ill defined. In the late 1960s, companies such as General Electric, Ford, and Exxon, set up venture capital programs to pursue diversification, in the 1980s, companies were looking for 'windows on new technology', however, most of these programs did not live up to expectations and were short-lived.[319]

During the late 1990s corporate venture capital experienced its latest and most extreme boom. In 1997, 24% of all dollars committed to venture capital funds came from corporations.[320] Including direct investment programs, it was estimated that corporate venture capital controls three times as much money as independent venture capitalists do.[321] High-tech companies such as Intel, Cisco, and Microsoft, realized huge investment profits, and in 2000 Intel became the single largest venture capital investor.

A recent empirical study shows that most corporate venture capitalists invest directly (78%) and are actively involved with their investments (80%). Their strategic goals can be categorized into accelerated market entry (e.g. Microsoft), demand enhancement (e.g. Intel), and external R&D (e.g. Cisco). The strategic orientation of corporate investors gives rise to fears of expropriation and of a limitation of strategic options on the side of the startup venture. Successful programs need to be designed to take account of this issue. It seems

---

317 Section 1045 of the Internal Revenue Code, enacted as part of the Taxpayer Relief Act of 1997, which -- after lobbying by the venture capital industry – was clarified in 1998 to include investments through partnerships. Cf. Seth A. Fineberg (1998), "Congress Approves Revised Rollover Law," *Venture Capital Journal*, August 1, 1998.

318 Antje Kann (2000), "Strategic Venture Capital Investing by Corporations: A Framework for Structuring and Valuing Corporate Venture Capital Programs," *Ph.D. dissertation*, Stanford University, p. 4.

319 Banatao/Fong (2000), op. cit., p. 308. Cf. Thomas Hellmann (1998b), "Some Thoughts on the Theory of Corporate Venture Investing," *Corporate Governance Today*, Columbia Law School, May 1998: 37-43.

320 Venture Economics. Kingley (1999), op. cit.

321 Brian E. Taptich (1998), "The New Startup," *Red Herring*, October, 1998, available at URL: http://www.redherring.com, retrieved: August 6, 1999.

advisable for corporations to structure their early stage investment as direct investments if market entry is the goal or if R&D is the goal and the venture has strong enough intellectual property rights not to fear expropriation. Indirect investment should be preferred if demand enhancement is the objective or if R&D is the objective but the venture's formal IP protection is weak.[322]

However, the volatility of corporate venture capital volumes suggests that the bulk of it is opportunistic, financially motivated investment that makes use of the fact that corporations can easily increase the value of complementary startups during boom times. As one corporate investor states, "if we increase the entrepreneurial firm's valuation by placing a large order, why wouldn't we want to participate in the financial upside?"[323] As the investment climate cools down and corporations face earnings pressure, they sharply reign in these venture investment programs. Empirical analysis shows that in particular purely financially motivated programs cannot sustain industry downturns and are more short-lived that strategically motivated initiatives.[324] A case in point is Apple's strategic investment group that was discontinued in the 1980s due to a lack of strategic focus, despite excellent financial returns. However, financially oriented corporate programs are also less tolerant of market downturns than the independent venture capital firms whose partnership structure isolates them somewhat from the swings of public equity markets. Moreover, they are usually less profitable, because corporate venture capitalists invest in startups at valuations that are some 20% higher than in the case of their independent counterparts.[325]

---

[322] Kann (2000), op. cit, pp. 14, 91, 105, 139-145.

[323] Ibid., p. 25.

[324] Paul A. Gompers and Joshua Lerner (1998b), "The Determinants of Corporate Venture Capital Success: Organizational Structure, Incentives, and Complementarities," *NBER Working Paper*, No. 6725, September 1998.

[325] Gompers/Lerner (1998b), op. cit., p. 29.

The diversity of corporate venture capital programs implies that some are in direct competition to independent venture capitalists, while others are complementary. If corporations decide to strategically 'outsource' business development and R&D through venture capital investing, the overall venture capital industry grows and benefits. On the other hand, the fickle nature of opportunistic corporate venture capital drives up startup valuations during boom times, exacerbates valuation cycles and thereby reduces investment returns.

Chapter 7. Venture Capital-backed Startups in Silicon Valley

Following the description of key characteristics of Silicon Valley's regional economy and of the functioning of the professional venture capital firms that finance startups, this chapter analyses the organization of startup companies in Silicon Valley. The analysis applies the comparative corporate governance framework developed in chapter four and is guided by the research issues identified there, which can be grouped into the areas as of initiation, resource gathering (financing and human resources), market strategy, and professionalization.

7. 1. Initiation

We can think of the initiation of a venture capital-backed startup company as a two-step process. First, an individual or group of individuals decides to start a business and to seek venture capital financing. Second, a venture capitalist agrees to finance the business.

As a rule of thumb, only a business that can be expected to achieve revenues of some $50 million after five years and offers its investors an expected rate of return of some 50-70% (approximately 10 times payback) within a time horizon of some five to seven years is suited for venture capital finance.[326] These requirements (high hurdle rate and sizable investment volume) limit startup venture capital financing to businesses that offer the prospect of transforming several million dollars of initial investment into some hundred million dollar of corporate value within a few years. Consequently, few startup companies are suited for venture capital and venture capitalists are highly selective, funding only about one percent of the investment proposals they receive. Studies show that the venture capitalist' due diligence process consists of an evaluation of people (execution skill), product (technology, patents, production), market (size, growth, competition), and financial factors (valuation, capital requirement). The investment decision is usually regarded as a non-compensatory decision process.[327] Human capital evaluation is a major element of the analysis and typically involves a very time-intensive examination of the startup's incumbent management. Geoffrey Smart finds that venture capitalists spend a mean of 120 hours on human capital evaluation and his survey documents a large variety of more or less systematic approaches that are being applied by venture capitalists to evaluate human capital. These range from the 'art critic' type of VC who judges quickly and intuitively to the 'airline captain' VC who aims for an objective evaluation using systematic checklists.[328] Venture capitalists usually do not want to compromise in this area and good management is regarded as essential for success. However, Smart's study shows that many early-stage venture capitalists take a different approach. They focus on promising technologies and markets, accept founders who possess some critical resource but are not experienced managers, and regard the need to upgrade management as the company grows as inevitable.[329] Therefore, founders are not necessarily expected to be managers. Rather than focusing on the evaluation of one dominant founder, the

---

[326] Daunt (1997), op. cit., p. 11. Russell Siegelman (1998), "Venture Capital 101," *Mimeo.*

[327] I. C. MacMillan, L. Zemann, and P. N. Subba Narasimha (1987), "Criteria distinguishing successful from unsuccessful Ventures in the Venture Screening Process," *Journal of Business Venturing*, 2: 123-137.

[328] Geoffrey H. Smart (1998), *Management Assessment Methods in Venture Capital: Toward a Theory of Human Capital Valuation*, Ph.D. dissertation, Claremont Graduate University, p. 133.

[329] Banatao/Fong (2000), op. cit., pp. 298-304.

complementarity of the different members in the founding team is emphasized.[330] Venture capitalists either make their funding contingent on bringing in professional management, or they accept the risk of having to change the management team later on. Well connected early-stage venture capitalists can afford to be less scrutinizing because they can quickly gather information on the management's performance and are able to find rapid replacement if necessary.[331] Apple, Cisco, and Yahoo are prominent examples of venture capital financed startups that have been initiated by inexperienced founders who were soon replaced or complemented by experienced executives.[332]

The objective of a startup is to create corporate value by commercializing a technology or business concept by means of building a business organization. Therefore we can analytically distinguish the realization of a technology/business concept, organization building, or the creation of financial value as possible motivations. Indeed, empirical observations suggest that there is a wide variety of reasons for people to initiate a startup venture. Among these, the 'technology implementer', the 'human capitalist', and the 'organization builder' can be identified as stylized types of initiators that can be frequently observed in Silicon Valley.

The *'technology implementer'* comes from a technical background. He has made some invention or discovered some new application of a technology that he wants to see put into practice. His goal is not necessarily to set up a company; he would be willing to have an existing company implement his technology. From the venture capitalists perspective, this type of initiator is only financable if the commercialization of his technology – the technology represents the critical resource – is extremely promising and the technical knowledge of the initiator can be complemented with professional management.

---

[330] Homa Bahrami and Stuart Evans (2000), "Flexible Recycling and High-Tech Entrepreneurship," Martin Kenney (ed.), *Understanding Silicon Valley*, Stanford: Stanford University Press: 165-189, p. 174.

Examples for this type of initiation include Apple Computer and Silicon Graphics. Both companies were started because existing companies were not willing to commercialize the technology. Apple is technically an Hewlett-Packard offspring, because its founder, Stephen Wozniak, worked as an HP engineer in the 1970s and used the company's accessible spare parts to build the Apple I personal computer. When he showed his creation to Hewlett, he couldn't get him interested in manufacturing it. Therefore he and Jobs set up Apple with venture capital funding from venture capitalist Arthur Rock and brought in professional management.[333] In the case of Silicon Graphics, Jim Clark first tried to license the 3-D imaging technology that he developed at Stanford, but existing companies were unwilling to commercialize it.[334]

The *'human capitalist'* is a highly successful industry specialist in an executive position. He feels that he does not obtain an adequate share of the corporate value that he creates or he is discontent with his superiors and decides to break out on his own. From the venture capitalists perspective, this type is most attractive because the initiator's industry insight and leadership experience let expect a sound business concept and good execution skills.[335] This group of people includes 'serial entrepreneurs' who have started a venture before.

Many companies in the semiconductor industry have been established this way. Robert Noyce and Gordon Moore were senior executives at Fairchild semiconductors but did not have a stake in the company.[336] Annoyed by the frequent management turnover at Fairchild,

---

[331] Smart (1998), op. cit., p. 138. Steven N. Kaplan, and Per Strömberg (2000), "How Do Venture Capitalists Choose Investments?" *Mimeo*, August 2000, University of Chicago.
[332] Cf. Rich Karlgaard (1997), "Present at Creation," *Forbes*, July 1997.
[333] David Jacobsen (1998), "Founding Fathers," *Stanford Magazine*, July/August 1998. Arthur Rock (1992), "Strategy vs. Tactics from a Venture Capitalist," Sahlman, William A., and Stevenson, Howard H. (eds.), *The Entrepreneurial Venture*, Boston: Harvard Business School Publications: 215-221. Tajnai, (1996), op. cit.
[334] Tajnai (1996), op. cit., p. 10.
[335] Banatao/Fong (2000), op. cit., p. 303.
[336] Kenney/Florida (2000), op. cit., p. 111.

they decided to leave the company and set up Intel with venture capital financing.[337] Some observers suggest that they also took some intellectual property from Fairchild.[338] Moore comments with regard to this type of startup: "that was a time period where it seems like every new idea that came along spawned one to five new companies. It really was the period of time when the 'silicon valley effect' of all the spin-offs really blossomed."[339] Examples of successful 'serial entrepreneurs' are Jim Clark or Dr. Pehong Chen who founded both Gain Technology and Broadvision.[340]

As a variety of the above type, we can identify the 'excluded human capitalist' in order to refer to the many immigrant entrepreneurs. Almost a quarter of Silicon Valley high-technology firms are started by Chinese and Indians.[341] Saxenian argues that part of the reason for this high share is that immigrants experience glass ceilings in existing organizations and therefore choose to start their own companies.[342] Another variety could be labeled 'opportunistic human capitalist' referring to the 'get-rich-quick' crowd of people who are attracted to entrepreneurship only in boom times.[343]

---

337 Moore (1995), op. cit.

338 Lester C. Hogan (1995), "Interview with Lester C. Hogan," *Silicon Valley Project*, Stanford University Libraries, available at URL: http;//www-sul.Stanford.edu/depts./hasrg/histsci/silicon genesis/hogan-ntb.html, retrieved: November 20, 2000. Federico Faggin (1995), "Interview with Federico Faggin," *Silicon Valley Project*, Stanford University Libraries, available at URL: http;//www-sul.Stanford.edu/depts./hasrg/histsci/silicon genesis/faggin-ntb.html, retrieved: November 20, 2000. Marcian Hoff (1995), "Interview with Marcian (Ted) Hoff," *Silicon Valley Project*, Stanford University Libraries. Available at URL: http;//www-sul.Stanford.edu/depts./hasrg/histsci/silicon genesis/hoff-ntb.html, retrieved: November 20, 2000.

339 Moore (1995), op. cit.

340 Banatao/Fong (2000), op. cit. p. 303.

341 Saxenian (1999b), op. cit.

342 Annalee Saxenian (1998), "Reflections of Silicon Valley and the American Economic Renaissance: Lessons Learned and Myths Dispelled," Keynote Address presented at the Conference "What We Can Learn from Silicon Valley" June 9, 1998 at the U.S. Embassy in Stockholm, available at URL: http://www.usemb.se/Silicon, retrieved November 20, 2000.

343 Anthony B. Perkins (2000), "Can the market get any uglier?" *Red Herring*, December 6, 2000, available at URL: http://www.redherring.com, retrieved December 6, 2000.

The absence of covenants not to compete under Californian law makes it easier for 'human capitalists' to initiate a business than in other parts of the country and at the same time makes it harder for companies to protect their trade secrets and critical information assets.[344]

The *'organization builder'* is an industry professional who wants to build an organization that suits his own values, or an executive that wants to build and lead an organization according to his concept of leadership. From the venture capitalist's perspective this type of initiator is only attractive if the content of the business is promising, and the initiator has sufficient leadership experience. A certain counterculture orientation has always been part of Silicon Valley and many companies emphasize their distinctive corporate culture. An example of a founder who stressed the wish to build an organization as main intention for starting his company is Federico Faggin who was a senior R&D executive at Intel. He left to found Zilog because Intel "was getting too big for [his] taste" and he wanted to work in an environment that was more "to [his] liking." [345]

Regardless of the founder's initial motivation, his business proposal will only be able to obtain funding if he possesses some valuable critical resource. Figure 16 shows the social network formed by the founders of the semiconductor industry in Silicon Valley. Each point (node) stands for a person and each line (tie) connects two people who co-founded a company. Each person in the network is connected to four others on average. The remarkable network density that characterizes the evolution of Silicon Valley suggests that the critical resource is typically leadership experience going along with industry expertise and the knowledge of a new niche business opportunity that arises from some new technology and lies outside the focus of existing companies.[346]

---

[344] Miller (2000), op. cit. Gilson (1999), op. cit.
[345] Faggin (1995), op. cit.
[346] Castilla/Hwang/Granovetter/Granovetter (2000), op. cit., p. 223.

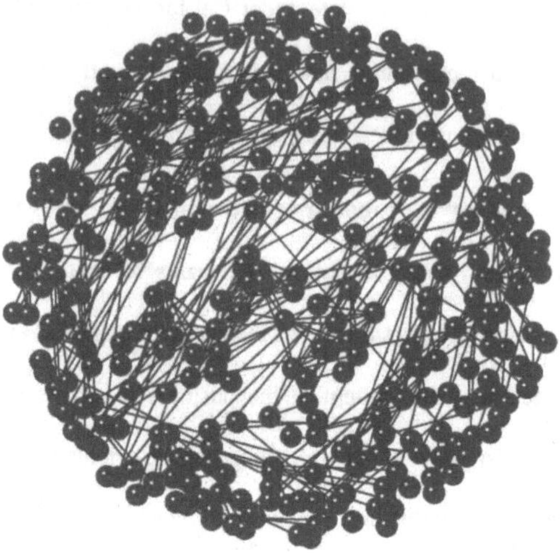

Figure 16: The Founders of the Semiconductor Industry[347]

The critical resource can be regarded as an information asset possessed by the initiator. As such it is hard to protect, unless the founder holds intellectual property rights (patent protection) to it, or its application requires extremely deep knowledge that makes the information almost inalienable ('rocket science').[348] However, more commonly the critical resource is just a piece of information that is hard to protect, and in fact, seizing the opportunity and building a business around it is the only way to realize its value. When seeking startup funding, the initiator needs to expose his critical resource to the venture

[347] Ibid., p. 228.

[348] Cf. for the role of 'star scientists' in the biotechnology industry, Lynne G. Zucker and Michael R. Darby (1996), "Star Scientists and Institutional Transformation: Patterns of Invention and Innovation in the Formation of the Biotechnology Industry," Paper presented at a colloquium entitled "Science, Technology, and the Economy," organized by Ariel Pakes and Kenneth L. Sokoloff, held October 20-22, 1995, at the National Academy of Sciences in Irvine, CA. Proc. Natl. Acad. Sci. USA, Vol. 93, November 1996: 12706-12716. Lynne G. Zucker, Michael R. Darby and Maximo Torero (1997), "Labor Mobility from Academe to Commerce," *NBER Working Paper*, No. 6050, May 1997, Cambridge, Mass.: NBER. Lynne G. Zucker, Michael R. Darby, and Marilynn B. Brewer (1996), "Intellectual Human Capital and the Birth of U.S Biotechnology Enterprises," *Mimeo*, forthcoming in the American Economic Review.

capitalist.[349] Consequently, only initiators that do not have to fear expropriation (e.g because they hold patents or are rocket scientists), or those who are sure that they are the best people to execute the business (experienced executives), will have reasonable cause to seek venture capital financing.

7. 2. Financing

Startup companies that plan to raise venture capital usually incorporate as C (or normal) corporations. The corporation forms a legal entity that is separate from the people who own and run it. Its shareholders elect a Board of Directors, which governs the corporation and appoints its officers. The shareholders' liability for corporate obligations is generally limited to the investment in their shares. Corporations can issue different classes of stock with different rights. With the incorporation, common stock is issued to the founders at a nominal price or a valuation set in correspondence with property contributed in exchange for the stock. In order to raise funds from outsiders, the corporation creates a two-tiered capital structure of common and preferred stock. Venture capitalists invest in a startup venture by purchasing preferred stock that is higher priced than common stock but comes with a number of preferences, covenants and special rights attached (see Table 4 and Table 5).[350] These provisions as well as the number and price of shares to be offered are specified in the financing contract or term sheet ('memorandum of terms of private placement of equity securities').[351] The term sheet serves as the basis for the fundraising negotiation between the company and the venture capitalist. The main negotiation item is the company's valuation and

[349] Alex Gove (1999c), "Full Disclosure," *Red Herring*, August 11, 1999, available at URL: http://www.redherring.com, retrieved: November 8, 1999.

[350] Daunt (1997), op. cit., pp. 6-7.

[351] See Appendix for a sample term sheet prepared by law firm Wilson Sonsini Rodrich Rosati.

the amount of investment, as this determines how much dilution the holders of founders' stock[352] have to accept.

Preferred Stock Characteristics

Dividend Preference	Most preferred stock is given a dividend preference over the common stock. There are two types of dividend preferences. A "when, as if declared, noncumulative" dividend preference means that the company cannot declare dividends on the common stock until a specified dividend is paid on the preferred stock. By contrast, a "mandatory, cumulative" dividend preference is more like an interest provision, since it requires the company to set aside dividends and pay dividends on the preferred stock at a designated rate. Most high tech companies adopt the first-mentioned provision and do not pay dividends.
Liquidation Preference	Upon liquidation of the company, the preferred stock has the right to receive a fixed dollar amount before any assets can be distributed to the holders of common stock. Typically, the liquidation preference is the purchase price plus accrued but unpaid dividends. A "participating" preferred stock also participates with the common stock in the distribution of any assets left after payment of the liquidation preference. In addition to actual liquidations, venture capitalists frequently want to receive their liquidation preference on a company merger. This provision will give the preferred shareholders the right to receive at least their original investment back in the event of a merger.
Redemption	There are two kinds of redemption provisions. An "optional" redemption provision lets the company repurchase or redeem the stock at its purchase price plus a redemption premium. The company can thus force the preferred stock to convert to common stock or face redemption. A "mandatory" redemption provision lets the investors require the company to repurchase the investors' preferred stock at its purchase price plus a redemption premium. Although disliked by companies, it gives investors the right to recover their initial investment, plus a profit, if the company fails to meet expectations.
Conversion Rights	Preferred stock issued in venture financings is almost always convertible into common stock at the holder's option. There is also a provision for automatic conversion upon the initial public offering of the company's stock. As a mechanism to encourage investors to support the company when it is forced to raise money at a lower price than its previous round, there may be a provision that automatically converts preferred stock to common if the holder declines to purchase his or her pro rata share of a lower priced offering. Typically, the preferred stock will be initially convertible on a one-by-one ratio.
Antidilution Protection	Convertible preferred stock always contains provisions protecting it against dilution from stock splits and stock dividends sometimes called "event protection." Moreover, there frequently are provisions protecting it against future sales of stock at lower prices, called "price protection." The most common price protection and that most favorable to the founder is a "weighted average" adjustment of the conversion price. The weighted average formula adjusts the conversion price by means of a weighted formula based upon both the sale price and number of shares sold. By contrast, some investors insist on "ratchet" antidilution protection, which drops the conversion price to the most recent lower price at which stock was sold, regardless of how many shares were sold at that price. This protects investors who decline to participate in lower priced offerings.
Voting Rights	Preferred stock typically votes with the common stock, on an "as if converted" into common stock basis. In addition, the preferred stock may be given the right to elect a certain number of directors to the company's Board of Directors, with the common stock electing the remainder.

Table 4: Legal Provisions in a Typical First Round Financing (I)[353]

---

[352] The term 'founders' stock' is used in a loose way, as there is no legal significance to being a founder. Founders' stock is the same as common stock purchased by employees who join later, however as the first

These innovative legal provisions specified in the financing contract evolved to become industry conventions. They trace their roots to early financings in the semiconductor industry and were shaped by Silicon Valley lawyers such as John Wilson. Before the development of venture capital, firms such as Shockley and Fairchild Semiconductors, had to turn to corporate investors for funding. These financing arrangements often failed to reflect the founders' contribution to the development of the company and caused successful companies to break apart.[354] Nowadays, room for negotiation in financing agreements is usually limited to a few specific issues concerning the design of antidilution protection, redemption provisions, dividend policy, and covenants regarding postfinancing management.

Special Rights, Covenants, and other Provisions	
Registration Rights	Registration rights give the investors the right to require the company to go public and register its shares with the SEC. These registriation rights are called "demand rights." The investor may also have the right to require the company to register their shares with the SEC when the company decides to go public. These rights are referred to as "piggyback rights."
Lock-up	Investors usually agree to a lock-up of 180 days after the closing of the IPO.
Information Rights	Affirmative covenants require the company to provide the investors with ongoing financial information and access to the company's records and management and may grant the investors the right to board representation.
Right of First Refusal	Typically, these provisions will give the investors the right to buy their proportionate share of any new stock offerings for a specified period. This right terminates upon a public offering.
Co-Sale Agreement	A co-sale agreement gives the investor the right to participate in any proposed sale of the founder's stock to third parties. Thereby, investors prevent that founders "cash out" without giving the investors the same opportunity.
Vesting Schedules and Buy Back Rights	Because founders buy their common stock at a cheaper price than investors buy preferred stock, they should "earn" their stock over a four year "vesting" period. A typical vesting arrangement might provide that no shares vest for the first year of employment, 25 percent of the share vest at the end of that year, with two percent of the shares vesting monthly thereafter. Since there is a risk of job loss in an acquisition, some vesting arrangements accelerate vesting by 12 month if the company is acquired. The company retains the right to repurchase an employee's unvested shares at the original purchase price on termination of employment.

Table 5: Legal Provisions in a Typical First Round Financing (II)[355]

stock being sold, it is usually sold at a much lower price and sometimes on more favorable vesting terms.

353 Adapted from Daunt (1997), op. cit., pp. 14-16.

354 Kenney/Florida (2000), op. cit., p.111.

355 Adapted from Daunt (1997), op. cit., pp. 16-17.

Far reaching provisions are included to give the venture capitalists the legal basis for the monitoring and control exercised in the post-financing phase. The financing contract gives the investor substantial control rights, including the right to dismiss the founder and have the company buy back the founder's non-vested shares at cost. These arrangements help to alleviate the adverse selection problem of precontractual opportunism, and separate the 'people risk' from the 'business risk'.

The board of directors of a startup company has typically not more than five members - the CEO, one or two investor representatives, one or two outside directors with relevant experience and possibly one of the non-CEO founders. There is a clear empirical relationship between venture capital financing and a board structure dominated by outsiders.[356]

Another characteristic of financing arrangements is the staged capital commitment. As startup companies accomplish certain milestones in their development (e.g. successful prototype, first customer, senior executive hire, etc.) they reduce risks and thereby increase their value. Accordingly, venture capital investments in seed and startup stage companies have a much higher risk-return profile than later stage investments. (See Figure 17.)

Venture capitalists make investments in stages and supply the finance needed in order to achieve such a step-up in the startup company's valuation. However, they do not provide all the capital that the company needs in order to become a going-concern at once. Thereby they reduce their exposure to any single project and force the company to come back periodically and convince investors of its virtue. At each stage, the company usually brings in additional investors, while the existing investors make a pro-rata follow-on investment. Stage financing and syndication leads to a regular evaluation by outsiders that prevents inefficient continuation and reduces hold up problems for both company and investor (the company can bring in another investor and get a 'fair market' valuation, the investor can abandon the project).[357] Control rights, board representation, as well as the threat of hold-up that comes with stage financing implies that venture capitalists can control both business strategy and personnel appointments in the startup venture.

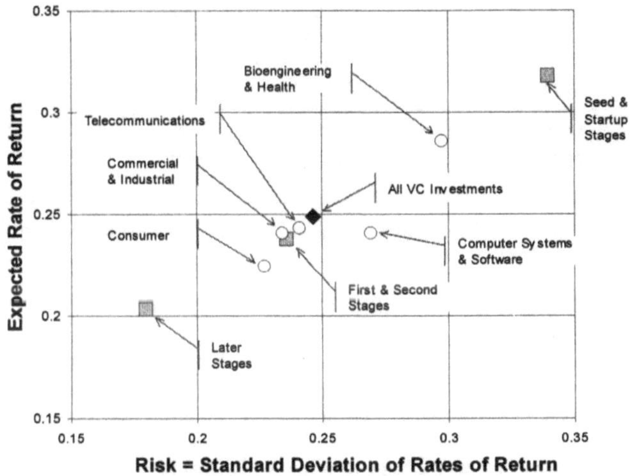

Figure 17: Venture Capital Risk-Return Profile by Stage and Industry[358]

Following is an example of a step-financing scenario that could apply to a highly successful startup venture. It involves a first round of financing from angel or seed venture capital investors, and two further rounds from professional venture capitalists. It shows that by raising capital in different rounds at increasing valuations of the company, the founders can make sure to retain a significant share while committing only a nominal amount of cash. (See Table 6.)

---

[356] Malcolm Baker and Paul A. Gompers (2000), "The Determinants of Board Structure and Function at the Initial Public Offering," *Mimeo*, Harvard University, June 2000.

[357] Cf. Anat R. Admati, and Paul Pfleiderer (1994), "Robust Financial Contracting and the Role of Venture Capitalists," *Journal of Finance*, 49: 371-402. Malcolm Baker (2000), "Career Concerns and Staged Investment: Evidence from the Venture Capital Industry," *Mimeo*, Harvard University, July 2000. Oliver Hart and John Moore (1994), "A Theory of Debt Based on the Inalienability of Human Capital," *Quarterly Journal of Economics*, Vol. 109, Issue 4, Nov. 1994: 841-879.

Shareholders	No. Shares	Purchase Price	Dollars Invested	Ownership % at Investment	Step-up	Company Valuation	Ownership % at IPO
Founders (Common)	2,500,000	$.01	$25,000	100%		$25,000	23%
Angel Investors (Preferred)	500,000	.20	$100,000	17%	20	$600,000	5%
Round I VC (Preferred)	2,000,000	1.00	$2,000,000	40%	5	$5,000,000	18%
Employees (Common)	1,000,000	.10	$100,000	17%		$6,000,000	9%
Round II VC (Preferred)	3,000,000	2.50	$7,500,000	33%	2.5	$22,500,000	27%
Employees (Common)	1,000,000	.25	$250,000	10%		$25,000,000	9%
Public (Common)	1,000,000	13.00	$13,000,000	9%	5.2	$143,000,000	9%
Total	11,000,000		$22,975,000				100%

Table 6: Financing Scenario of a Highly Successful Startup[359]

In cases of seed financing as illustrated in the above example, the commitment of capital by the founder-entrepreneur is typically only nominal. By raising just enough funds to run the company up to the next milestone that allows for a higher valuation in the next financing round, the entrepreneur can manage to keep a significant ownership share. However, the share that founders are able to retain, depends on how the smoothly this step-wise increase in the company's valuation proceeds. This is illustrated by a comparison of founder ownership at IPO for the four U.S. net directory companies that went public in the 1990s. The founders of Lycos were holding 10 %, the founders of Excite 11%, while in the case of Infoseek they held 27%, and in the case of Yahoo even 34 %. These differences are to a large part due to differences in the founders' bargaining power and financing strategy. If a company gets

[358] Brophy (1996), op. cit., p. 49, based on survey data from Plummer (1987), op. cit.

[359] Daunt (1997), op. cit., p. 22, modified. Step-up refers to the ratio of pre-money valuation over post-money valuation of the previous financing round.

launched with a lot of money early on, step-ups in valuation are harder to realize and the ownership of the entrepreneur may decrease rapidly.[360]

The ability of a would-be entrepreneur to start a company contingent on the seed funding by a venture capitalist means that he does not have to assume the function and financial risk of a capitalist. By getting his share in the company almost for free, and making it subject to vesting schedules, the entrepreneur holds a residual cash flow claim that is contingent on him contributing to and remaining with the company. The ownership thus earned is often referred to as 'sweat equity'. By allocating extensive control rights to the venture capitalist, the financing contract separates the control and the cash flow aspect of ownership.

7. 3. Human Resources

Human resource management in Silicon Valley technology startups has been the subject of detailed empirical analysis as part of the Stanford Project on Emerging Companies.[361] This ongoing panel study of more than 170 young technology firms in the region has found a remarkable variety in employment models in this seemingly homogeneous group of high-tech firms.[362] When starting their businesses, founders embrace quite distinct organizational blueprints that differ with regard to the criteria of employee selection, the basis of employees'

---

[360] Anthony B. Perkins (1996), "You too can be a Winner!" Red Herring, June 1996, available at URL: http://www.redherring.com, retrieved October 18, 1998. Gompers (1999), op. cit., p. 217 and Sahlman (1990), op. cit., table 4 present stage financing examples, including cases of 'downrounds.'

[361] Cf. M. Diane Burton (1995), "The Evolution of Employment Systems in High Technology Firms," Ph.D. dissertation, Stanford University. Michael T. Hannan, M. Diane Burton and James N. Baron (1996), "Inertia and Change in the Early Years: Employment Relations in Young, High-Technology Firms," *Industrial and Corporate Change*, Vol. 5, 503-535. James N. Baron, M. Diane Burton, and Michael T. Hannan (1996), "The Road Taken: Origins and Evolution of Employment Systems in Emerging Companies," *Industrial and Corporate Change*, Vol. 5, No. 2, 239-275. James N. Baron, M. Diane Burton, and Michael T. Hannan (1998), "Engineering Bureaucracy: The Genesis of Formal Policies, Positions, and Structures in High-Technology Firms," *Industrial and Corporate Change*, Vol. 5, No. 2: 239-275. James N. Baron, M. Diane Burton, and Michael T. Hannan (1999), "Building the Iron Cage: Determinants of Managerial Intensity in the Early Years of Organizations," *Working Paper*, Stanford University, April 1999. James N. Baron, Michael T. Hannan, and M. Diane Burton (1999). "Labor Pains: Organizational Change and Employee Turnover in Young, High-Tech Firms." *Mimeo*, June 7, 1999.

[362] Burton (1995), op. cit., p. 152.

attachment to the firm, and the means of control and coordination within the organization. Along the lines of these three core dimensions, five basic types of employment models have been identified (see Table 7).

Employment Model	**Core Dimensions**		
	Basis of Attachment & Retention -Compensation ("money") -Qualities of the work ("work") -Work group as community ("love")	**Criterion for Selection** -Skills -Exceptional talent/potential -Fit with the team or organization	**Means of Control & Coordination** -Direct monitoring -Peer and/or cultural control -Reliance on professional standards -Formal processes and procedures
-Star	Work	Potential	Professional
-Engineering	Work	Skills	Peer/Cultural
-Commitment	Love	Fit	Peer/Cultural
-Bureaucracy	Work	Skills	Formal
-Autocracy or Direct Control	Money	Skills	Direct

Table 7: HR Models in Young Silicon Valley Technology Companies[363]

A majority of firms can be classified into one of these ideal-type models. The study also examined whether there is a relationship between venture capital funding and the organizational blueprints that founders adopt. Table 8 provides the descriptive statistics.

Venture Financing	Autocracy	Commitment	Star	Engineering	Bureaucracy	Hybrid	Total
	Founder's Organizational Model						
-None as of 1994-5	4	10	5	13	1	14	47
-Received within first two years	3	6	8	30	8	24	79
-Received after 2+ years	2	4	1	5	0	8	20
Total	9	20	14	48	9	46	146

Table 8: Founder's HR Model and Venture Capital Financing (No. of companies)[364]

Companies that receive venture capital early in their development are less likely to follow the 'commitment' model and somewhat more likely to adopt the 'bureaucracy' model. The 'star' and 'engineering' models are also frequently observed with venture capital funding. However, venture capital financing does not appear to reduce organizational diversity very

[363] Stanford Project on Emerging Companies, various publications, see fn. 361.
[364] Baron/Burton/Hannan (1998), op. cit., p. 58.

significantly. Baron et al. conclude, "having an early relationship with a venture capital firm was hardly determinative of the founder's organizational blueprint. [...] Rather, the influence of venture capitalists seemed to be confined to the realm of formal structures and policies."[365]

Some formal policies and practices in human resource management, such as the grant of stock options and the use of vesting schedules are prevailing standard in venture capital financed firms. The practice of giving stock options to employees goes far back in Silicon Valley history and local executives stress its importance.[366] Intel co-founder and EVP, Leslie L. Vadasz stresses the need to tie compensation to the success of the company as a way of balancing knowledge power and hierarchical power and rewarding cooperation.[367] Recent studies document the large share of equity-linked compensation (see Table 9).

Position	Base Salary ($000)	Bonus ($000)	Total ($000)	Average equity holdings (%)	Founder status
CEO	178	72	250	13.5%	65%
COO	152	53	205	8.1%	52%
CFO	143	40	183	2.3%	15%
CTO	147	48	195	4.5%	36%
Engineering	143	38	181	1.9%	24%
Marketing	140	46	186	1.7%	13%
Sales	148	54	202	1.6%	6%
Business Development	134	62	196	2.5%	25%
Human Resources	95	23	118	0.5%	8%

Table 9: Compensation in Venture Capital-backed Startups[368]

Employment contracts in California are peculiar for their absence of covenants not to compete. This increases the fluidity of the labor market. High fluidity in the labor market is a

---

[365] Ibid., p. 32.

[366] E. Floyd Kvamme (2000), "Life in Silicon Valley," Lee, Chong-Moon, Miller, William F., Gong Hancock, Marguerite, Rowen, Henry S. (eds.), *The Silicon Valley Edge*, Stanford: Stanford University Press: 59-80, p. 60.

[367] World Economic Forum (2001), "Talent Strategies for the New Economy," 2001 Annual Meeting, Session summary, available at URL: http://www.weforum.org, retrieved: January 30, 2001.

long-standing characteristic of Silicon Valley that goes along with the highly specialized but portable nature of skills in the semiconductor area.[369] Stock options that become exercisable according to a vesting schedule can be regarded as a bonding mechanism that ties employees to the firm and thereby induces their investment in firm-specific human capital. On the other hand, the Silicon Valley clustering of firms in the same industries has the effect of making even specialized skills portable. Therefore, in a sense, people are 'working for the valley' rather than for any particular company.[370] More than fixed compensation, stock options are used as the 'currency' in compensation negotiations and allow key employees to capture a share of the corporate value that is being created through their work. This leads to legally rather sophisticated employment contracts and frequent renegotiations. (See Appendix for an example employment contract.)

7. 4. Market Strategy

By accepting venture capital financing and thereby relegating control to outside investors, the creation of corporate value is adopted as the paramount goal of corporate strategy. This is reflected in the position of the founder who settles into the role of a professional, and accepts the risk of loosing his position and his ownership stake. While investors are involved in setting the strategic direction of the company, day-to-day execution is performed by management. Staged capital commitments that are tied to the arrival of new information about product development, market acceptance, competition, execution capability, preserve

---

[368] Data for 2000, based on a survey of over 1000 executives in 211 private companies in Hale & Dorr, Ernst & Young, and J. Robert Scott (2001), *2001 Internet Compensation Report*, available at http://www.compstudy.com, retrieved March 6, 2001. Cf. Po Bronson (1999), "Gen Equity." *Wired Digital Archive*, July 1999, available at URL: http://www.wired.com, retrieved August 11th, 1999. Edward O. Welles (1999), "In Search of Equity," *Inc.*, 20th Anniversary Issue: 145-146. Lisa K. Meulbroek (2000), "The Efficiency of Equity-Linked Compensation: Understanding the Full Cost of Awarding Executive Stock Options," *Working Paper*, Harvard University.

[369] Kenney/von Burg (1999), op. cit, p. 83.

[370] Hogan (1995), op. cit.

the venture capitalist's option to abandon or invest further. A thorough strategy reassessment takes place with each new financing round.

Market strategies of startup ventures are highly experimental.[371] As Gordon Moore formulates, "when you're a startup company you have to bet the company on a lot of the programs you do. When you get bigger you only want to bet half the company if you can do that."[372] Since venture companies adopt extremely experimental strategies, which can turn out to be misled, some ventures get aborted even before their resources are exhausted, and what is left of money in the bank is being returned to investors.[373]

Most Silicon Valley startups are technology companies that commercialize some cutting-edge technology. An innovative local customer base is an important benefit to these firms. Moreover, insiders stress the importance of informal talk even between competitors.[374] On the other hand there are only few examples of successful consumer companies in Silicon Valley (such as Apple, HP).[375] Investors typically try to define and analytically separate the different risks involved in a startup venture, such as market risk, technology/product risk, team risk, and financing risk.[376] Staged funding is then tied to the subsequent elimination of risks and a concurrent step-up in the venture valuation. Silicon Valley venture capital used to focus on financing technical risk involved in new product development with the aim of building niche monopolies based on cutting-edge technologies. However, as more funding became available, projects that involve considerable market risk, and require larger

---

[371] Thomas Hellmann and Manju Puri (1999), "The Interaction between Product Market and Financing Strategy: The Role of Venture Capital," *Working Paper*, Stanford University, Graduate School of Business, December 1999, provide empirical evidence of the interrelation between venture capital financing and 'innovator' type product market strategies.

[372] Moore (1995), op. cit.

[373] Julie Landry (2000), "Crosspoint Takes a Time Out on $1 Billion Fund," *Red Herring*, Dealflow, November 29, 2000, available at URL: http:///www.redherring.com/vc, retrieved November 29, 2000.

[374] Tajnai (1996), op. cit., p. 2.

[375] McKenna (1995), op. cit.

[376] Siegelman (1998), op. cit.

investments, because the proof of concept and elimination of risk takes place later, have received funding as well.[377]

By definition, the evolution of a startup venture into a going concern has to offer the venture capitalist a way to exit the investment. This process can follow very different paths, either involving a trade sale (M&A) or a public offering (IPO). Many startup ventures are actually better viewed as product development organizations, rather than companies. They do not strive to become viable independent economic units, but rather look to be acquired by a firm that complements their own organization, for example by providing distribution capability for a newly developed product.[378]

As outlined above, the venture capital financing arrangement typically provides the investor with the ability to influence the type of exit pursued. With regard to this decision, the venture capitalists, limited partners and company management do not always have congruent interests. Given the same valuation, a trade sale appears preferable to an initial public offering since it offers instant liquidity to investors. However, venture capitalists might value the reputation building effect of an IPO and due to the short-term overpricing phenomenon of newly listed shares, an IPO may maximize the venture capital funds internal rate of returns if an in-kind distribution of shares to the limited partners is possible. Yet, institutional investors may be unwilling to assume management responsibility for a newly issued stock that they do not follow and cannot sell because it is thinly traded.[379] Individual investors, on the other hand, may be eager to quickly receive their shares expecting to be able to sell their minor stakes easily. Management may also prefer an IPO for the sake of the prestige attached to it and the newly gained management independence that might be associated with replacing

---

[377] Kvamme (2000), op. cit., p. 77.
[378] Randy Komisar (2000), *The Monk and the Riddle*, Boston: Harvard Business School Press, p. 48.

venture capital investors with a more dispersed shareholder structure. Table 10 summarizes the different parties' considerations regarding the exit decision.

	Initial Public Offering	**Merger & Acquisition**
Venture Company Management	+ Option to regain control (by having VC replaced by dispersed shareholders) + Continuing management responsibility - Lock up and only gradual liquidity	+ Faster liquidity - Risk of loosing management responsibility
Venture Capitalist (General Partner)	+ Reputation building - Lock up and only gradual liquidity - Potential for conflict with LPs and management over distribution	+ Faster liquidity + No conflicts of interest in distribution because either cash or liquid shares are received as consideration
Institutional Investors (Limited Partners)	- In-kind distribution involves lack of instant liquidity, burden to manage the position - Performance of GP cannot be clearly evaluated because IRR looses meaning if illiquid shares are distributed	+ Faster liquidity because either cash or liquid shares of larger entity are received
Individual Investors (Limited Partners)	+ Sale of shares can be timed for tax efficiency + Small stake allows sale without driving down stock price	+ Faster liquidity

Table 10: Considerations regarding the Exit Decision

Studies have shown that venture capitalists play an important role in timing the public offering of shares. Issuing firms tend to prefer equity finance before periods of low returns and tend to shun equity, in favor of debt, before periods of high returns. That means to time the IPO market is an important managerial task, and part of venture capitalist's value added.[380]

---

[379] Standish M. Fleming (1999), "The Challenge of Distributing Thinly Traded Stocks," *Venture Capital Journal*, February 1, 1999.

[380] Malcolm Baker and Jeffrey Wurgler (2000). "The Equity Share in New Issues and Aggregate Stock Returns." *Journal of Finance*, Vol. LV, No. 5, 2219-2257. Luc Hatlestad (1999), "Diary of an Internet IPO," *Red Herring*, July 1999, available at URL: http://www.redherring.com, retrieved: July 20, 1999. Eric Moskowitz (2001), "Loudcloud sends smoke signals to IPO market," *Redherring.com*, February 21, 2001, available at URL: http://www.redherring.com, retrieved February 22, 2001. Price Waterhouse Coopers (PWC) (1999), *The Guide to Going Public*, Price Waterhouse Coopers.

7. 5. Professionalization

The strategic focus on the creation of corporate value and the control exercised by venture capitalists leads to a very rapid professionalization of startup firms. Professionalization in this context can be defined as increasing division of labor and allocation of specialialized tasks to qualified professionals. In the context of the entrepreneurial organization, the allocation of the functions initiation, coordination, and uncertainty-bearing is of particular interest. As described above, initiation is the key function performed by the founder of a startup. In addition, the founder often acts as the Chief Executive, at least during the early stages of the company's development. In this sense, he initially combines the function of initiation and coordination, before the coordinating function is assigned to specialized managers. However, there are also examples for venture capitalist-initiated startups, where venture capitalists initiate a startup company and staff it with 'founders' who are chosen for their management/execution skill. The entrepreneurial function of uncertainty-bearing in the sense of taking financial risks, is concentrated on the venture capitalists. Human resources share this risk to some extent if they accept below market fixed compensation with a large share of contingent compensation. The coordination function is usually rapidly professionalized, and management, as well as other positions, are staffed from the pool of highly specialized human resources available in the region. This feature is complementary with the specialized nature of resources and the continuous inter-firm mobility of human resources that characterizes the Silicon Valley region.[381]

Venture capitalists frequently need to intervene with management and key personnel appointment decisions. This was true for ARD, the first venture capital firm, founded in 1946 and is still the case today. In 1950, ARD founder Doriot noted "success would be attained

[381] Komisar (2000), op. cit., p. 46. Bahrami/Evans (2000), op. cit., p. 174.

more often if good idea men would entrust their ideas to good operating men"[382] and ARD had to make this happen by replacing management in several cases. Several studies indicate that venture capitalists play an active role in professionalizing human resources in startup ventures by using their control rights to actively intervene in appointment decisions. The panel study of Internet-related ventures quoted in Table 9 shows that some 35 % of CEOs in privately-held venture capital-backed companies are non-founders. The SPEC panel study finds that the likelihood of a non-founder being appointed CEO in the first 20 months of a company's life is around 10 %, after 40 months this likelihood increases to 40 % and after 80 month to over 80 %.[383] Steven Kaplan and Per Strömberg find that in more than 50% of investment situations, venture capitalists expect to change the management team with investment or expect to do so in the future.[384] Baker and Gompers examine the relationship between the venture capitalist's reputation and the likelihood of management professionalization. Their study finds that the probability that a founder remains CEO after the firm's IPO is decreasing in VC reputation. In other words, more reputable venture capitalists seem to be more active in professionalizing management.

Vesting arrangements and the control rights held and exercised by the venture capitalists, make the founder's stake in the startup contingent upon his staying with the company. In this sense the founders' share in a startup is often referred to as 'sweat equity' that has to be earned by doing a good job and staying with the company. Since ultimate control rests with the outside investors, the entrepreneur's sole incentive in this system is to increase the value of the venture and to make it attractive to the public market or a strategic investor. This arrangement has interesting implications for the attitude towards failure. In a system

---

[382] Liles (1977), op. cit., p. 69.
[383] Hannan/Burton/Baron (1996), op. cit.

characterized by value-oriented governance, the evaluation of human capital cannot be based on the success or failure of the venture. Failure becomes tolerable because observers then look at a startup as a legitimate, professionally pursued experiment that can work or go wrong. The performance of individuals cannot be judged by the performance of the venture alone, since a high, calculated technical or market risk has been consciously assumed. The close involvement of venture capitalists with the management of the firm, allows them to gain a closer insight into the performance of managers, which allows them to separate the execution and non-execution related causes for failure. There are various examples for founders who failed with one venture, and yet received funding for another project.[385]

---

[384] Kaplan/ Strömberg (2000), op. cit. Cf. Thomas Hellmann and Manju Puri (2000), "Venture Capital and the Professionalization of Startup Firms: Empirical Evidence," *Working Paper*, Stanford University, Graduate School of Business, September 2000.

[385] Miller (1998), op. cit.

III. Startup Ventures in Tokyo

Based on the research framework in Part I and its application to the analysis of the 'Silicon Valley Model' in Part II, Part III proceeds to analyze the governance of venture capital-backed startups in Tokyo.

In contrast to Silicon Valley, venture capital-backed startups are relatively new to Japan. Consequently, there are neither established ways of building these companies, nor is there a lot of information available on the few precedents. In this sense, there is no Tokyo equivalent to the 'Silicon Valley Model'. This study attempts to identify some key features of venture capital-financed startups in Tokyo and takes a snapshot of the organization of a sample of Internet-related startup ventures that were established in 1999 and 2000 and funded by professional venture capitalists. The analysis within the venture governance framework developed here allows a comparison with the established practice in Silicon Valley and the identification of key conceptual differences. Since this type of startup company has only been born recently and is rare in Japan, the research objective is accomplished through in-depth case studies based on interviews with the founders, managers, employees, and venture capital investors of a sample of venture capital-backed startups that has been observed over the period of 1999 to 2002.

The analysis of Tokyo startup ventures proceeds as follows. Chapter 8 gives an overview of some aspects of the general economic background in Japan, which are relevant to the understanding of startup ventures. Chapter 9. draws a picture of the indigenous Japanese venture capital industry contrasting it with the U.S. counterpart analyzed above and describes how providers of classic venture capital have emerged. Chapter 10. summarizes the results of the case studies of startup ventures.

Chapter 8. Economic Background

8. 1. Economic Slump and Corporate Governance Crisis

During the observation period (1999-2002), the overall economic situation in Japan and the United States was very different. The United States experienced an unprecedented economic upturn and stock market boom from the middle to the end of the 1990s, mainly driven by the information technology and Internet sector. On the other hand, the Japanese economy has been experiencing a period of prolonged economic slump and structural change since the burst of the Japanese bubble economy at the beginning of the 1990s. However, during this period of adjustment that is sometimes referred to as Japan's 'lost decade', there were several short periods of economic growth, during which the market sentiment became very bullish. In particular the period from the end of 1998 to the beginning of 2000, i.e. during the last phase of the U.S. and global IT/Internet bubble, the economic sentiment in the U.S. and Japan was aligned and both equity markets did grow in parallel until the burst of the IT/Internet bubble in early 2000 (see Figure 18).

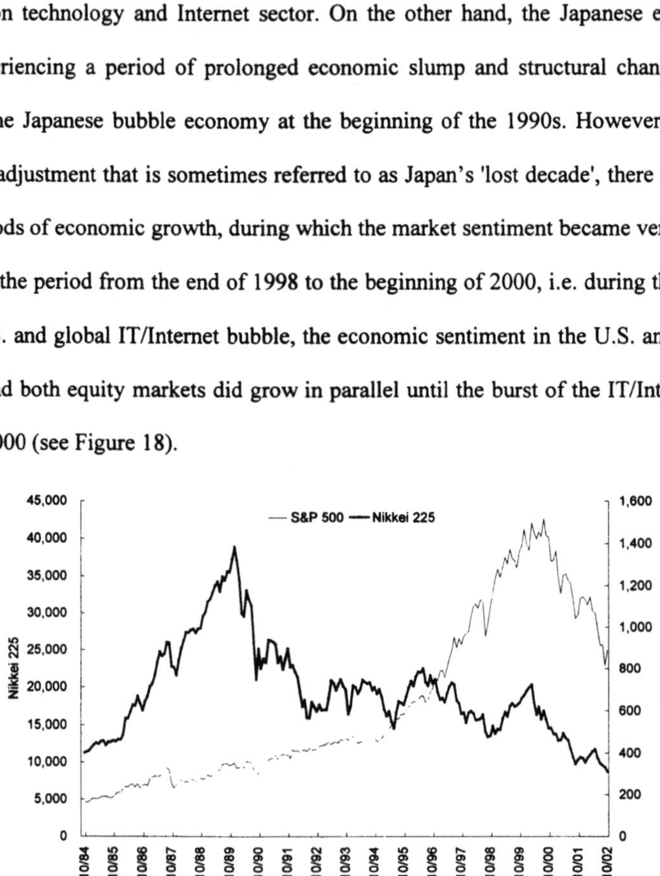

Figure 18: S&P 500 vs Nikkei 225 (1984-2002)[386]

[386] Source: Bloomberg.

At the heart of the structural recession in Japan is the breakdown of the economy's ability to allocate financial resources to areas of growth. In order to address these issues, structural policies that range from addressing the structure of households' asset holdings, to the workings of financial intermediaries and corporate governance are considered necessary and a variety of policies in this area, including the so-called Financial Big Bang deregulation,[387] are under consideration or have already been implemented.[388]

With the demise of the governance function of stakeholders such as main banks, labor-unions and the bureaucracy and the dissolution of cross-shareholding structures, large companies face the challenge of making themselves accountable to less stable shareholder's such as foreign and institutional investors.[389] Over the last several years some large corporations, for example Sony, have taken the lead in reforming their corporate governance and management structures. Corporate policies include the move to smaller and more independent boards of directors that include outside members. This goes along with a concentration of the board's function on control and strategy setting and the appointment of 'corporate executives' (Shikkoyakuin) for day-to-day management. The adoption of holding company structures and 'internal companies' aims at making different business units accountable for their results.[390]

Revisions of the Commercial Code have addressed these issues and a revision that takes effect in April 2003 will allow companies to make a choice between retaining the current

---

387 Cf. Tetsuro Toya (2000), *The Political Economy of the Japanese Financial Big Bang: Institutional Change in Finance and Public Policy Making*, Ph.D. dissertation, Stanford University.

388 MoF (2000a), "21 Seiki no Wagakunikeizai no jizokuteki Seichou wo kanou to surutame no kinyuumen no Shokadai ni tsuite," June 2000, *21 Seiki no Shikin no Nagare no Kouzouhenkaku ni kansuru Kenkyuukai*, Ministry of Finance, Japan. Katsuhiro Nakagawa (2000), "The Government's Role to Cultivate Entrepreneurs in Japan," CEO & Minister Forum at Stanford, June 1-2, 2000, prepared, unedited remarks, available at URL: http://aparc.stanford.edu/events/june2000/nakagawa/remarks.html, retrieved October 20, 2000.

389 MITI (2000a), "2001 Nen ni mukete Keizaisangyouseisaku: Aratana Keizaikouzou kaikaku wo mokushi shite," August 2000, Ministry of International Trade and Industry, Japan.

system in which companies employ a group of statutory auditors (Kansayaku) separate from the board itself or institute a U.S.-style board audit committee consisting of outside directors. Moreover, the separation of the roles of directors and corporate executives becomes legally codified, and large corporations are required to appoint at least one outside director.[391] These structures might help to restore the accountability of top management and restore shareholder's trust in the mangers' dedication to the creation of corporate value.

8. 2. Venture Business in Japan

Venture business in Japan is typically understood as a sub segment of the small and medium-sized enterprise sector with superior growth potential. Therefore, our definition of a venture, as venture capital-financed startup is more specific than the terminology commonly used in Japan. Compared with the U.S. economy, the Japanese industrial structure is heavily tilted towards SMEs in terms of number of companies and share of employment. Traditionally, a duality between large and SME enterprises has been observed in Japan, with regard to their value-added, compensation level, and business risk and therefore SME were regarded as being unable to hire the best human resources.[392] Due to their dependence on bank financing, the prolonged recession and the crisis of the financial sector affects SMEs strongly and their capital investment fell clearly below cash flow in 1999 and 2000.[393] A recent survey of technology-based venture businesses shows that the dependence on bank finance and public funds for the founders' procurement of capital applies to the venture sub segment of SMEs as

---

390 Cf. Asia/Pacific Research Center (1999), "Crisis and Aftermath: The Prospects for Institutional Change in Japan," Report of a Conference Held May 3, 1999, at Stanford University.

391 Makoto Komiyama and Yuinobu Masaoka (2002), "Corporate Governance: A New Phase for Japanese Companies." *NRI Papers*, No. 47, Nomura Research Institute. Zenichi Shisido (1999), "Japanese Corporate Governance: The Hidden Problems of the Corporate Law and Their Solutions," *Working Paper*, No. 153, Columbia Law School. Nikkei (2001a),"Shasetsu: Kigyoukachi takameru Torishimariyakukai wo tsukure," *Nikkei Shinbun*, April 18, 2001.

392 Tadao Kiyonari (1996), *Shinsangyou wo Soushitsusuru Kigyouka Shihonshugi*, Tokyo: Toyo Keizai, p. 175.

well. As such funding sources typically represent personal rather than corporate lending, the establishment of a venture business requires significant financial risk taking by the founder (see Table 11).

	Overall	Biotechnology	Internet-related
Banks	50.0%	51.7%	48.2%
Venture capital	0.7%	0.0%	1.3%
Public sources	15.8%	5.5%.	24.8%
Others	33.5%	42.8%	25.6%
Total	100.0%	100.0%	100.0%

Table 11: Sources of Funds for Japanese Venture Businesses[394]

In the case of large companies, the shift from main bank to market based governance still involves an important role for banks but also gradually recognizes a market for corporate control. Large companies diversify funding to include financial market products and move from an implicit contract with the main bank as lender of last resort to explicit arrangements such as commitment lines, small companies on the other hand even seek to strengthen their ties to main banks in the absence of other alternatives (see Figure 19).

In this system the governance of venture businesses is centered on the founder-manager and the availability of risk capital is limited. Government research panels have recognized that in order to make new sources of funds available to venture startups, a reassessment of its governance system and in particular, the relationship between founders/management and the suppliers of finance is required. [395] Stimulated by the demands of the venture capital community,[396] the Commercial Code is lately undergoing major revisions to enable tailor

---

393 METI (2002), "2002 Nenhan Chuushokigyouhakusho no pointo," April 2002, *SME Agency*, Ministry of Economy, Trade and Industry, Japan. Cf. Cornelia Storz (1997), *Der mittelständische Unternehmer in Japan*, Baden-Baden: Nomos.

394 Kiyonori Sakakibara, Tadahisa Koga, Yuji Honjo, and Kazunori Kondo (2000), *Nihon ni okeru gijutsukei Benchakigyou no Keieijittai to Sougyousha ni kansuru Chousakenkyuu*, Tokyo: National Institute of Science and Technology, Table 13.

395 MoF (2000a), op. cit.

396 Cf. Venture Business Petition for Commercial Code Changes, URL: http://www.venture-business.org/petition.html. Corporate Governance Forum of Japan (1998), "Corporate Governance Principles - A Japanese View - (Final Report)," *Mimeo*, Corporate Governance Committee, May 26, 1998.

made investment contracts and a differentiation of governance arrangements depending on whether the company is private or public and whether it expects high or low future growth rates.

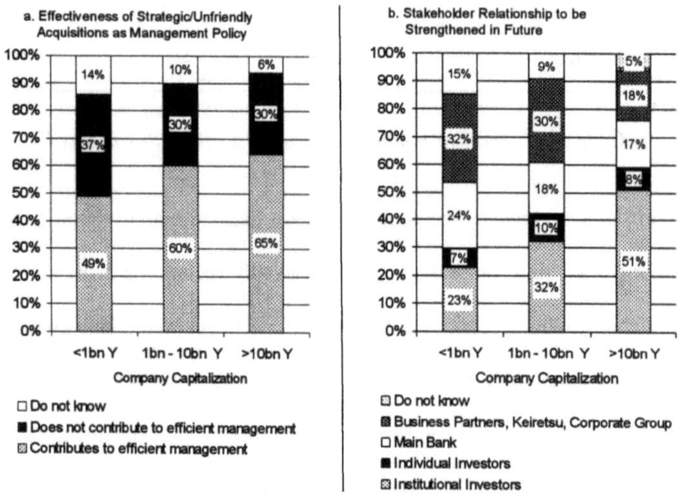

Figure 19: Governance Attitude and Policy Priorities Depending on Company Size[397]

8. 3. A New Breed of Internet Ventures

With the Internet boom in the late 1990s, a new breed of Internet ventures did emerge which realized previously unthinkable growth and creation of value. These ventures did not fit the stereotype of the 'underdog' disadvantaged venture startup that was common in Japan. Companies, such as Softbank, Rakuten, Monex, Cyberagent were established by entrepreneurs who are untypical because they are young and they did hail from career positions with large well-established companies. The sense of business opportunity created by these role models and the perceived prospects of Internet technology did give birth to a wave of interest in entrepreneurship and the 'Bitvalley' phenomenon. Bitvalley refers to Tokyo's Shibuya area that is home to a disproportionate share of its Internet-related venture companies (see Figure 20). This agglomeration in an urban area characterized by mixed business and residential use shows parallels to New York's Silicon Alley or the South of Market area of San Francisco.[398] The new breed of young and qualified entrepreneurs and the popular interest in entrepreneurship sets this generation of startups apart from previous generations.

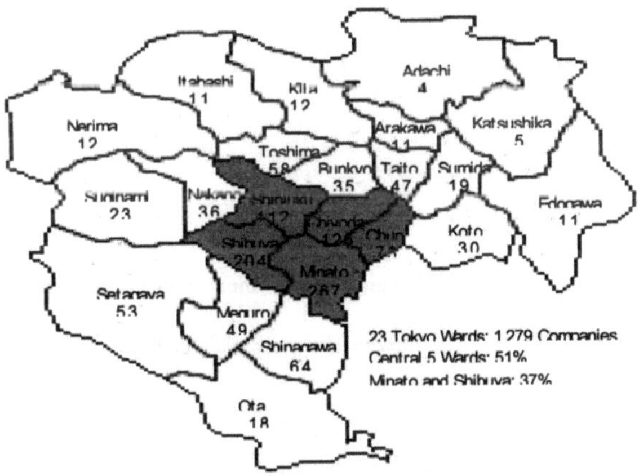

Figure 20: Urban Clustering of Internet Ventures in Tokyo[399]

---

[397] MoF (2000b), "Wagakunikigyou no fainansushisutemu to koporeetogabanansu ni kansuru Ankeeto Chousa: Shoukeikekka to bunseki no chuukan houkokusho," October 20, 2000, Ministry of Finance, Japan, based on a survey of 1,219 publicly traded companies in Japan.

[398] Cf. Matthew A. Zook (2000), "Grounded Capital: Venture Capital's Role in the Clustering of Internet Firms in the U.S.," *Mimeo*, November 1, 2000.

[399] Fujitsu Research Institute (2000). *Tokyo ni okeru Kigyou Shuuseki*. Tokyo: Fujitsu Research Institute. Cf. also URL: http:www.bitvalley.org. Hisashi Arai (2000), *Bitbare no Kodou*, Tokyo: Nikkei BP. Yuko Aoyama (2001), "The Information Society, Japanese Style: Corner Stores as Hubs for E-Commerce Access," *Mimeo*, forthcoming in Leinbach, Thomas, and Brunn, Stanley (eds.). *Worlds of Electronic Commerce*, London: Wiley. The Bitvalley phenomenon attracted many students and youngsters interested in pursuing an entrepreneurial career and at its peak in February 2000 the craze of popularity around the Bitvalley networking association drew more than 2000 attendants to a networking event in Tokyo's Velfarre dance club.

Chapter 9. Emerging Classic Venture Capital

9. 1. Evolution of Venture Capital in Japan

Historical Development

There are about 200 established venture capital firms in Japan. The largest ones are Jafco, Japan Investment & Finance, Japan Asia Investment Corp, and the newcomer Softbank Investment. Some pioneering private venture capital firms were established during the 'first venture boom' of 1970-73, the vast majority of firms were set up during the 'second venture boom' in 1982-86, and another smaller wave followed since 1995.[400] More than 80 % of firms are affiliate companies of banks, security firms, insurance companies, trading companies or industrial corporations.[401]

Organization of Venture Capital Firms

Venture capitalists are not so different from other 'salaryman' employees in Japanese financial institutions. The largest players are publicly listed or seek a listing, which they regard as necessary in order to be able to attract qualified staff. Most venture capital firms invest both on their own account and by establishing, investing in and managing so-called Investment Enterprise Partnership (IEP, Toushi Jigyou Kumiai) funds (see Figure 21). The corporate organizational structure leads to a less high-powered incentive system than in the U.S. partnership structure.

---

[400] Masato Ono (1997), *Benchaa Kigyou to Toushi no Jissaichishiki*, Tokyo: Touyou Keizai Shinbunsha, p. 163.

[401] In this respect, the origins of venture capital in Japan share similarities with the history of venture capital in Germany. Cf. Horst Albach, Detlef Hunsdiek, and Ljuba Kokalj (1986), *Finanzierung mit Risikokapital*, Stuttgart: C.E. Poeschel. Holger Frommann and Günter Leopold (1998), *Eigenkapital für den Mittelstand. Venture Capital im In- und Ausland*, Munich: C.H. Beck. Horst Albach, and Dieter Köster (1997), "Risikokapital in Deutschland," *Discussion Paper*, FS IV 97 – 17, Wissenschaftszentrum Berlin für Sozialforschung.

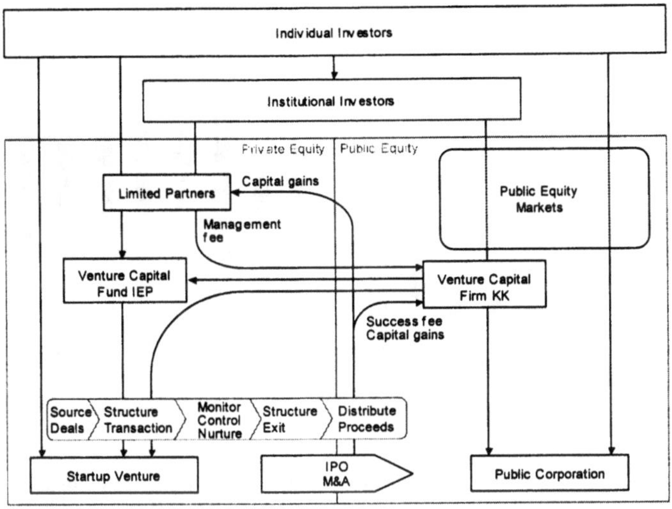

Figure 21: Venture Capital Fund/Corporate Hybrid Structure

The State of Venture Capital

Even though annual investment amounts showed cyclical declines in 1993 and 1998, the Japanese venture capital industry was characterized by a rather stable balance of outstanding investments during much of the 1990s. However, in 1999 and 2000 the industry grew significantly. With an investment balance in excess of one trillion yen, the Japanese venture capital industry reached its historical record in 2001. Since then investments have dropped sharply as a result of the downturn of equity markets.[402] (See Figure 22.)

[402] Nikkei (2002), "Benchaa Kyapitaru Chousa 2001 Nendo," *Nikkei Shinbun*, July 5, 2002. There are two principal sources of data on the Japanese venture capital industry: The annual survey of the METI-affiliated Venture Enterprise Center (VEC) and the annual survey of the Nihon Keizai Shinbun (Nikkei). Both surveys do not capture Japanese investments by foreign funds and therefore do not fully reflect the boom that occurred in 2000.

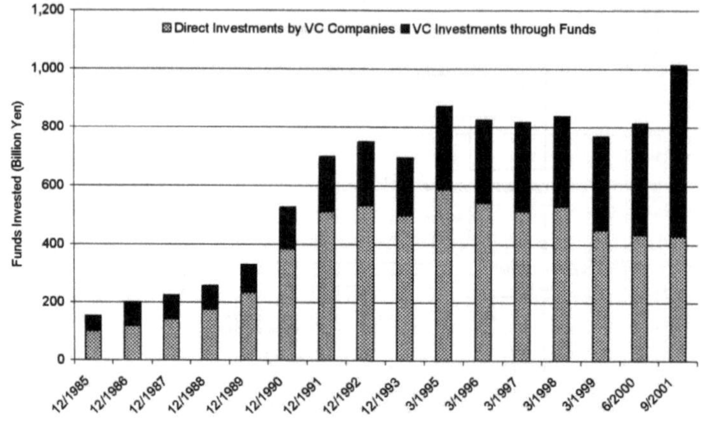

Figure 22: Venture Capital Investments and Loans Outstanding[403]

Even though the limited quality of data does not allow for a direct comparison, it is clear that the relative size of the industry is a mere fraction of the U.S. industry. However, more importantly, fundamental structural differences exist. While the average U.S. fund invests some $5 million in six companies, the average Japanese fund invests some $ 500 thousand in thirty companies. I.e. broadly speaking Japanese venture capital has traditionally been characterized by small and scattered investments in relatively old and well-established companies briefly before their IPO, while U.S. funds take larger stakes in younger companies and exercise more control. [404]

Banks and trust banks are the largets contributors to venture capital funds (33%) followed by industrial corporations (26%), and insurance companies (14%). Pension funds that are the largest venture capital investor in the U.S. supply only 2% of the funds invested in Japanese venture capital. In the year ending September 2001, Japanese venture capitalists covered by

---

403 Venture Enterprise Center.

404 MITI (2000b), "Puraibeetoekuitifainansu Jigyoukankyouseibikenkyuukai Taigen: Puraibeetoekuitifainansu no kankyou to sono fukyuu ni muketeno kadai," *Industrial Policy Bureau*, November 2000, Ministry of International Trade and Industry, Japan, p. 9.

the Venture Enterprise Center (VEC) survey, did invest JPY 283 billion in 3,736 companies (see Figure 23).

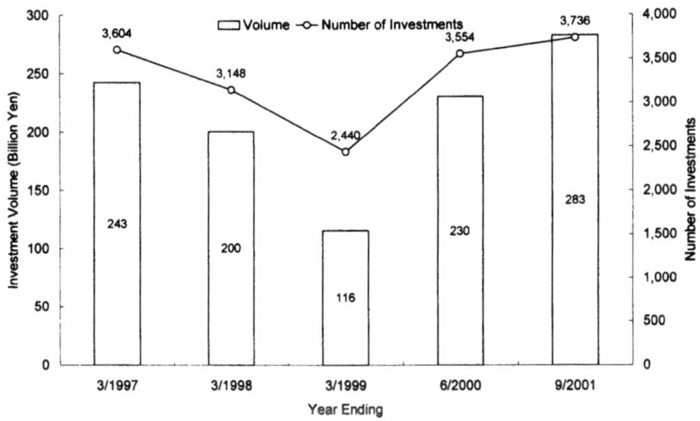

Figure 23: Annual Venture Capital Investments[405]

17% of the investment amount did go to Semiconductor-related targets, 15% to Internet-related companies and 15% to Computer-related companies. With 48%, almost half the investment volume did go to target companies located in Tokyo. In the same period 1,153 exit events occurred which is twice the number of the previous year. 40% of all exits were IPOs. Japanese venture capital firms do usually not engage in early-stage 'classic venture capital' investing. However, they are actively supplying funds to established growth businesses that are planning a public listing in the foreseeable future and more than 70% of IPOs are venture capital-backed.[406] Jafco, alone has backed some 30% of all IPOs over the last years.

According to a 1998-benchmark study on VC fund performance, returns of Japanese funds have been disappointingly low, averaging an IRR of 5.5%, with more than half of the funds showing a negative IRR. Fully invested funds, on the other hand, showed a return of 10.3 %, which compares favorably with the 3.4 % increase of the Topix over the same period.[407] Two more recent attempts to measure IRR of Japanese venture capital funds are consistent in finding that funds that were established in the late 1990s yield higher average returns than older funds, due to their ability to make some profitable exits in the boom of 1999/2000, however rates of return are significantly lower than in the U.S.[408]

9. 2. Birth of Classic Venture Capital

The Internet Bubble as Catalyst

With the global Internet and technology boom during the latter half of the 1990s not only the investment volume increased, but also the structure of the industry began to change. Large incumbent firms had to suffer defections and small independent venture capital firms sprang up. At the same time foreign buyout and venture capital firms set up shop in Japan. More than half of the funds formed in 2000 and 2001 were raised to target seed and early stage investments. Major incumbents also shifted their focus to this area. Jafco took the lead in the 'old guard' and reorganized the company into small semi-autonomous investment teams that share in the capital gain of their investments. At the same time, Jafco announced to move to a hands-on 'build-the-company' approach. Moreover, in order to address resentments by foreign investors, they decided to move closer to the U.S: partnership model by channelling all their investments through funds and have Jafco contribute up to 50% of the funds capital. In spite of these adjustments, Jafco President Mitsumasa Murase is proclaiming that the U.S. venture

---

405 Venture Enterprise Center.
406 Nakagawa (1999), op. cit., p. 10.
407 MITI (1998), "1998 Nen Benchaa Kyapitaru Fando (Toushijigyoukumiai) Pafoomansu Benchimaaku," December 1998, Ministry of International Trade and Industry, Japan. European Venture Capital Association (EVCA) (1998), "New Pan-European Performance Study," *Europe Private Equity Update*, January 1998.
408 VEC and Thomson Venture Economics (2002), *Japanese VC Survey*, September 3, 2002.

capital partnership model is not necessarily the best and is committed to further develop what he regards as a Japanese-style corporate model.[409]

Within the context of the boom of the Japanese stock markets during 1999, and the improved prospects for venture companies to go public a new breed of independent venture capital firms with a hands-on approach played an increasing role.[410] Moreover, corporates increased their venture investments. Some of the heaviest venture capital Internet investors in Japan were 'nouveau riche' companies, such as Softbank and Hikari Tsushin, that have in 1999 been dignified by x-fold increases in their market capitalization (see Table 12).

Company Name	Increase in Market Capitalization (¥100 million)	Market Capitalization at '99 End (¥100 million)	Stock Price at '99 End (Yen)	Stock Price at '98 End (Yen)	Market Capitalization 98' End/99' End
Hikari Tsushin Inc.	61,368	63,419205,0	00	6,950	30.9
Fast Retailing Co.	10,503	11,027	41,600	1,998	21.0
Trans Cosmos Inc.	9,935	10,614	43,600	3,180	15.6
Softbank Corp.	100,393	107,44497,80	0	6,800	15.2

Table 12: Japanese Internet Bubble Stocks

The recovery that the Japanese stock markets have experienced in 1999 was driven by a small group of telecommunications and technology stocks that were sporting rather optimistic valuations. Yahoo Japan, for instance, was trading on nearly 300 times sales. On the newly established Mothers segment, valuations were equally extreme. The first stock to be listed on Mothers was a consultancy called the Internet Research Institute. The institute, established three years before, employed 45 people and generated annual sales of only $7 million. But after its Dec. 22 1999 debut on Mothers, the institute's market value has soared to more than $10 billion – $3 billion of which was held by founder Hiroshi Fujiwara. These and similar companies tried to sustain their valuations by investing in ventures. However, this proved

---

409 Nikkei (2001b), "Nihon Dokuji VC Moderu Mezasu," *Nikkei Shinbun*, Febuary 20, 2001.

410 Wako Securities (2000), "Aratana kigyoukachisouzou wo mezashite," *Research Report*, February 3, 2000. Nikkei (2000), "Koujinsekinin de bencha wo ikkanikusei, NTVP Muraguchi Daihyou," *Nikkei Shinbun*, November 30, 2000.

unsustainable and with the burst of the bubble most of this investment frenzy came to an end. Some other children of the Internet bubble, such as Rakuten and Cyberagent that raised a lot of cash in their IPOs have since actively engaged in acquisitions of venture capital-funded startups in related areas and have thereby provided an exit channel for venture capitalists.

Regulatory Changes Fostering Classic Venture Capital

Apart from the favorable equity market environment at the end of the 1990s, classic venture capital investing received a more fundamental boost through the relaxation of listing requirements at the traditional venture stock market, the JASDAQ (OTC market), at the end of 1998, and the establishment of TSE MOTHERS (Market of the High-growth and Emerging Stocks) in 1999 and NASDAQ Japan (in 2000) as new markets for growth companies (see Table 13).

	NASDAQ Japan (Venture Standard)	**Tokyo Stock Exchange (MOTHERS)**	**JASDAQ (2nd Standard)**
Established	June 2000	November 1999	December 1998
Shareholders' Equity (Net Asset)	¥ 400 million of paid-in capital (upon listing); OR	N.A.	N.A.
Market Cap	¥5 billion of market cap; OR ¥ 75 million of before-	¥ 500 million or more upon listing	¥ 500 million or more upon listing
Before-Tax Profit	tax profit	N.A.	N.A.
Number of Floating Shares	1,000	Must offer 1,000 shares or more by offering new shares upon listing	N.A.
Number of Shareholders	300 or more	Additional 300 upon listing	300-500 (depending on the number of outstanding shares)
Operating History	If operating history is 1 year or less, ¥ 5 billion market cap is required.	N.A.	10 years or less; or R&D per revenue is 3% or more
Liquidity (% of stocks traded)[411]	81.2	92.1	68.5
No. of Companies Listed (Dec. 2000)	40	29	887 (both standards)

Table 13: Listing Requirements and Characteristics of Japanese Growth Markets[412]

---

[411] TSE (2001), "Mothers Statistics," *Mimeo*, February 2001, Tokyo Stock Exchange. Calculated as monthly average of no. of listed companies whose stocks are traded on that day/ no. of listed companies on that day.

[412] Tokyo Stock Exchange.

Traditionally, stock market listing standards used to be very strict and required at least a two-year track record of profitability. For example, the largest stock market in Japan, the Tokyo Stock Exchange (TSE), has traditionally required all companies listing on its First Section to have shareholders' equity of at least JPY1 billion, before-tax profits of at least JPY600 million over the previous three years (or over JPY400 million for the last year and JPY100 million or more the previous year), and an operating history of at least three years. Furthermore, the initial listing fee has been JPY120 million. The traditional requirements of the over-the-counter market (JASDAQ) have been less demanding, but still far more restrictive than requirements in their counterpart markets overseas. Under traditional JASDAQ requirements, a listing company must have shareholders' equity of JPY200 million, net profits in each of the past two years, and at least 300 shareholders.

In addition to the initiatives by the Japanese stock markets to relax listing standards, the Japanese government has over the last years adopted a number of legislative measures that improved the regulatory framework for classic venture capital. Most notable are regulatory changes with regard to limited partnerships, stock options, and angel investing.

In November 1998, the Limited Partnership Act (LPA, Toushi Jigyou Yugen Sekinin Kumiai Hou) was adopted providing for the equivalent of a U.S. limited partnership structure for VC funds. Under the previously available partnership structures investors had to accept the disadvantage of general liability for all partners (Minpoujou Kumiai) or corporate tax-liability (Tokumei Kumiai). The new limited partnership structure remedies these disadvantages and provides for limited liability, 'pass through' tax treatment, and financial disclosure requirements. Along with other recent reforms in the pension fund industry (e.g. the relaxation of investment policies with the adoption of the 'prudent investor rule', and the introduction of 'defined contribution' plans), the adoption of the LPA is expected to encourage Japanese pension funds to participate more actively in venture capital funds, and indeed some Japanese corporate pension funds began to invest in venture capital funds, both in Japan and even more so, abroad.[413]

Until recently, stock options were not available under Japanese law. The New Business Promotion Act in 1995 provided for the limited grant of stock options by start-up companies under narrowly restricted circumstances subject to approval by the Ministry of International Trade an Industry. In 1997, the Diet amended the Commercial Code to allow corporations generally to provide stock options to their own directors and employees – but not to any other parties (including employees of subsidiaries). The total of all such options was not allowed to exceed 10% of the outstanding shares of the company, and the maximum exercise period was 10 years. Subsequent legislation expanded the availability of stock options further to include grants to outside professionals (such as business consultants or patent attorneys). Not only venture companies, but also major industrial corporations such as, Sony, NEC, Matsushita, Fujitsu, Nissan, Fuji Heavy Industries, and others have introduced stock options as part of their compensation systems since. A recent survey of Japanese CEOs showed that 49% of them are planning to introduce stock options, whereas 0% are planning to maintain a seniority-based compensation system.[414]

Under the Angel Tax Incentive introduced in 1997, individual investors who have made qualifying investments are permitted to carry forward the losses on such investments for a period of up to three years. In order for an investment to qualify for such treatment, among other requirements, the company in which the investment is made must have been in

---

[413] Nikkei (2001c), "Nenkin no VB Toushi Hirogaru," *Nikkei Shinbun*, April 15, 2001. David Snow (2000), "Japanese Pensions Tap U.S. Market," *Venture Capital Journal*, March 1, 2000.

[414] Nikkei (2001d), "Shachou 100 Nin Ankeeto," *Nikkei Shinbun*, Nikkei Chousa, January 25, 2001.

operation for less than 5 years, and its R&D expenses must be equal to at least 3% of its revenue.

Other amendments to the Commercial Code that went into effect in 2001 and 2002 included:

- the removal of restrictions on acquisition of treasury stock;
- abolition of par value shares;
- abolition of net asset requirement for stock splits;
- introduction of new rules for unit and fractional shares;
- changes to capital reserve requirements;
- simplification of procedures for issuing new shares;
- the introduction of a new 'stock subscription option';
- the introduction of more flexible share classification rules; and
- the introduction of electronic voting, notices and financial disclosure.

Most of these reforms have been motivated by the intention to facilitate U.S. style venture capital investing in Japan, and while there is still little experience in their application they can be expected to make the structuring of investments significantly more flexible in the future.

New Sources of Classic Venture Capital at the End of the 1990s

The favorable stock market conditions in 1999 and the described improved prospects for liquidity have really 'kick-started' classic venture capital in Japan. The most active investors can be broadly divided into three groups: The 'old guard' (affiliates of Japanese financial institutions or corporations), the 'nouveau riche' (investment vehicles of the likes of Softbank, Hikari Tsushin), and the 'independents' (mostly newcomer VCs, often spin-offs from the old-guard; foreign VCs). These groups differ considerably with regard to their organization, investment stance, and cash at hand. The exact size of Japan's classic venture-capital pool is difficult to determine. Most established VCs invest only in rare cases opportunistically in newly established firms. The segment of early-stage IT/Internet-targeted funds only came into existence in the late 1990s. Industry experts estimate that the available funds in this segment have grown from less than $200 million in 1998 to about $500 million in 1999, probably rising to more than $2 billion in 2000. The 'nouveau riche' companies are the largest investors in this segment, with more than $1bn at hand, however they combine financial and strategic investment objectives and therefore fall outside our definition of classic venture capital. The 'independents' are a diverse group. Some of them have not more than some $10 million under management, and tend to make small investments of typically less than $1 million. However, there is also a number of larger firms with fund volumes of $30 million to $200 million. Foreign-affiliated firms often invest from global or regional funds and have much more capital at hand than Japanese independents. With that much new capital flowing into the early stage Internet and technology segment, informed observers unanimously agree that there was too much money chasing too few investment opportunities in 1999 and 2000. This is reflected in the VEC survey data which shows that the proportion of investment target companies less than five years old has increased considerably and amounted to 62% in 2000 (see Figure 24).

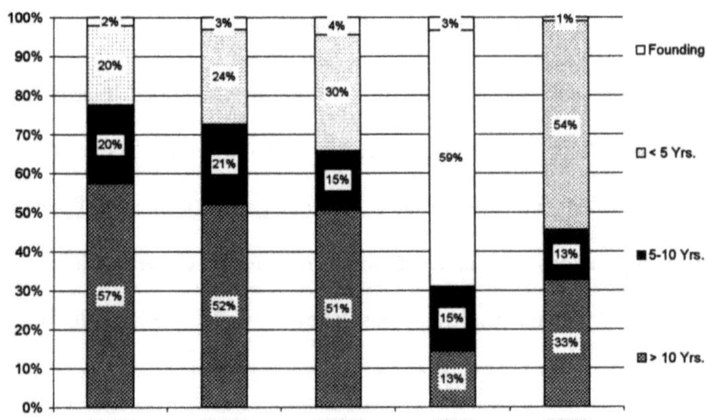

Figure 24: Age Structure of Companies Receiving Venture Capital[415]

[415] Venture Enterprise Center.

After the burst of the Internet bubble in the spring of 2000, the situation changed. While capital is still available waiting to be invested, investors have become much more scrutinizing and valuations have come down. During the first quarter of 2000, 25 companies going public on one of the three Japanese growth markets raised more than $700 million, one year later IPOs are priced much lower and 24 companies raised only some $200 million during the first quarter of 2001.

Nevertheless, several of the new Japanese independents have successfully brought their first investments public, and there is still a steady stream of companies going public.[416] While the market downturn in 2000 has hit the new venture capital firms rather hard, some of them will probably succeed and drive the evolution of classic venture capital in Japan.[417] Similarly, some foreign-affiliated venture capital firms remain committed to classic venture capital in Japan and have set annual investment targets of some $100 million.[418] Softbank Investments has established itself as the largest venture capital investor with an investment volume of JPY 68 billion in the year ending March 2002, which amounts to more than three times the investment amount of now number two Jafco.

Chapter 10. Venture Capital-backed Internet Startups in Tokyo

10. 1. Survey Design

Venture capital-backed startups are new to Japan; there are neither established ways of building these companies, nor is there a lot of information available on the few precedents. Therefore, in the case of Japan, the research objective is accomplished through in-depth case

---

[416] Yasushi Hamao, Frank Packer, and Jay R. Ritter (1999), "Institutional Affiliation and the Role of Venture Capital: Evidence from Public Offerings in Japan," *Mimeo*, September 1999, find that firms backed by independent venture capitalists are more successful than those backed by captive investors.

[417] Nikkei (2001e), "ShinkouVC Toushisaki Kabushikikoukai Hajimaru," *Nikkei Shinbun*, January 18, 2001.

[418] Nikkei (2001f). "Gaishikei VC, Nihonde Benchaatoushi Kakudai." *Nikkei Shinbun*, March 25, 2001.

studies based on interviews with the founders (Founder Survey), managers (CEO Survey), employees (Employee Survey), and venture capital investors (VC Survey) of a sample of venture capital-backed startups in Tokyo.

The findings are based on semi-structured interviews with the founders, managers, employees, and venture capital investors of a sample of ten venture capital-backed startups that were observed over the period from October 1999 to October 2002. Survey questionnaires were structured according to the venture governance framework and research questions developed in Part I. (See Appendix for survey questionnaires and aggregate results.)

All companies surveyed are newly established (in 1999 or 2000), operate in an Internet-related business, and have received seed/startup financing from professional, financially-motivated venture capital investors. Companies that fit these criteria are rare. A bustling scene of Internet startups has emerged since 1998 in Tokyo, however, promising startups that are self-financed and grow organically, or startups that are initiated together with corporate partners are much more common than companies backed by purely financially motivated professional venture capitalists. It is estimated that during 1999 and 2000, there were less than one hundred companies that fit our criteria. We owe a lot of gratitude to the founders, investors and employees of the ten companies for participating in the survey. They all did embark on an adventure at a time when the world economy was characterized by 'irrational exuberance' and they all did have to adjust to a much harsher environment since. In exchange for their frankness in sharing their experiences and providing privileged information, we did commit not to disclose the identity of the participating companies.

Following a brief profile of the survey companies in 10. 2. the different elements of the venture governance framework are analyzed in 10. 3. to 10. 7.

10. 2. Case Study Profiles

Table 14 provides an overview of the companies participating in the survey.

VB1	VB2	VB3	VB4	VB5	VB6	VB7	VB8	VB9	VB10
Business Content									
Online media	Online service	E-commerce intermediary	Online education	E-commerce intermediary	Marketing services	Online and marketing services	Media/ Publishing	B to B E-commerce	Media and system design
Initiation How was the venture initiated?									
Two journalists hook up with seed investor via mailing list	Spin-off from incubator to commercial-ize new business model	Started as non-commercial project to use newly available Internet technology	Spin-off from education/ training company	Investor-led initiation, copy of US business model	Started by business school graduate to introduce technology of US company to Japan	Spin-off from incubator to commercial-ize new business model	Started by executive from unrelated field in order to pursue personal interest in industry	Spin-off from incubator to commercial-ize new business model	Started by freelance designer
What is the nature of the critical resource that the venture is based on, and what is its relationship to the initiator?									
Ability to produce high quality content	Business idea that was made possible by Internet technology	Application of generic Internet technology to Japan-specific market	Industry knowledge, business knowledge, idea of applying Internet technology	Knowledge of US business model, capital	Business and technology knowledge, access to US technology provider	Technology and market knowledge	Business skills, leadership, application of new business model to old industry	Technology knowledge	Technology/ design skills
How does the initiator envision complementing and capturing the value of the critical resource?									
Leading organization building, set up functional hierarchy	Professional, first-mover commercial-ization	Raised capital when commercial prospect of business became apparent, first mover in niche market	Raise a lot of capital upfront and quickly grow the company	Use capital to build professional organization	Use capital to build professional organization	Use capital to build professional organization, first-mover commercial-ization	Build professional organization raise capital on project basis	Use capital to build professional organization	Use capital to grow organization
Resource Gathering How are relationships to potential resource providers established?									
Network of industry professionals, introductions by VC	Professional recruiting, incubator support	Founder's network, introductions by VC	Professional recruiting	Professional recruiting	Professional recruiting, founder's network	Founder's network, introductions by VC	Professional recruiting, founder's network	Incubator support	Founder's industry network
What rationale (increase overall value of the project/retain large share/avoid stand-still) does the sequencing of gathering resource commitments follow?									
Capital commitment was secured before initiation, focus on increasing overall value, but retain control	Capital secured before initiation, increase overall value of the project	Raise professional VC to be able to attract qualified human resources	Raise a lot of capital to grow fast, accept ownership dilution	Build professional organization to grow fast	Raise capital to be able to grow fast	Raise capital step-wise, increase overall value while maintaining share	Build self-sustainable organization, retain control	Raise capital to develop product	Retain control and profitability

VB1	VB2	VB3	VB4	VB5	VB6	VB7	VB8	VB9	VB10
What are the arrangements between the firm and its providers of finance/venture capital? How are investors attracted to the firm, how are control and cash flow rights allocated?									
No formal control rights, initial seed finance from US VC, next round Japanese corporate VC without strategic interest	Founder comes from incubator/ investor firm, no formal control rights	Founder is initiator and CEO, VC is involved in corporate governance	Investors control majority, but are dispersed therefore founder retains effective control	Investor-initiated, i.e. controlled by investor	No formal control rights, but influence on exit	No formal control rights, but influence on exit	No formal control rights, capital raised on non-recourse basis for project purpose	No formal control rights	No formal control rights
What are the arrangements between the firm and its employees? How are human resources attracted to the firm, how are effort and firm-specific investments induced?									
Recruitment from industry contacts, corporate culture, largely portable skills	Professional recruitment, strong incentives, largely portable skills	Initially based on attraction of founder, after VC professional recruitment	Professional recruitment, strong incentives	Professional recruitment, strong incentives	Professional recruitment, strong incentives, corporate culture	Initially based on attraction of founder, after VC professional recruitment, corporate culture	Founder's contacts, corporate culture	Professional recruitment, strong incentives	Founder's contacts, corporate culture
Market Strategy What are the product and market strategies, how are they adjusted over time?									
Focus on building service and brand, getting users, providing high quality	Focus on getting users, offer service for free	Established strong market position/ proof of concept before VC funding, use capital to grow business	Developed service and launched aggressive marketing campaign	Copy US business model and introduce it to Japanese market	Superior technology, but market found to be smaller than expected	Become dominant player in niche service category	Introduce new business model to old industry, become self-sustainable	Develop service and use capital to build customer base	Grow spectrum of services and customer base
In which way does the startup venture evolve into a going concern?									
Strategic relationship and shareholding by media company, self-sustainable	Was aborted due to lack of revenue prospects before resources exhausted	Acquired by major e-commerce company	Was aborted after having spent capital on marketing without much success	Envisioned future sale to US company with the same business model	When growth plans proofed elusive fire sale to company in related field, return of remaining cash to investors	Acquired by major e-commerce company	Build self-sustainable core business and pursue growth projects by raising capital on a project basis	Aborted after conflict between founder and investor	Capital returned to investor and pursuit of organic growth with internal financing
Professionalization How are the entrepreneurial functions of initiation, coordination, and uncertainty bearing allocated to different members of the firm? How does this allocation change with the growth of the firm?									
Founder is initiator and CEO, growing functional hierarchy	Founder is initiator, and CEO, as well as investor, project organization	Founder is initiator and CEO, growing functional hierarchy	Founder is only initiator, professional CEO	Initiated by investor, professional CEO	Founder is initiator and CEO, growing functional hierarchy	Founder is initiator and CEO, growing functional hierarchy	Founder is initiator and CEO, functional hierarchy	Founder is initiator and CEO	Founder is initiator and CEO, as well as investor, project organization
Investment performance at the end of observation period									
Living Dead	Aborted	Trade sale	Aborted	Living Dead	Fire sale	Trade sale	Living Dead	Aborted	Capital returned

Table 14: Case Study Profiles

10. 3. Initiation

The Founder Survey shows that startup founders are strongly motivated by the wish to build an organization. They recognize market opportunities based on their superior industry insights. They perceive almost no personal career risk and limit their financial risk. Some view their company as a lifetime mission; others view it more like a project. Most founders strive for a public offering within three years (see Table 15).

N=10

How would you describe the following aspects of your previous position?	Very Bad			Very Good
Compensation.		10%	40%	50%
Working Time.	40%	10%	10%	40%
Relationship with Co-workers.			10%	90%
Relationship with Superiors.	10%		10%	80%
Ability to influence the direction of the company.	20%	30%	10%	40%
Ability to share in the success of the company	40%		40%	20%
Overall quality of your previous company		10%	40%	50%

How important were the following factors in your decision to establish this company?	Not important			Very Important
Design an organization that suits my own work style and values.			10%	90%
Make more money than as an employee.	50%	30%	20%	
Work in the area that I find most interesting.			20%	80%
Have nobody who tells me what to do.	30%	30%	20%	20%
Have a chance to become really rich.	10%	10%	40%	40%
Do less or more enjoyable work than as an employee.	80%			20%
Gain the respect of others.	30%	50%	10%	10%

How important were the following factors in developing your business idea?	Not important			Very Important
Do the same business as in my previous position.	38%	25%	25%	13%
Commercialize an invention that I developed in an academic context.	88%			13%
Commercialize a technology that I developed in my previous position.	63%		38%	
Make use of a new technology that is generally available.	25%		38%	38%
Satisfy a market need that nobody had identified so far.	13%			88%
Copy the business model of another company.	50%		38%	13%
Enter an existing market and design an organization that is more efficient than incumbent competitors.	38%	13%	13%	38%

How did you perceive the following risks at the time of establishment?	Not high			Very high
Risk that the product/service/technology fails.	44%	11%	44%	
Risk that the market for the product/service is too small.	50%	30%		20%
Risk that the company will not be profitable.	20%		30%	50%
Risk that the company will become bankrupt.	20%	10%	40%	30%
Personal career risk of not finding a good job if the company fails.	100%			
Personal financial risk of loosing significant share of personal assets.	40%	20%		40%

How did you perceive the following possibilities at the time of establishment?	Not high			Very high
Possibility of creating a company that I can lead for the rest of my professional career.	44%	22%	22%	11%
Possibility of changing my lifestyle by earning more money.	20%	20%	40%	20%
Possibility of becoming very rich, and be able to retire early.	20%	10%	40%	30%
Possibility of leading the company to a public offering within 3 years.	10%	10%	10%	70%
Possibility of leading the company to a public offering within 10 years.	30%	10%	10%	50%
Build a respected and sustainable company and remain its sole owner.	75%	25%		

Table 15: Startup Initiation (Founder Survey)

Most startups have made detailed plans before beginning business operations. Some have secured customers before starting operations. They aim to secure their intellectual property by gaining patent protection (see Table 16).

When, in relation to the beginning of business operations did you accomplish the following?

	Never	Prior	After
Secure first customers	13%	38%	50%
Secure employees		38%	63%
Secure technology/know how		88%	13%
Legally establish the company		75%	25%
Prepare a business plan		75%	25%
Retain an attorney	25%	25%	50%
Establish an accounting system		13%	88%
Obtain external equity financing	13%	25%	63%
Obtain external debt financing	100%		
Write a mission statement	25%	63%	13%
Hire an employee		13%	88%
Hire a full-time personnel specialist	88%		13%
Develop a marketing plan	13%	75%	13%
Announce a product	25%	25%	50%
File a patent application	38%		63%
Sell first product	13%	13%	75%

Table 16: Sequencing (Founder Survey)

10. 4. Financing

All survey companies are established as joint stock corporations (Kabushiki Kaisha) and have authorized only one class of stock. Survey companies received seed/startup financing from independent Japanese and foreign-affiliated venture capital firms. Investors purchased common stock in the form of a third party share allotments and did not receive significant preferences, rights, or covenants that would give them strong control rights. The only provision that was made in some of the contracts is a liquidity preference that gives the venture capital investor senior claims in case of business failure. As the investor survey shows, investors do not expect to exercise control in an informal way either (see Table 17).

Please answer the following questions regarding your involvement in the management of the company.

	On an ongoing basis			If demanded/necessary		
	Never	Sometimes	Regularly	Never	Sometimes	Regularly
Do you provide advice on strategic management issues?	25%		75%			100%
Do you provide advice on day-to-day management issues?	25%		75%	25%		75%
Do you provide accounting and tax advice?	25%		75%	25%		75%
Do you introduce advisors to the company?	33%	33%	33%		50%	50%
Do you introduce customers to the company?	25%	25%	50%	33%		67%
Do you introduce suppliers to the company?	25%	25%	50%	33%		67%
Do you introduce employees to the company?	25%	25%	50%	33%		67%
Do you introduce other investors to the company?	25%	50%	25%		50%	50%

Please comment on the likelihood of the following action being taken, depending on the company's performance and your control rights.

	If things go well			If the company is in trouble		
	Likely	Possible	Unthinkable	Likely	Possible	Unthinkable
Do you exercise a right of approval for appointment of new employees?			100%	25%	50%	25%
Do you exercise a right of approval for appointment of senior management positions?		75%	25%	25%	75%	
Do you exercise a right of approval for large investments?	25%	25%	50%	50%	50%	
Do you exercise a right to replace current management?			100%		75%	25%
Do you exercise a right to replace the founder-manager?			100%		50%	50%
Do you exercise a right to check the company's books	75%	25%		75%	25%	

Table 17: Financing – Role of Venture Capitalist (Venture Capitalist Survey)

Only in cases where the investors hold a majority of stock, did they regard a replacement of the founder as possible in case of severe problems. Investors stress the fact that holding formal control rights would not be worth much, because the prospects of finding qualified replacement for the management of a faltering startup company were dim, and replacing the founder would cause a major upheaval or falling apart of the organization. While not exercising control, many investors are active in providing advice and introducing business partners. They also usually join the company's board of directors.

All survey companies are entirely equity-financed. Only one entrepreneur strategically used the practice of step financing, tied to milestones of company development. Investors either make it clear that they do not want to participate in a follow-on round and expect the company to turn to other investors for the later financing rounds, or the funding is expected to bring the company to a stage where it can embark on a public offering. In two cases management decided to raise capital from a number of venture capitalists in order to avoid that any single investor obtains a large stake.

10. 5. Human Resources

The most important recruitment channels are referrals from current employees and business contacts. Moreover, companies make extensive use of employment agencies and search firms for both technical and management positions. Nevertheless, recruiting qualified personnel is perceived as the largest challenge by all companies. Founders expect to use their ability to raise venture capital as a form of external validation which makes it easier to attract qualified resources (see Table 18).

Which of the following recruitment channels do you use?

	Promote from within	Advertise in the newspaper	Advertise on the web site	Get referrals from current employees	Get referrals from business contacts	Recruit at schools or colleges	Use employment agencies or search firms
Senior Management	30%	10%	40%	80%	60%		60%
Other Administrative & Managerial	40%	10%	40%	60%	30%		40%
Engineering & Science		20%	50%	70%	50%	10%	60%
Sales & Marketing	10%	30%	60%	70%	30%	10%	70%
Clerical	10%	30%	40%	80%	20%	20%	30%
Skilled labor		10%	20%	40%	10%		30%
Unskilled labor		10%	20%	40%	10%	10%	10%

Table 18: Recruitment Channels (Founder/CEO Survey)

In the hiring decision experience and skills and motivation are most highly valued. Formal credentials, such as university degrees, are eschewed, which reflects a certain 'counterculture' mentality of wanting to break with the established norms of large companies (see Table 19).

How important are the following criteria in determining whom your company hires for various positions?

	Most important				Least important		
	Company or Group Fit	Industry/ Business Experience	Specialize d Skills	Overall Motivation or Drive	Credential s	Industry/ Business Experience	Specialize d Skills
Senior Management	13%	63%	25%		75%		25%
Other Administrative & Managerial		38%	38%	25%	88%		13%
Engineering & Science			100%		88%	13%	
Sales & Marketing		13%	13%	75%	88%		13%
Clerical	25%	13%	13%	50%	100%		
Skilled labor			100%		100%		
Unskilled labor	33%			67%	100%		

Table 19: Hiring Decision (Founder/CEO Survey)

Compensation structures are oriented at the individual's performance. Companies make use of stock options, however some CEOs report that non-executive employees do take little interest in stock options. Equity ownership is heavily concentrated in the hands of the founder-CEO and is with the exception of one case not even significantly diluted in order to attract key employees (see Table 20).

Which best describes your company`s compensation structure?

	Fixed Salary			Individual Performance-based Bonus			Stock Options			Hourly Wage		
	Never	Sometimes	Regularly	Never	Sometimes	Regularly	Never	Sometimes	Regularly	Never	Sometimes	Regularly
Senior Management			100%	30%	20%	40%	10%	20%	70%	100%		
Other Administrative & Managerial			100%	40%	30%	20%	11%	33%	56%	89%	11%	
Engineering & Science			100%	50%	30%	20%	11%	33%	56%	67%	22%	11%
Sales & Marketing		10%	90%	30%	30%	40%	22%	22%	56%	89%		11%
Clerical	10%	10%	80%	60%	20%	10%	38%	38%	25%	56%	22%	22%
Skilled labor	33%		67%	67%		33%	50%		50%	50%	50%	
Unskilled labor	50%		50%	50%			50%		50%		50%	50%

How important are the following criteria in determining increases in annual compensation?

	Most important						Least important					
	Individual Performance	Group Performance	Firm Performance	Rank	Seniority	Adjusting to Market Wager	Individual Performance	Group Performance	Firm Performance	Rank	Seniority	Adjusting to Market Wager
Senior Management	38%	13%	50%								88%	13%
Other Administrative & Managerial	38%	13%	38%								88%	13%
Engineering & Science	86%					14%				13%	75%	13%
Sales & Marketing	50%		25%							13%	75%	13%
Clerical	50%		25%				14%				71%	14%
Skilled labor	100%										67%	33%
Unskilled labor	50%		50%								100%	

Table 20: Compensation (Founder/CEO Survey)

How would you describe the following aspects of your previous position?

	Very Bad			Very Good
Compensation.	13%		75%	13%
Working Time.	25%	38%	13%	25%
Relationship with Co-workers.			25%	75%
Relationship with Superiors.	13%	38%	25%	25%
Ability to influence the direction of the company.	13%	63%	13%	13%
Ability to share in the success of the company.	38%	38%	25%	
Overall quality of your previous company	25%	25%	25%	13%

How important were the following factors in your decision to join this company?

	Not important			Very Important
Work in an organization that suits my own work style and values.			25%	75%
Make more money than in my previous position.	13%	50%	38%	
Work in the area that I find most interesting.			13%	88%
Be able to work independently.		13%	25%	63%
Have a chance to become rich.			88%	13%
Do less or more enjoyable work than as an employee.	50%	25%	25%	
Gain the respect of others.	13%	13%	75%	

How did you perceive the following risks at the time of joining this company?

	Not high			Very high
Risk that the product/service technology fails.	25%	13%	63%	
Risk that the market for the product/service is too small.	63%	38%		
Risk that the company will not be profitable.	13%	13%	50%	25%
Risk that the company will become bankrupt.	25%	38%	38%	
Personal career risk of not finding a good job if the company fails or getting fired.	63%	13%	13%	13%
Personal financial risk of loosing significant share of personal assets.	63%	38%		

How did you perceive the following possibilities at the time of joining this company?

	Not high			Very high
Possibility of working in this company for the rest of my professional career.	25%	50%	13%	13%
Possibility of changing my lifestyle by earning more money.	13%	13%	25%	50%
Possibility of becoming very rich, and be able to retire early.	13%	38%	25%	25%
Possibility of being promoted as the company grows.		38%	38%	25%
Possibility of being promoted due to my personal performance.		50%	13%	38%

Table 21: Employee's Motivation (Employee Survey)

Employees are attracted to the firm by the wish to be able to work in the area that they find most interesting and by the wish to work in an organization that suits their work style and values. Many of them expect to – in the medium to long run – rise in the organization and make more money than in their previous position, thus becoming able to change their lifestyles. In other words, they expect to participate in the success of the company, however not in an explicit formally specified manner. Most employees do not perceive a high career risk in case of failure of the venture. However, they feel more such risk than the founders do. On the other hand, employees do perceive a lower risk of failure of the company than the founders do (see Table 21).

10. 6. Market Strategy

Companies plan up-front investment in technology/operations (50%) and marketing/advertising (40%) during the early periods of growth, going along with increasing rates of revenue growth. Market strategies involve an expected break-even after one to two years (ranging from 6 to 26 months, average 16 months). Most survey companies have chosen to bring in corporate partners in later financing rounds in order to build or strengthen business partnerships.

During the observation period, three of the ten companies were aborted because their business did not develop according to expectations, another three companies can be qualified as 'Living Dead' from the investor's point of view, since they emerged into a going concern, but can not be expected to create significant investment returns. In one case, exit took the form of a fire sale (sale at a loss) to a competitor, and in another case the entrepreneur did return the capital to the investor after changing the company's growth strategy. In two cases a successful exit to a trade buyer took place.

10. 7. Professionalization

In two cases, non-founders act as CEO. In one case because the company is part of an 'incubator' type organization, and in another case in order to professionalize management ahead of fundraising. Most companies cite problems in hiring qualified people in both technical and managerial positions. The corporate organization is set up as a functional hierarchy, however with an average staff count of 22, companies are still small enough for pervasive information sharing. In order to prepare for an eventual public listing companies have retained external auditors. The functions of initiation and coordination are mostly integrated in the person of the founder/CEO, however by limiting the commitment of personal financial resources, the function of uncertainty bearing is concentrated in the venture capitalist.

IV. Comparative Venture Governance

While classic venture capital has received a significant boost during the Internet bubble of the late 1990s and did spread from the U.S. to many other countries including Japan as a result, the above analysis has made it clear that 'venture capital' is not the same in Silicon Valley and Japan. Chapters 11 and 12 summarize the stylized venture governance systems of startups in the Silicon Valley Model and startups in Tokyo, based on the analysis presented in Parts II and III within the framework developed in Part I. Chapter 13 presents the main conclusions of the study.

Chapter 11. Silicon Valley Venture Governance

11. 1. Stylized Governance System

It can be said that in Silicon Valley, raising startup venture capital finance amounts to selling the company with an option to earn it back. The financing contract de-bundles control and cash flow rights. Control is made contingent and if need arises, the venture capitalist is in control. The founders, as well as other employees earn cash flow claims as 'sweat equity' and if everything goes well, founders may even regain some control when the company goes public.

The salient features of the financing, human capital and market strategies that characterize this governance system are embedded in the financial, labor and product market environment of the regional economy where uncertainty bearing and contingent control is assumed by the venture capitalist and labor markets allow for rapid professionalization through job-based contingent hiring (see Figure 25).

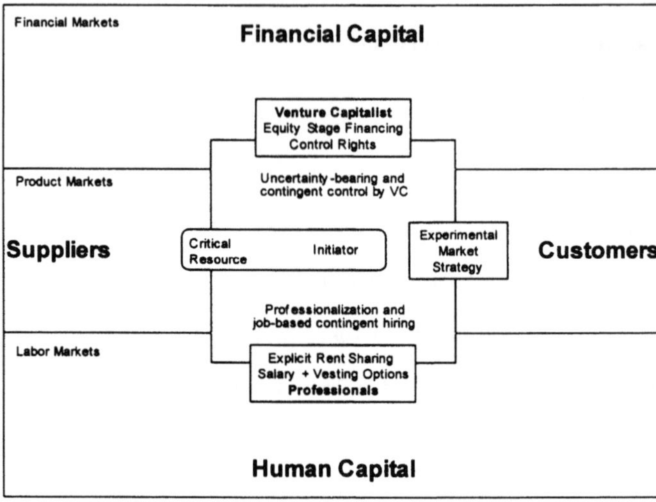

Figure 25: Silicon Valley Venture Governance

The Silicon Valley system is contributing to economic growth along two channels. First, by providing a distinct governance system that makes it possible for the entrepreneur to reduce his role to the function of initiating the venture, the group of potential entrepreneurs and the set of potential business concepts is expanded. Second, by being subject to governance by the venture capitalist, the management of emerging firms is professionalized, execution risk is reduced and the success of the company is separated from the dependence on the qualities of the specific founder/entrepreneur. Thereby, more experimental market strategies are enabled.

11. 2. De-bundling Entrepreneurship

Redefining the Role of the Entrepreneur

What does this governance system imply for the role of the entrepreneur? More than one hundred years ago, John Bates Clark wrote: "It is a matter of common knowledge that an entrepreneur cannot, by any ordinary method, borrow all of his capital."[419] Nowadays, venture capital startup financing does provide a method for entrepreneurs to limit their investment to a nominal amount of money. The funds that they can acquire are of course not 'borrowed', but come as equity with strong control rights. Therefore, at the same time as the entrepreneur can rid himself from taking the financial risk of the capitalist and concentrate on his functions as innovator and/or leader; the capitalist assumes some of the control rights traditionally held by the entrepreneur. Moreover, employees of venture capital-funded startup firms are to a considerable extent compensated by stock options, therefore, they become capitalists to a degree, too. In this sense, the Silicon Valley system, de-bundles much of the "personal union of the entrepreneur's function with a certain part of the functions of the capitalist and the directive worker"[420] that Clark regarded as being called for.

Observing the rise of the corporation at the end of the nineteenth century, John Bates Clark acknowledged its fundamental strength of enabling initiative action that he regarded as the "essence of social progress."[421] He continued to state: "More and more important therefore will be hereafter the devices that reduce the true value of the risks of initiation."[422] And the best type of enterprise "must have good risk-makers in its entrepreneurs, and good risk-reducers in its management; but it must have, in addition to these, good loss-bearers in its capitalists. In this last fact lies the unanalyzed influence that favors corporations. Business losses need to be located where they will do the smallest amount of personal harm"[423] Venture capital-backed startup ventures certainly represent a type of enterprise that matches these criteria, and in this sense their rise provokes associations with the rise of the large

---

419 Clark (1892), op. cit., p. 47.
420 Ibid., p. 48.
421 Ibid., p. 52.
422 Ibid., p. 54.
423 Ibid., p. 50.

corporation as a new type of business venturing organization at the end of the nineteenth century.

As functions traditionally united in the entrepreneur become de-bundled, firm formation increasingly becomes a task of organizational design. This task is at the core of the entrepreneurial function, and is in the Silicon Valley model jointly assumed by the entrepreneur and the venture capitalist.

Raising the Seeds of Innovation

By enabling the initiator who possesses a critical resource such as a technology or idea to get directly in touch with the capitalist, seeds of innovation that would otherwise remain unpursued, since they are out of the focus of the existing organization, get a chance to be evaluated in an outside context.

The evolution of the semiconductor industry is abundant of examples where a given company had to make a certain decision with regard to a technological trajectory to pursue and spin-offs were created to pursue a different trajectory. By enabling this diversity of opinion highly experimental market strategies are enabled and the overall system's capacity for innovation in highly uncertain environments increases.

Professionalizing the Entrepreneurial Process

The venture capitalist as powerful outside team monitor can make sure that the resources are adjusted to the technology/market strategy pursued rather than having existing resources limit the strategic choices.

Explicit rent-sharing, e.g. in the form of stock options combined with a fluid market that values even highly specialized skills, ensures that providers of human capital get rewarded for their skills. The vesting feature of options acts like a bonding mechanism that makes sure that employees remain with the firm as long as they expect its value to increase.

11. 3. Innovating Corporate Governance

Governing Human Capital and Information-Intensive Team Production

Silicon Valley Venture Governance makes innovation in newly established firms financable and copes with technological uncertainty, human capital intensity, and information intensity. The system is characterized by complementarities between financing, human resource and market strategies: outside monitoring makes professional recruitment and explicit rent-sharing credible and a professional organization enables outside financing. Professionalization reduces the resource constraint and enables highly experimental strategies.

Financing and human resource strategies are dependent on fluid local markets and increasing corporate activity deepens these markets. In this sense the elements of the system are interconnected, complementary and sustain each other.

The continued long-term growth of venture capital suggests that the governance arrangements that have evolved make startup companies increasingly more financable. However, the reduction of agency costs does not seem to be the main point, because if this were the case we would have to see a trend back to the founder-owner-manager entrepreneur, rather specialization, division of labor and the virtue of an outside team monitor appear to be the key features to understand the system.

If so, we should ask why a regional cluster of small firms can be a more effective innovator than one large corporation. One aspect is that the corporation would not be able to retain the valuable human resources, another aspect is that a cluster might make better use of information that sometimes needs to be shared but also needs to be protected and encapsulated in order to prevent information overflow or expropriation.

Information Systemic Aspects of 'Governance by Tournament'

For the entrepreneurial company, the VC is an important source of various kinds of information. Especially in regional clusters, such as Silicon Valley, the VC is a node in the network of personnel and information flows between companies, universities, professional service firms, etc. He assists the entrepreneur in finding key personnel, suppliers, customers, and partners. An illustrative example for this is the venture capital firm Kleiner Perkins Caufield & Byers that prides itself to have facilitated more than 100 alliances among the network of their investee companies. They go as far as to refer to their investment companies as a "keiretsu" [424] where insights, knowledge and information among more than 175 companies and thousands of executives are shared consistently.

By abstracting from the dyadic system of investor and entrepreneurial company, and looking at a regional system of many investors and many ventures, such as Silicon Valley, additional factors for its success can be identified. Saxenian argues that Silicon Valley's success and the relative decline of Massachusetts' Route 128 has to do with the fact that despite of similar histories and technologies, Silicon Valley developed a decentralized but cooperative industrial system while Route 128 came to be dominated by independent, self-sufficient corporations.[425]

Aoki stresses the fact that in Silicon Valley, multiple firms compete for the completion of similar products. They may be initiated simultaneously and are gradually screened as information, such as on technological standards, is evolving. In order to restrain duplicated

---

[424] Kleiner, Perkins, Caufield & Byers (1999), *Company Web Site*, URL: http://www.kpcb.com, retrieved: January 2, 1999.

financing, financing is made step-wise. He refers to this governance mechanism as "governance by tournament" and argues that information sharing among firms about the emergent industrial systemic environment is mediated by the venture capitalist. While on the other hand, "technological information that are necessary for product design is generated within individual firms in an integrative manner and hidden from others until the completion of product design."[426] This VC-mediated information system gains informational efficiency with the emergence of de facto standardized interfaces of design products. The circulation of information by the VC helps this kind of modularization to evolve. In this sense the system is self-reinforcing.[427]

11. 4. The Hazards of the Venture Capital Cycle

Venture capital is inherently cyclical, because it 'serves' the cyclical public equity markets. Cyclicality means that a certain kind of issuer, e.g. a startup, does not continuously have the same access to a certain kind of investor, e.g. venture capitalist. During boom times, barely started unprofitable companies are able to go public, whereas in periods of slow markets, even a solid company may have problems accessing the public markets.[428]

As a result, all kinds of investors are attracted to invest in startups during boom times, and companies are pressured to use a lot of capital to grow quickly and access the public markets.[429] On the other hand during periods of cooldown, investors move out of classic venture capital, ventures are likely to pursue slower and less capital intensive growth paths in order to reach break-even as soon as possible (see Figure 26).

---

[425] Saxenian (1994), op. cit.

[426] Masahiko Aoki (1999a), "Information and Governance in the Silicon Valley Model," *Working Paper*, Stanford University, p. 12.

[427] Cf. Masahiko Aoki (1999b), "An Information Theoretic Approach to Comparative Corporate Governance," *Working Paper*, Stanford University.

[428] Cf. Anthony B. Perkins and Michael C. Perkins (1999), *The Internet Bubble*, New York: Harper Collins.

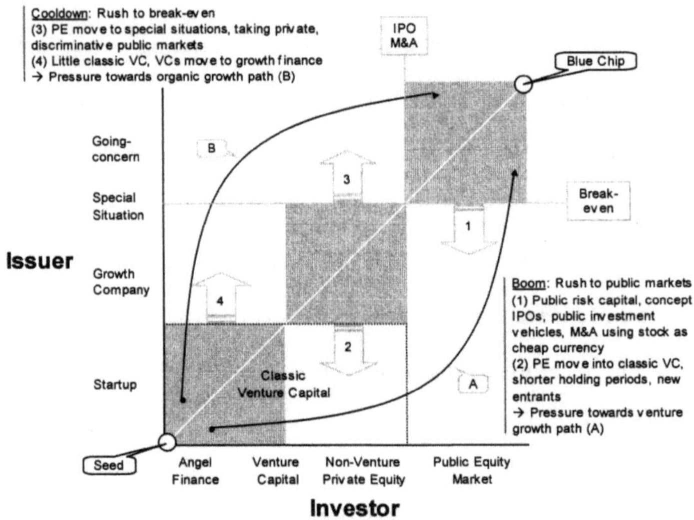

Figure 26: Classic Venture Capital in Boom and Cooldown

It is questionable whether this unsteady supply of risk capital corresponds to real cycles in business opportunity, and therefore initiatives to smoothen these cycles might be regarded as desirable. It remains to be seen how the 'institutionalization' of venture capital funds, i.e. the dominant role that pension funds have come to play in the supply of capital, will influence the cyclicality of the industry.[430] It may contribute to a more steady supply of venture capital and a smoother transition between private and public equity markets because institutional investors and pension funds invest both in public markets and in private equity funds and therefore would be able to hold, whether directly or indirectly, a company from the startup stage throughout its public listing.[431]

---

[429] Cf. Ralph King (2001), "Bonehead Safari – My Hunt for America's Dumbest VC," *Ecompany.com*, January 2001. Available at URL: http://www.ecompany.com, retrieved January 22, 2001.
[430] Cf. Alissa Leibowitz (2000), "VC Goes Institutional," *Venture Capital Journal*, October 1, 2000.
[431] Cf. Alex Gove (2000). "VCs to Limited Partners: Take a Hike!" *Red Herring*, July 28, 2000, available at URL: http://www.redherring.com, retrieved November 20, 2000.

Chapter 12. Emerging Venture Governance in Tokyo

12. 1. Stylized Governance System

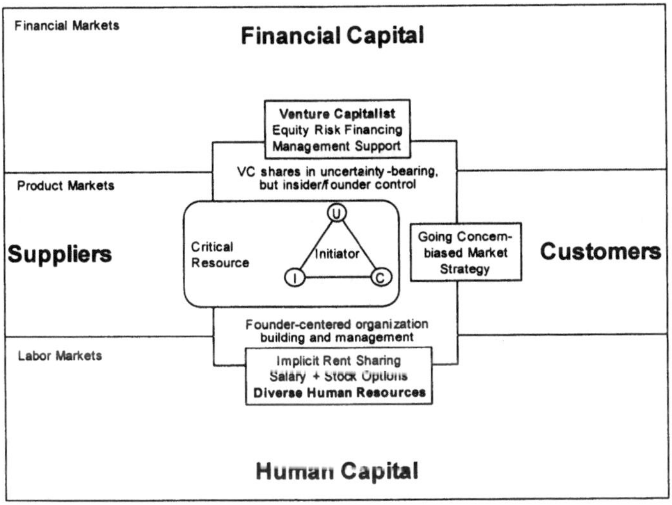

Figure 27: Venture Governance in Tokyo

The venture capital-backed startups observed in Tokyo do not conform to this Silicon Valley model. Raising startup venture capital financing in Tokyo can be described as selling part of the company to an outsider who gets a share of cash flow rights in exchange, but does not take control. Most founders are leaders who want to build an organization. Their investors do their best to support them, but capabilities of the founder may limit the prospects of the company. Human resources, as well as other resource providers, rely in their commitment decision on their evaluation of the founder (see Figure 27).

Startup venture capital in Tokyo helps cash-constrained qualified founders to initiate a company. Venture capitalists share risk and increase the chances of success by providing various kinds of assistance. However, 'people risk' and 'business risk' are not separated.

Moreover, the founder carries more responsibility for his employees, and therefore there is a bias for the venture to adopt a less experimental market strategy and become a mediocre going-concern rather than an outstanding success or a clear failure. The role of the initiator is critical for the success of the venture. As founder-manager, he integrates much of the entrepreneurial functions of initiation, coordination, and uncertainty-bearing.

12. 2. Trajectories of Organizational Innovation

The examined venture governance system in Tokyo is therefore not fundamentally different from the traditional concept of the entrepreneurial startup company. The system is characterized by complementarities between financing, human resource and market strategies: insider control makes implicit rent sharing credible and founder-centered organization building leads to a going concern bias which again enables the maintenance of insider control and implicit rent sharing. The lack of an outside monitor limits the ability to attract resources and does not allow for highly experimental strategies.

Shareholder Control

The described system has been characterized by a large number of venture capital investments that can be referred to as 'Living Dead', i.e. companies that evolve into going concerns but to not produce attractive returns for investors. Therefore, Japanese venture capital investors are demanding increasingly strong control rights in startup investments. The revised Commercial Code that allows for different classes of stock, facilitates this process.[432] Moreover venture capital companies have introduced a structure whereby one team remains responsible over the entire investment lifecycle. Recently, there have been some cases of stage financing and active exercise of control. The announcement of a foreign-affiliated firm to apply stage-financing contingent on operational milestones made news headlines.[433] In another remarkable instance, one independent Japanese VC moved in as CEO of a portfolio company and replaced the incumbent founder manager even though he was holding a 50% stake in the company.[434] Related developments such as the stronger voice of shareholders in general, the increasing mobility of labor, the move of large companies to more modular structures and the use of M&A to restructure and grow their business can be expected to develop in a complementary fashion and lead to a more professional, outsider-controlled type of venture governance.

Chapter 13. Conclusions

Business venturing is risky and needs to be financed with equity. Suppliers of equity finance receive ownership in exchange. Ownership is a bundle of cash flow claims and control rights. Cash flow claims can be divided – we can share the profit - control rights cannot – only one of us can have the last say-. The large corporation emerged by splitting its equity in many shares, selling it off to often dispersed shareholders, pretending that ownership could actually be shared. However, as Berle and Means pointed out, dispersed shareholders had really acquired something else, they were relegated to become beneficial owners, not having any say in how the company is run. Cash-flow claims and control rights were de-facto separated. However, as beneficial shareholders enjoy the right to sell their shares on the public market, the emergence of a M&A market and of specialists in corporate control, such as raiders, became possible. Their activities of aggregating dispersed, beneficial ownership to gain

---

[432] Cf. John Sasaki and Hajime Tanahashi (2002). "Shirikon Baree Moderu toha Nanika." [What is the Silicon Valley Model?] *Mimeo*, May 2000 and Update October 2002.

[433] Nikkei (2001g), "VC ni Bunkatsu Shuhou hirogaru," *Nikkei Shinbun*, Mach 3, 2001.

[434] Nikkei (2001h), "NTVP, Toushisakikigyoushachou ni Daihyou wo Haken," *Nikkei Shinbun*, January 17, 2001.

control, and more importantly the sheer threat of it holds executives accountable to fulfill the return requirements that shareholders demand.

Startup ventures also need to bring in outside equity investors to finance their market strategy. However, the threat of the market for corporate control does not exist in privately held companies, where shareholders do not have liquidity. Therefore, when external capital is raised, cash flow claims and control rights either become de-facto separated (as in the case of the founder-controlled company, where outside equity investors are beneficial owners without any market for corporate control to protect their interests), or they are explicitly separated, as in the case of the investor-controlled venture capital-financed startup company, where the delegation of control rights to management is contingent, and the outside investor acts as a team monitor, reallocating resources.

Investor control makes implicit rent sharing incredible, because the company is not a going concern, and human resource allocation is market-based; founder-control makes experimental strategies less credible because there is a going concern bias, and human resource allocation is hierarchical.

The Silicon Valley system is contributing to economic growth along two channels. First, by providing a distinct governance system that makes it possible for the initiator of a startup to reduce his role to a specific aspect of the entrepreneurial function, the group of potential entrepreneurs and the set of potential business concepts is expanded. The system enables holders of valuable human capital to realize its value, i.e. it is characterized by a high cost of human capital orientation, which leads to focused organizations. Second, by being subject to governance by the venture capitalist, the management of emerging firms is professionalized, and execution of the strategy does not depend on the qualities of the specific founder/entrepreneur.

Considering the described facets of venture capital as source of funds, incentive system, control system, and information system, it is fair to say that it constitutes an idiosyncratic governance system that is different from the traditional notion of the founder-owner-entrepreneur. This governance system expands the array of business concepts that can be commercialized through two channels. First, more projects are initiated and, second, a larger proportion of them is successfully completed.

1. Initiation

Expanding the group of potential entrepreneurs and the set of potential business concepts expands the array of ventures that become initiated. By reducing the risk and the scope of functions that an initiator has to assume, people who lack sufficient own funds or are unwilling to become entrepreneurs in the traditional sense are enabled to initiate a company. This may be particularly relevant for science-driven breakthrough technologies such as biotechnology that heavily depend on knowledge embodied in a small number of people. Star scientists have played a critical role in the formation of the biotechnology industry in the U.S.[435] The venture governance system allows the scientist to get involved in a venture business without taking the risks or assuming the functions traditionally associated with being an entrepreneur.

2. Completion

Through the separation of various risks associated with a new venture, the described governance system increases the likelihood of successful completion. If an entrepreneurial company is perceived as the nexus of concept, people, and capital, it is obvious that problems

---

[435] Zucker/Darby (1996), op. cit. Michael R. Darby and Lynne G. Zucker (1997), "Star Scientists, Institutions, and the Entry of Japanese Biotechnology Enterprises," *Mimeo*, Revision of National Bureau of Economic Research Working Paper No. 5795, revised May 1997.

in any of these spheres can potentially lead to failure. It can be argued that the described governance system allows for the flexible recombination of those elements, while on the contrary, the owner-founder-entrepreneur embodies all three elements in person. The venture capitalist's monitoring function is critical in adjusting the business concept, and in making sure that limited management capacity of the founding team does not hamper the success of the business concept. Moreover, through pure equity financing, the risk of the venture is limited to the business risk. Thereby, this governance system reduces the risk that viable concepts fail.

Through both channels the array of business concepts that become commercialized is expanded. By enabling more people to start businesses and by enabling aggressive strategies to secure first-mover advantages more concepts become initiated. And through effective monitoring and professional execution, the full potential of the business concept is being realized.

In the Silicon Valley venture governance system both channels are at work and venture capital-backed startups are characterized by an innovative governance system that makes them distinct from traditional archetypes of business venturing. In the current Japanese system, on the other hand, the economic contribution of classic venture capital is still focused on reducing the risks of initiation for traditional entrepreneurs.

Bibliography

Admati, Anat R., and Pfleiderer, Paul (1994). "Robust Financial Contracting and the Role of Venture Capitalists." *Journal of Finance*, 49: 371-402.

Albach, Horst (1981). "On the Re-Discovery of the Entrepreneur in Economic Policy Discussion." Engels, Wolfram, and Pohl, Hans (eds.). *German Yearbook on Business History 1981*. Berlin: Springer: 11-26.

Albach, Horst (1984). "Die Rolle des Schumpeter-Unternehmers Heute." Bös, Dieter, and Stolper, Hans-Dieter (eds.). *Schumpeter oder Keynes? Studies in Contemporary Economics*, Vol. 12, Berlin: Springer: 125-146.

Albach, Horst (2000). "Globalisierung und Organisationsstruktur mittelständischer Unternehmen: Eine Analyse aus europäischer Sicht." Schneider, Uwe H, Hommelhoff, Peter, and Schmidt, Karsten (eds.). *Deutsches und europäisches Gesellschafts-, Konzern- und Kapitalmarktrecht - Festschrift für Marcus Lutter zum 70. Geburtstag.* Köln: Verlag Dr. Otto Schmidt.

Albach, Horst (2002). "Der Unternehmer als schöpferischer Zerstörer – Ein Kolloquium mit Joseph A. Schumpeter." Schweickart, Nikolaus (ed.). *Unternehmertum am Beginn des 21. Jahrhunderts*. Munich: Piper: 81-96.

Albach, Horst (ed., 1989). *Zur Theorie der Unternehmung. Schriften und Reden von Erich Gutenberg. Aus dem Nachlaß*. Berlin: Springer.

Albach, Horst, and Köster, Dieter (1997). "Risikokapital in Deutschland." *Discussion Paper*, FS IV 97 – 17, Wissenschaftszentrum Berlin für Sozialforschung.

Albach, Horst, Detlef Hunsdiek, and Ljuba Kokalj (1986). *Finanzierung mit Risikokapital.* Stuttgart: C.E. Poeschel.

Alchian, Armen A. (1950). "Uncertainty, Evolution, and Economic Theory." *Journal of Political Economy*, 58: 211-221.

Alchian, Armen A., and Demsetz, Harold (1972). "Production, Information Costs, and Economic Organization." *American Economic Review*, 62: 777-795.

Allen, Franklin, and Gale, Douglas (2000). *Comparing Financial Systems*. Cambridge: MIT Press.

Anand, Bharat N., and Piskorski, Mikolaj Jan (2000). "(Why) Are Networks Important?" *Working Paper*, Harvard University.

Aoki, Masahiko (1984). *The Co-operative Game Theory of the Firm*. Oxford: Clarendon Press.

Aoki, Masahiko (1988). *Information, Incentives & Bargaining in the Japanese Economy.* Cambridge: Cambridge University Press.

Aoki, Masahiko (1990). "Toward an Economic Model of the Japanese Firm." *Journal of Economic Literature*, Vol. XXVIII, March 1990: 1-27.

Aoki, Masahiko (1994). "The Contingent Governance of Teams: An Analysis of Institutional Complementarity." *International Economic Review*, 35: 657-675.

Aoki, Masahiko (1995). "An Evolving Diversity of Organizational Mode and Its Implications for Transitional Economies." *Journal of the Japanese and International Economies*, 9: 330-353.

Aoki, Masahiko (1999a). "Information and Governance in the Silicon Valley Model." *Working Paper*, Stanford University.

Aoki, Masahiko (1999b). "An Information Theoretic Approach to Comparative Corporate Governance." *Working Paper*, Stanford University.

Aoki, Masahiko (2001). *Toward a Comparative Institutional Analysis*. Cambridge: MIT Press.

Aoki, Masahiko, and Patrick, Hugh (eds., 1994). *The Japanese Main Bank System: Its Relevance for Developing and Transforming Economies.* New York: Oxford University Press.

Aoyama, Yuko (2001). "The Information Society, Japanese Style: Corner Stores as Hubs for E-Commerce Access." *Mimeo*, forthcoming in Leinbach, Thomas, and Brunn, Stanley (eds.). Worlds of Electronic Commerce, London: Wiley

Arai, Hisashi (2000). *Bitbare no Kodou.* Tokyo: Nikkei BP.

Arrow, Kenneth J. (1962). "Economic Welfare and the Allocation of Resources for Invention." Richard R. Nelson (ed.). *The Rate and Direction of Inventive Activity.* Princeton: Princeton University Press.

Arrow, Kenneth J. (1971). *Essays in the Theory of Risk Bearing.* Chicago: Markham.

Asia/Pacific Research Center (1999). "Crisis and Aftermath: The Prospects for Institutional Change in Japan." Report of a Conference Held May 3, 1999, at Stanford University.

Bahrami, Homa, and Evans, Stuart (2000). "Flexible Recycling and High-Tech Entrepreneurship." Martin Kenney (ed.). *Understanding Silicon Valley*. Stanford: Stanford University Press, 165-189.

Baker, Malcolm (2000). "Career Concerns and Staged Investment: Evidence from the Venture Capital Industry." *Mimeo*, Harvard University, July 2000.

Baker, Malcolm, and Gompers, Paul A. (2000). "The Determinants of Board Structure and Function at the Initial Public Offering." *Mimeo*, Harvard University, June 2000.

Baker, Malcolm, and Wurgler, Jeffrey (2000). "The Equity Share in New Issues and Aggregate Stock Returns." *Journal of Finance*, Vol. LV, No. 5: 2219-2257.

Bakos, Yannis, and Brynjolfsson, Erik (1997). "Organizational Partnerships and the Virtual Organization." C. Kemerer (ed.). *The Future of Markets and Organizations: How IT Shapes Competition*. Kluwer Acacemic Press.

Banatao, Dado P., and Fong, Kevin A. (2000). "The Valley of Deals." Lee, Chong-Moon, Miller, William F., Gong Hancock, Marguerite, and Rowen, Henry S. (eds.). *The Silicon Valley Edge*. Stanford: Stanford University Press.

Baron, James N., Burton, M. Diane, and Hannan, Michael T. (1996). "The Road Taken: Origins and Evolution of Employment Systems in Emerging Companies." *Industrial and Corporate Change*, Vol. 5, No. 2: 239-275.

Baron, James N., Burton, M. Diane, and Hannan, Michael T. (1998). "Engineering Bureaucracy: The Genesis of Formal Policies, Positions, and Structures in High-Technology Firms." *Industrial and Corporate Change*, Vol. 5, No. 2: 239-275.

Baron, James N., Burton, M. Diane, and Hannan, Michael T. (1999). "Building the Iron Cage: Determinants of Managerial Intensity in the Early Years of Organizations." *Working Paper*, Stanford University, April 1999.

Baron, James N., Hannan, Michael T., and Burton, M. Diane (1999). "Labor Pains: Organizational Change and Employee Turnover in Young, High-Tech Firms." *Mimeo*, June 7, 1999.

Bartlett, Joseph W. (1999). *Fundamentals of Venture Capital*. Lanham: Madison Books.

Baudeau, Nicolas (1910, first published 1767). *Première introduction à la philosophie économique*. Ed. A. Dubois. Paris: P. Geuthner.

Becht, Marco (1999). "European Corporate Governance: Trading Off Liquidity Against Control." *European Economic Review*, June 1999.

Becker, Gary (1962). "Investment in Human Capital: A Theoretical Analysis." *Journal of Political Economy*, LXX: 9-49.

Bentham, Jeremy (1952). *Jeremy Bentham's economic writings*. Ed. W. Stark. London: Allen & Unwin.

Berglof, Erik, and von Thadden, Ernst-Ludwig (1999). "The Changing Corporate Governance Paradigm: Implications for Transition and Developing Countries." Paper prepared for the *Annual World Bank Conference on Development Economics*, Washington, D.C., April 28-30, 1999.

Berle, Adolf A., and Means, Gardiner C. (1930). "Corporations and the Public Investor." *The American Economic Review*, Vol. 20, Issue 1, Mar. 1930, 54-71.

Berle Adolf A., and Means, Gardiner C. (1967). *The Modern Corporation and Private Property*. Revised edition (first edition 1932). New York: Harcourt, Brace & World.

Bhidé, Amar V. (2000). *The Origin and Evolution of New Businesses*. Oxford: Oxford University Press.

Black, Bernard S., and Gilson, Ronald J. (1998). "Venture Capital and the Structure of Capital Markets: Banks versus Stock Markets." *Journal of Financial Economics*, 47: 243-277.

Blair, Margaret M., and Kruse, Douglas L. (2000). "Worker Capitalists?" *Leading Companies*, Online Magazine of the Foundation for Enterprise Development, available at: http://www.fed.org/onlinemag/Mar00/trends.htm, Reprinted from Brookings Review, Fall 1999.

Blair, Margaret M., Stout, Lynn A. (1999). "A Team Production Theory of Corporate Law." *Virginia Law Review*, Vol. 85, No. 2, March 1999: 247-328.

Boehmer, Ekkehart (1999). "Corporate Governance in Germany: Institutional Background and Empirical Results." *Arbeitspapier*, Nr. 78, Humboldt University Berlin, March 24, 1999.

Brockman, John (1997). "John Doerr: The Coach." *Edge*. Available at URL: http://www.edge.org, retrieved: March 28, 2000.

Bronson, Po (1999). "Gen Equity." *Wired Digital Archive*, July 1999. Available at URL: http://www.wired.com, retrieved August 11th, 1999.

Brophy, David (1996). "United States Venture Capital Markets: Changes and Challenges." OECD. *Venture Capital and Innovation*. OCDE/GD(96)168, Paris: OECD.

Brown, John S., and Duguid, Paul (2000a). *The Social Life of Information*. Harvard: Harvard Business School Press.

Brown, John S., and Duguid, Paul (2000b). "Mysteries of the Region: Knowledge Dynamics in Silicon Valley." Available at URL: http://www.slofi.com/mysteries.htm, retrieved: Novermber 20, 2000.

Brynjolfsson, Erik (1993). "An Incomplete Contracts Theory of Information, Technology and Organization." *Mimeo*, revised June 1993.

Bryjolfsson, Erik, Hitt, Lorin M., and Yann, Shinkyu (2000). "Intangible Assets: How the Interaction of Computers and Organizational Structure Affects Stock Market Valuations." *MIT Working Paper*, July 2000.

Burton, M. Diane (1995). "The Evolution of Employment Systems in High Technology Firms." *Ph.D. dissertation*, Stanford University.

Bygrave, William D. (1997). *The Portable MBA in Entrepreneurship*. Second Edition. New York: John Wiley.

Bygrave, William D., and Timmons, Jeffry A. (1992). *Venture Capital at the Crossroads*. Boston: Harvard Business School Press.

Cable, Daniel M., and Shane, Scott (1997). "A Prisoner's Dilemma Approach to Entrepreneur-Venture Capitalist Relationships." *Academy of Management Review*, Vol. 22, No.1: 142-175.

California Public Employees' Retirement System (1998). *Corporate Governance Core Principles & Guidelines (The United States)*. April 13, 1998, Sacramento: Calpers.

Carey, David (1999). "The Year in Deals: Buyout Firms Take to Venture Capital." *The Daily Deal*, December 29, 1999. Available at URL: http://www.thedailydeal.com, retrieved February 21, 2000.

Castilla, Emilio J., Hwang, Hokyu, Granovetter, Ellen, and Granovetter, Mark (2000), "Social Networks in Silicon Valley," Lee, Chong-Moon, Miller, William F., Gong Hancock, Marguerite, and Rowen, Henry S. (eds.), *The Silicon Valley Edge*, Stanford: Stanford University Press.

Chandler, Alfred Dupont (1977). *The Visible Hand*. Cambridge, Mass.: The Belknap Press.

Cheung, Steven N. S. (1983). "The Contractual Nature of the Firm." *Journal of Labor and Economics*, 26: 1-24.

Christopher, Allistair (2000). "Piecing Together Limited Partner and General Partner Relations." *Venture Capital Journal*, August 1, 2000.

Clark, J. M. (1942). "Relations of History and Theory." *Journal of Economic History*, Vol. 2, Issue Supplement: The Tasks of Economic History, Dec. 1942: 132-142.

Clark, John B. (1892). "Insurance and Business Profit." *The Quarterly Journal of Economics*, Vol. 7, Issue 1, Oct. 1892: 40-54.

Coase, Ronald H. (1937). "The Nature of the Firm." *Economia*, November 1937: 386-405.

Cohen, Allan R., and Bradford, David L. (1989). "Influence Without Authority: The Use of Alliances, Reciprocity, and Exchange to Accomplish Work." *Organizational Dynamics*, 17: 4-17.

Cole, Arthur H. (1942). "Entrepreneurship as an Area of Research." *Journal of Economic History*, Vol. 2, Issue Supplement: The Tasks of Economic History, Dec. 1942: 118-126.

Cole, Arthur H. (1946). "An Approach to the Study of Entrepreneurship: A Tribute to Edwin F. Gay." *Journal of Economic History*, Vol. 6, Issue Supplement: The Tasks of Economic History, May 1946: 1-15.

Corporate Governance Forum of Japan (1998). "Corporate Governance Principles - A Japanese View - (Final Report)." *Mimeo*, Corporate Governance Committee, May 26, 1998.

Darby, Michael R., and Zucker, Lynne G. (1997). "Star Scientists, Institutions, and the Entry of Japanese Biotechnology Enterprises." *Mimeo*, Revision of National Bureau of Economic Research Working Paper No. 5795, revised May 1997.

Daunt, Jacqueline A. (1997). "Venture Capital: A Strategy for High Technology Companies." Palo Alto: Fenwick & West LLP.

Davenport, Herbert (1913). *Economics of Enterprise*. New York: Macmillan.

David, Paul A. (2000). "The Digital Technology Boomerang: New Intellectual Property Rights Threaten Global 'Open Science'." *Working Paper*, Stanford University, October 2000.

Department of Commerce (1998). *The Emerging Digital Economy*. Washington D.C.: Department of Commerce.

Department of Special Collections (1989). "Frederick Emmons Terman Biography." *Frederick Emmons Terman Papers*, SC160, Stanford University Archives: Stanford. Available at URL: http://www.oac.cdlib.org/dynaweb/ead/stanford/sc0160, retrieved: November 20, 2000.

Easterbrook, W.T. (1949). "The Climate of Enterprise." *The American Economic Review*, Vol. 39, Iss. 3, May 1949: 322-335.

Eisenberg, Melvin A. (1999). "The Conception that the Corporation is a Nexus of Contracts, and the Dual Nature of the Firm." *Working Paper*, Columbia Law School, May 12, 1999.

Emerson, Richard M. (1962). "Power-Dependence Relations." *American Sociological Review*, Volume 27, Issue 1, Feb. 1962: 31-41.

European Association of Securities Dealers (2000). *EASD Corporate Governance Principles and Recommendations*. Brussels: EASD.

European Venture Capital Association (EVCA) (1998). "New Pan-European Performance Study." *Europe Private Equity Update*, January 1998.

Evans, George Heberton (1949). "The Entrepreneur and Economic Theory: A Historical and Analytical Approach." *The American Economic Review*, Vol. 39, Issue 3, May 1949: 336-348.

Evans, Herberton G. Jr. (1959). "Business Entrepreneurs, Their Major Functions and Related Tenets." *Journal of Economic History*, Vol. 19, Issue 2, Jun. 1959: 250-270.

Faggin, Federico (1995). "Interview with Federico Faggin." *Silicon Valley Project*, Stanford University Libraries. Available at URL: http;//www-sul.Stanford.edu/depts./hasrg/histsci/silicon genesis/faggin-ntb.html, retrieved: November 20, 2000.

Fama, Eugene F. (1980). "Agency Theory and the Theory of the Firm." *The Journal of Political Economy*, Vol. 88, Issue 2, Apr. 1980: 288-307.

Fama, Eugene F., and Jensen, Michael C. (1983). "Separation of Ownership and Control." *Journal of Law and Economics*, 26 (June): 301-325.

Fenn, George W., Liang, Nellie, and Prowse, Stephen (1996). "The Economics of the Private Equity Market." Extended version of a staff study published in the *Federal Reserve Bulletin*, January 1996: 26-27. Available at URL: http://www.imdr.com/venture/preqmkt.htm, retrieved: February 9, 1998.

Fineberg, Seth A. (1998). "Congress Approves Revised Rollover Law." *Venture Capital Journal*, August 1, 1998.

Fleming, Standish M. (1999). "The Challenge of Distributing Thinly Traded Stocks." *Venture Capital Journal*, February 1, 1999.

Fujitsu Research Institute (2000). *Tokyo ni okeru Kigyou Shuuseki*. Tokyo: Fujitsu Research Institute

Gannon, Michael (1999a). "Financing in Purgatory." *Venture Capital Journal*, May 1, 1999.

Gannon, Michael (1999b). "M&A Deals Gain Cachet." *Venture Capital Journal*, October 1, 1999.

Garrison, Jayne (1998). "Doctor Stock." *Wired Digital Archive*, October 1998. Available at URL: http://www.wired.com, retrieved: March 20, 1999.

Gilson, Ronald J. (1999). "Silicon Valley's Idiosyncratic Legal Infrastructure." Presented at the Conference "*Silicon Valley: Center of Innovation*" June 3, 1999 at Stanford University. Available at URL: http://aparc.stanford.edu/events/june1999/index.html, retrieved November 22, 1999.

Gilson, Ronald J. (2000). "Globalizing Corporate Governance: Convergence of Form or Function." *Working Paper*, No. 192, Stanford Law School, John M. Olin Program in Law and Economics.

Goldberg, Michael (1994a). "Fire in the Valley." *Wired Digital Archive*, January 1994. Available at URL: http://www.wired.com, retrieved: March 20, 1999.

Goldberg, Michael (1994b). "Why Jim Clark Loves Mosaic." *Wired Digital Archive*, October 1994. Available at URL: http://www.wired.com, retrieved: March 20, 1999.

Gompers, Paul A. (1994). "The Rise and Fall of Venture Capital." *Business and Economic History*, Vol. 23, No. 2, Winter 1994: 1-26.

Gompers, Paul A. (1999). "Resource Allocation, Incentives and Control: The Importance of Venture Capital in Financing Entrepreneurial Firms." Acs, Zoltan J., Carlsson, Bo, and Karlsson, Charlie (eds.). *Entrepreneurship, Small and Medium-Sized Enterprises and the Macroeconomy.* Cambridge: Cambridge University Press: 206-235.

Gompers, Paul A., and Lerner, Joshua (1998a). "What Drives Venture Capital Fundraising?" *Working Paper*, Harvard University, August 1998.

Gompers, Paul A., and Lerner, Joshua (1998b). "The Determinants of Corporate Venture Capital Success: Organizational Structure, Incentives, and Complementarities." *NBER Working Paper*, No. 6725, September 1998.

Gompers, Paul, and Lerner, Joshua (2000). "Money Chasing Deals? The Impact of Fund Inflows on Private Equity Valuations." *Journal of Financial Economics*, 55: 281-325.

Gove, Alex (1999a). "Those Pesky Entrepreneurs." *Red Herring*, July 10, 1999. Available at URL: http://www.redherring.com, retrieved: July 12, 1999.

Gove, Alex (1999b). "Head's Up." *Red Herring*, July 14, 1999. Available at URL: http://www.redherring.com, retrieved: July 20, 1999.

Gove, Alex (1999c). "Full Disclosure." *Red Herring*, August 11, 1999. Available at URL: http://www.redherring.com, retrieved: November 8, 1999.

Gove, Alex (2000). "VCs to Limited Partners: Take a Hike!" *Red Herring*, July 28, 2000. Available at URL: http://www.redherring.com, retrieved November 20, 2000.

Granovetter, Mark S. (1985). "Economic Action and Social Structure: The Problem of Embeddedness." *American Journal of Sociology*, 91 (3): 481-510.

Green, Milford B. (ed., 1991). *Venture Capital: International Comparisons*. London: Routledge.

Greif, Avner (1997). "Economic History and Game Theory: A Survey." *Mimeo*, Draft June 25, 1997.

Grossman, Sanford J., and Hart, Oliver (1986). "The Costs and Benefits of Ownership: A Theory of Vertical and Lateral Integration." *Journal of Political Economy*, Vol. 94, Issue 4, Aug. 1986: 691-719.

Grover, Mary B. "Starting a Company is like going to War." *Forbes*, November 2, 1998: 184-193.

Haberler, Gottfried (1950). "Joseph Alois Schumpeter 1883-1950." *The Quarterly Journal of Economics*, Vol. 64, Issue 3, Aug. 1950: 333-372.

Hale & Dorr, Ernst & Young, and J. Robert Scott (2001). *2001 Internet Compensation Report.* Available at http://www.compstudy.com, retrieved March 6, 2001.

Hall, Brian J., and Liebman, Jeffrey B. (1997). "Are CEOs Really Paid Like Bureaucrats?" *NBER Working Paper*, No. W6213.

Hamao, Yasushi; Packer, Frank; and Ritter Jay R. (1999). "Institutional Affiliation and the Role of Venture Capital: Evidence from Public Offerings in Japan." *Mimeo*, September 1999.

Hamilton, Joan O' C., and Himelstein, Linda (1997). "A Wellspring Called Stanford." *Business Week*, August 25 1997.

Hannan, Michael T., Burton, M. Diane, and Baron, James N. (1996). "Inertia and Change in the Early Years: Employment Relations in Young, High-Technology Firms." *Industrial and Corporate Change*, Vol. 5, 1996: 503-535.

Hart, Oliver (1983). "The Market Mechanism as Incentive Scheme." *Bell Journal of Economics*, 14: 366-382.

Hart, Oliver (1995). *Firms, Contracts, and Financial Structure.* Oxford: Clarendon Press.

Hart, Oliver, and Moore, John (1990). "Property Rights and the Nature of the Firm." *Journal of Political Economy*, Vol. 98, Issue 6, Dec. 1990: 1119-1158.

Hart, Oliver, and Moore, John (1994). "A Theory of Debt Based on the Inalienability of Human Capital." *Quarterly Journal of Economics*, Vol. 109, Issue 4, Nov. 1994: 841-879.

Hatlestad, Luc (1999). "Diary of an Internet IPO." *Red Herring*, July 1999. Available at URL: http://www.redherring.com, retrieved: July 20, 1999.

Hawley, Frederick B. (1893). "The Risk Theory of Profit." *The Quarterly Journal of Economics*, Vol. 7, Issue 4, Jul. 1893: 459-479.

Hawley, Frederick B. (1900). "Enterprise and Profit." *The Quarterly Journal of Economics*, Vol. 15, Issue 1, Nov. 1900: 75-105.

Hawley, Frederick Barnard (1927). "The Orientation of Economics on Enterprise." *The American Economic Review*, Vol. 17, Issue 3, Sep. 1927: 409-428.

Hayek, Friedrich August von (1944). *Road to Serfdom*. Chicago: University of Chicago Press.

Hayek, Friedrich August von (1945). "The Use of Knowledge in Society." *American Economic Review*, Vol. 35, Issue 4, Sep. 1945: 519-530.

Haynes, John (1895). "Risk as an Economic Factor." *The Quarterly Journal of Economics*, Vol. 9, Issue 4, Jul. 1895: 409-449.

Hébert, Robert F., and Link, Albert N. (1988). *The Entrepreneur: Mainstream Views and Radical Critiques*. Second edition. New York: Praeger.

Hellmann, Thomas (1998a). "The Allocation of Control Rights in Venture Capital Contracts." *Rand Journal of Economics*, Vol. 29, No. 1, Spring 1998: 57-76.

Hellmann, Thomas (1998b). "Some Thoughts on the Theory of Corporate Venture Investing." *Corporate Governance Today*, Columbia Law School, May 1998: 37-43.

Hellmann, Thomas (1998c). "Discussion of 'What Drives Venture Capital Fundraising?' by P. Gompers and J. Lerner." M. Bailey, P. Reiss and C. Winston (eds.), *Brookings Papers on Economic Activity: Microeconomics:* 197-203.

Hellmann, Thomas (2000). "Entrepreneurship and the Process of Obtaining Resource Commitments." *Mimeo*, February 2000.

Hellmann, Thomas, and Puri, Manju (1999). "The Interaction between Product Market and Financing Strategy: The Role of Venture Capital." *Working Paper*, Stanford University, Graduate School of Business, December 1999.

Hellmann, Thomas, and Puri, Manju (2000). "Venture Capital and the Professionalization of Startup Firms: Empirical Evidence." *Working Paper*, Stanford University, Graduate School of Business, September 2000.

Hellwig, Martin (1998). "On the Economics and Politics of Corporate Finance and Corporate Control." *Mimeo*, University of Mannheim.

Hermann, Thomas (1994). *Zur Theoriengeschichte des dispositiven Faktors*. Stuttgart: Schäfer-Poeschel.

Hirschman, Albert O. (1970). *Exit, Voice and Loyalty: Responses to Decline in Firms, Organizations, and States*. Cambridge: Harvard University Press.

Hoff, Marcian (1995). "Interview with Marcian (Ted) Hoff." *Silicon Valley Project*, Stanford University Libraries. Available at URL: http;//www-sul.Stanford.edu/depts./hasrg/histsci/silicon genesis/hoff-ntb.html, retrieved: November 20, 2000.

Hogan, Lester C. (1995). "Interview with Lester C. Hogan." *Silicon Valley Project*, Stanford University Libraries. Available at URL: http;//www-sul.Stanford.edu/depts./hasrg/histsci/silicon genesis/hogan-ntb.html, retrieved: November 20, 2000.

Itami, Hiroyuki (1994). "The 'Human-Capital-ism' of the Japanese Firm as an Integrated System." Imai, Kenichi, and Komiya, Ryutaro (eds.). *Business Enterprise in Japan: Views of Leading Japanese Economists*. Cambridge: MIT Press: 73-88.

Itami, Hiroyuki (1999). "Concept of the Firm and Corporate Governance in Japan." *Mimeo*, Hitotsubashi University.

Itoh, Hideshi (1994). "Japanese Human Resource Management from the Viewpoint of Incentive Theory." Aoki, Masahiko, and Dore, Ronald (eds.). *The Japanese Firm: The Sources of Competitive Strengths*. New York: Oxford University Press: 233-284.

Iwata, Ryushi (1992). "The Japanese Enterprise as a Unified Body of Employees." Shumpei Kumon, and Henry Rosovsky (eds.). *The Political Economy of Japan, Volume 3, Cultural and Social Dynamics*. Stanford: Stanford University Press: 170-197.

Jacobsen, David (1998). "Founding Fathers." *Stanford Magazine*, July/August 1998.

Jensen, Michael C. (1993). "The Modern Industrial Revolution, Exit, and the Failure of Internal Control Systems." *Journal of Finance*, Vol. XLVIII, No. 3: 831-879.

Jensen, Michael C. (2000). "Value Maximization, Stakeholder Theory, and the Corporate Objective Function." *Working Paper*, No. 00–58, Harvard Business School, April 2, 2000.

Jensen, Michael C., and Meckling, William H. (1976). "Theory of the Firm: Managerial Behavior, Agency Costs and Capital Structure." *Journal of Financial Economics*, 3: 305-360.

Joint Venture (1999). *Joint Venture's Internet Cluster Analysis*. San Jose: Joint Venture: Silicon Valley Network.

Joint Venture (2000). *Joint Venture's 2000 Index of Silicon Valley.* San Jose: Joint Venture: Silicon Valley Network.

Joint Venture (2001). *Joint Venture's 2001 Index of Silicon Valley.* San Jose: Joint Venture: Silicon Valley Network.

Joint Venture (2002). *Joint Venture's 2002 Index of Silicon Valley.* San Jose: Joint Venture: Silicon Valley Network.

Kagono, Tadao, and Kobayashi, Takao (1994). "The Provision of Resources and Barriers to Exit." Kenichi Imai, and Ryutaro Komiya (eds.). *Business Enterprise in Japan: Views of Leading Japanese Economists*. Cambridge: MIT Press: 89-104.

Kagono, Tadao, Nonaka, Yujiro, Sakakibara, Kiyonori, and Okumura, Akihiro (1985). *Strategic vs. Evolutionary Management: A US-Japan Comparison of Strategy and Organization*. New York: North-Holland.

Kaldor, Nicholas (1975). "What is Wrong With Economic Theory." *Quarterly Journal of Economics*, Vol. 89, Issue 3: 347-357.

Kanda, Hideki (1998). "Comparative Corporate Governance Country Report: Japan." Hopt, Klaus J, Kanda, Hideki, Roe, Mark J., Wymeersch, Eddy, and Prigge, Stefan (eds.). *Comparative Corporate Governance: The State of the Art and Emerging Research.* Oxford: Clarendon Press.

Kann, Antje (2000). "Strategic Venture Capital Investing by Corporations: A Framework for Structuring and Valuing Corporate Venture Capital Programs." *Ph.D. dissertation*, Stanford University.

Kanter, Larry (1999). "Jim Clark." *Salon.com*, November 24, 1999. Available at URL: http://www.salon.com, retrieved: March 21, 2000.

Kaplan, Steven N. (1997). "The Evolution of U.S. Corporate Governance: We Are All Henry Kravis Now." *Mimeo*, November 1997, University of Chicago.

Kaplan, Steven N. (1998). "Top Executive Incentives in Germany, Japan and the U.S.: A Comparison." *Mimeo*, February 1998, University of Chicago.

Kaplan, Steven N., and Strömberg, Per (2000). "How Do Venture Capitalists Choose Investmens?" *Mimeo*, August 2000, University of Chicago.

Karlgard, Rich (1997). "Present at Creation." *Forbes*, July 1997.

Kenney, Martin, and Florida, Richard (2000). "Venture Capital in Silicon Valley: Fueling New Firm Formation." Kenney, Martin (ed.) *Understanding Silicon Valley*. Stanford: Stanford University Press: 89-123.

Kenney, Martin, and von Burg, Urs (1999). "Technology, Entrepreneurship and Path Dependence: Industrial Clustering in Silicon Valley and Route 128." *Industrial and Corporate Change*, Vol. 8, No. 1: 67-103.

Keynes, John Maynard (1964). *The General Theory of Employment, Interest, and Money*. New York: Harcourt, Brace & World.

King, Ralph (2001). "Bonehead Safari – My Hunt for America's Dumbest VC." *Ecompany.com*, January 2001. Available at URL: http://www.ecompany.com, retrieved January 22, 2001.

Kingsley, Daniel T. (1999). "The State of the Venture Capital Industry and its Impact on the U.S. Economy." *Mimeo*, Speech before the Conference on Corporate Governance and Equity Offerings, February 24, 1999.

Kirzner, Israel M. (1973). *Competition and Entrepreneurship*. Chicago: University of Chicago Press.

Kiyonari, Tadao (1996). *Shinsangyou wo Soushitsusuru Kigyouka Shihonshugi*. Tokyo: Toyo Keizai.

Kleiner, Perkins, Caufield & Byers (1999). *Company Web Site*, URL: http://www.kpcb.com, retrieved: January 2, 1999.

Knight, Frank H. (1942). "Profit and Entrepreneurial Functions." *Journal of Economic History*, Vol. 2, Issue Supplement: The Tasks of Economic History, Dec. 1942: 126-132.

Kohn, Meir (1999). "The Capital Market Before 1600." *Working Paper*, No. 99-06, Department of Economics, Dartmouth College.

Komisar, Randy (2000). *The Monk and the Riddle*. Boston: Harvard Business School Press.

Komiyama, Makoto, and Masaoka, Yukinobu (2002). "Corporate Governance: A New Phase for Japanese Companies." *NRI Papers*, No. 47, Nomura Research Institute.

Kortum, Samuel, and Lerner, Joshua (2000). "Assessing the Contribution of Venture Capital to Innovation." *Mimeo*, Harvard University.

Kotter, John P. (1996). *Matsushita Leadership: Lessons from the 20th Century's Most Remarkable Entrepreneur*. New York: Free Press.

Krackhardt, David (1992). "The Strength of Strong Ties." Nohria, Nitin, and Eccles, Robert G. (eds.). *Networks and Organizations: Structure, Form, and Action*. Boston: Harvard Business School Press: 220-239.

Kreps, David (1984). "Corporate Culture and Economic Theory." *Mimeo*, May 1984.

Kvamme, E. Floyd (2000). "Life in Silicon Valley." Lee, Chong-Moon, Miller, William F., Gong Hancock, Marguerite, and Rowen, Henry S. (eds.). *The Silicon Valley Edge*. Stanford: Stanford University Press, 59-80.

La Porta, Rafael, Lopez-de-Silanes, Florencio, and Shleifer, Andrei (1998). "Corporate Ownership Around the World." *Mimeo*, October 1998.

La Porta, Rafael, Lopez-de-Silanes, Florencio, Shleifer, Andrei, and Vishny, Robert W. (1998). "Law and Finance." *Journal of Political Economy*, Vol. 106, No. 1: 1113-1155.

La Porta, Rafael, Lopez-de-Silanes, Florencio, Shleifer, Andrei, and Vishny, Robert (2000). "Investor Protection and Corporate Governance." *Mimeo*.

Lazear, Edward P. (1979). "Why is there Mandatory Retirement?" *Journal of Political Economy*, 89: 841-864.

Lazear, Edward P. and Moore, Robert L. (1984). "Incentives, Productivity, and Labor Contracts." *Quarterly Journal of Economics*, 99: 275-295.

Leibowitz, Alissa (2000). "VC Goes Institutional." *Venture Capital Journal*, October 1, 2000.

Lerner, Joshua. (1995). "Venture Capitalists and the Oversight of Private Firms." *Journal of Finance*, Vol. L, No. 1, March 1995: 301-318.

Levin, Jack S. (1998). *Structuring Venture Capital, Private Equity, and Entrepreneurial Transactions*. 1999 Edition. Gaithersburg: Aspen Publishers.

Lewis, Ben W. (1937). "The Corporate Entrepreneur." *The Quarterly Journal of Economics*, Vol. 51, Issue 3, May 1937: 535-544.

Liles, Patrick R. (1977). *Sustaining the Venture Capital Firm*. Cambridge, Mass.: Management Analysis Center.

MacMillan, I. C., Zemann, L., and Subba Narasimha, P. N. (1987). "Criteria distinguishing successful from unsuccessful Ventures in the Venture Screening Process." *Journal of Business Venturing*, 2: 123-137.

Mangoldt, Hans von (1855). *Die Lehre vom Unternehmergewinn*. Leipzig.

Marshall, Alfred (1920). *Principles of Economics*. 8th edition. London: Macmillan.

Matsushita Electric Industrial Co., Ltd. (1989). Annual Report 1989 (for the year ending March 31, 1989).

Matsushita, Konosuke (1975). *Ningen wo Kangaeru*. Tokyo: PHP Institute.

Matsushita, Konosuke (1982). *Thoughts on Man*. Tokyo: PHP Institute.

Matsushita, Konosuke (1988). *Quest for Prosperity*. Tokyo: PHP Institute.

McCormick, Jim (1998). "Silicon Valley History." *Silicon Valley Online*. Available at URL: http://www.silvalonline.clever.net/history.html, retrieved November 22, 2000.

McKenna, Regis (1995). "Interview with Regis McKenna." *Silicon Valley Project*, Stanford University Libraries. Available at URL: http;//www-sul.Stanford.edu/depts./hasrg/histsci/silicon genesis/regis-ntb.html, retrieved: November 20, 2000.

METI (2002). "2002 Nenhan Chuushokigyouhakusho no pointo." April 2002, *SME Agency*, Ministry of Economy, Trade and Industry, Japan.

Meulbroek, Lisa K. (2000). "The Efficiency of Equity-Linked Compensation: Understanding the Full Cost of Awarding Executive Stock Options." *Working Paper*, Harvard University.

Meyerson, Debra, Weick, Karl A., and Kramer, Roderick M. (1996). "Swift Trust and Temporary Groups." Kramer, R. M., and Tyler, T. (eds.). *Trust in Organizations: Frontiers of Theory and Research*. Tousand Oaks: Sage: 166-195.

Milgrom, Paul R. (1988). "Employment Contracts, Influence Activities, and Efficient Organization Design." *The Journal of Political Economy*, Vol. 96, Issue 1, Feb. 1988: 42-60.

Milgrom, Paul R., and Roberts, John (1990). "The Economics of Modern Manufacturing: Technology, Strategy, and Organization." *American Economic Review*, Volume 80, Issue 3: 511-528.

Milgrom, Paul, and John Roberts (1994). "Complementarities and Systems: Understanding Japanese Economic Organization." *Estudios Económicos*, Vol. 9, No. 1, 1994: 3-42.

Mill, John Stuart (1848). *Principles of Political Economy with Some of Their Applications to Social Philosophy*. London.

Miller, William F. (1998). "Stanford's Role in Silicon Valley." Presented at the Conference "What We Can Learn from Silicon Valley" June 9, 1998 at the U.S. Embassy in Stockholm. Available at URL: http://www.usemb.se/Silicon, retrieved November 20, 2000.

Miller, William F. (2000). "The 'Habitat' for Entrepreneurship." *Silicon Valley Networks Project*, July 2000, Stanford University.

Mises, Ludwig von (1949). *Human Action: A Treatise in Economics*. New Haven: Yale University Press.

MITI (1998). "1998 Nen Benchaa Kyapitaru Fando (Toushijigyoukumiai) Pafoomansu Benchimaaku." December 1998, Ministry of International Trade and Industry, Japan.

MITI (2000a). "2001 Nen ni mukete Keizaisangyouseisaku: Aratana Keizaikouzou kaikaku wo mokushi shite." August 2000, Ministry of International Trade and Industry, Japan.

MITI (2000b). "Puraibeetoekuitifainansu Jigyoukankyouseibikenkyuukai Taigen: Puraibeetoekuitifainansu no kankyou to sono fukyuu ni muketeno kadai." *Industrial Policy Bureau*, November 2000, Ministry of International Trade and Industry, Japan

Miwa, Yoshiro (1997). "The Economics of Corporate Governance in Japan." *Working Paper*, University of Tokyo.

MoF (2000a). "21 Seiki no Wagakunikeizai no jizokuteki Seichou wo kanou to surutame no kinyuumen no Shokadai ni tsuite." June 2000, *21 Seiki no Shikin no Nagare no Kouzouhenkaku ni kansuru Kenkyuukai*, Ministry of Finance, Japan.

MoF (2000b). "Wagakunikigyou no fainansushisutemu to koporeetogabanansu ni kansuru Ankeeto Chousa: Shoukeikekka to bunseki no chuukan houkokusho." October 20, 2000, Ministry of Finance, Japan

Moore, Andrew (2001). "Angel Investing Is Up According to Survey." *Angel Society*, available at URL://www.angelsociety.com, retrieved January 8, 2001.

Moore, Gordon E. (1995). "Interview with Gordon E. Moore." *Silicon Valley Project*, Stanford University Libraries. Available at URL: http;//www-sul.Stanford.edu/depts./hasrg/histsci/silicon genesis/moore-ntb.html, retrieved: November 20, 2000.

Moskowitz, Eric (2001). "Loudcloud sends smoke signals to IPO market." *Redherring.com*, February 21, 2001. Available at URL: http://www.redherring.com, retrieved February 22, 2001.

Nakagawa, Katsuhiro (1999). "Japanese Entrepreneurship: Can the Silicon Valley Model Be Applied to Japan?" *Silicon Valley Networks Project*, December 1999, Stanford University.

Nakagawa, Katsuhiro (2000). "The Government's Role to Cultivate Entrepreneurs in Japan." CEO & Minister Forum at Stanford, June 1-2, 2000, prepared, unedited remarks. Available at URL: http://aparc.stanford.edu/events/june2000/nakagawa/remarks.html, retrieved October 20, 2000.

Nakane, Chie (1967). *Tate Shakai no Ningen Kankei*. Tokyo: Kodansha.

Naughton, John (1999). "The Billion Dollar Man who put us on the Web." *The Guardian*, December 19, 1999. Available at URL: http://www.newsunlimited.co.uk, retrieved: March 21, 2000.

Neidorf, Shawn (1999a). "Terms Tango." *Venture Capital Journal*, June 1, 1999.

Neidorf, Shawn (1999b). "L.P.s Weigh the Pros and Cons of Venture Capital Investing." *Venture Capital Journal*, July 1, 1999.

Neumann, Manfred J.M. (1997). "Wagniskapital." Gutachten des Wissenschaftlichen Beirats beim Bundesministerium für Wirtschaft [Report of the Council of Academic Advisers to the German Ministry of Economics], May 23, 1997, Bonn: Bundesministerium für Wirtschaft [German Ministry of Economics].

Nikkei (2000). "Koujinsekinin de bencha wo ikkanikusei, NTVP Muraguchi Daihyou." *Nikkei Shinbun*, November 30, 2000.

Nikkei (2001a). "Shasetsu: Kigyoukachi takameru Torishimariyakukai wo tsukure." *Nikkei Shinbun*, April 18, 2001.

Nikkei (2001b). "Nihon Dokuji VC Moderu Mezasu." *Nikkei Shinbun*, Febuary 20, 2001.

Nikkei (2001c). "Nenkin no VB Toushi Hirogaru." *Nikkei Shinbun*, April 15, 2001.

Nikkei (2001d). "Shachou 100 Nin Ankeeto." *Nikkei Shinbun*, Nikkei Chousa, January 25, 2001.

Nikkei (2001e). "ShinkouVC Toushisaki Kabushikikoukai Hajimaru." *Nikkei Shinbun*, January 18, 2001.

Nikkei (2001f). "Gaishikei VC, Nihonde Benchaatoushi Kakudai." *Nikkei Shinbun*, March 25, 2001.

Nikkei (2001g). "VC ni Bunkatsu Shuhou hirogaru." *Nikkei Shinbun*, Mach 3, 2001.

Nikkei (2001h). "NTVP, Toushisakikigyoushachou ni Daihyou wo Haken." *Nikkei Shinbun*, January 17, 2001.

Nikkei (2002). "Benchaa Kyapitaru Chousa 2001 Nendo." *Nihon Keizai Shinbun*, July 5, 2002.

Nohria, Nitin (1988). *Creating New Business Ventures: Network Organization in Market and Corporate Contexts. Ph.D. dissertation*, Massachusetts Institute of Technology.

Nohria, Nitin, and Eccles, Robert G. (eds., 1992). *Networks and Organizations: Structure, Form, and Action*. Boston: Harvard Business School Press.

O'Brien, Tia (1998). "Feasting on Failure." *Upside*, June 29, 1998. Available at URL: http://www.upside.com, retrieved July 13, 1998.

OECD (1995). *National Systems for Financing Innovation*. Paris: OECD.

OECD (1996a). "Special Feature: Venture Capital in OECD Countries." *Financial Market Trends*, No. 62, February 1996: 15-39.

OECD (1996b). "Venture Capital and Innovation." OCDE/GD(96)168, Paris: OECD.

OECD (1996c). "The Knowledge-based Economy." OCDE/GD(96)102, Paris: OECD.

OECD (1997). "Special Feature: Shareholder Value and the Market in Corporate Control in OECD Countries." *Financial Market Trends*, No. 69, February 1998: 15-37.

OECD (1998). *Small Business, Job Creation and Growth.* Paris: OECD.

OECD (1999). "OECD Principles of Corporate Governance." Ad Hoc Task Force on Corporate Governance, SG/CG(99)5, Paris: OECD.

OECD (2000). "Is There a New Economy? First Report on the OECD Growth Project." Paris: OECD.

Ono, Masato (1997). *Benchaa Kigyou to Toushi no Jissaichishiki*. Tokyo: Touyou Keizai Shinbunsha.

Osnabrugge, Mark van, and Robinson, Robert J. (1999a). "Do Venture Capitalists Behave Differently When Investing In High Tech Ventures?" *Working Paper*, Harvard Business School, March 1999.

Osnabrugge, Mark van, and Robinson, Robert J. (1999b). "A Comparison of Business Angel and Venture Capitalist Investment Procedures: An Agency Theory-Based Analysis." *Working Paper*, Harvard Business School, March 1999.

Osnabrugge, Mark van, and Robinson, Robert J. (1999c). "The Influence of a Venture Capitalist's Source of Funds." *Working Paper*, Harvard Business School, March 1999.

Perkins, Anthony B. (1996). "You too can be a Winner!" Red Herring, June 1996. Available at URL: http://www.redherring.com, retrieved October 18, 1998.

Perkins, Anthony B. (2000). "Can the market get any uglier?" *Red Herring*, December 6, 2000. Available at URL: http://www.redherring.com, retrieved December 6, 2000.

Perkins, Anthony B., and Perkins, Michael C. (1999). *The Internet Bubble*. New York: Harper Collins.

Pfirrmann, Oliver, Wupperfeld, Udo, and Lerner, Joshua (1997). *Venture Capital and New Technology Based Firms: An US-German Comparison*. Heidelberg: Physica-Verlag.

Pigou, A. C. (1929). *Industrial Fluctuations*. 2nd edition. London: Macmillan.

Plummer, James L. (1987). "QED Report on Venture Capital Financial Analysis." Palo Alto: QED Research.

Poterba, James (1989). "Venture Capital and Capital Gains Taxation." Summers, Lawrence (ed.). *Tax Policy and the Economy*. Cambridge: MIT Press.

Price Waterhouse Coopers (PWC) (1999). *The Guide to Going Public*. Price Waterhouse Coopers.

Price Waterhouse Coopers (PWC) (2000b). "Global Private Equity 2000." Available at URL: http://www.pwcmoneytree.com, retrieved: November 20, 2000.

Private Equity Investors (2001). "Brief History of Secondary Purchases." *Private Equity Investors*, available at URL: http://www.pei.com, retrieved February 20, 2001.

Quesnay, Francois (1888). *Oeuvres économiques et philosophiques*. Ed. A. Oncken. Frankfurt: M. J. Baer.

Raik-Allen, Georgie (1999). "Venture Capitalists Feel the Heat." *Red Herring*, July 10, 1999. Available at URL: http://www.redherring.com, retrieved: July 12, 1999.

Rajan, Raghuram G., and Zingales, Luigi (1998a). "The Governance of the New Enterprise." *Mimeo*, University of Chicago, December 8, 1998.

Rajan, Raghuram G., and Zingales, Luigi (1998b). "Power in a Theory of the Firm." *Mimeo*, University of Chicago, forthcoming in the Quarterly Journal of Economics.

Rajan, Raghuram G., and Zingales, Luigi (2000). "The Firm as a Dedicated Hierarchy: A Theory of the Origin and Growth of Firms." *Mimeo*, University of Chicago, May 5, 2000.

Rajgopal, Shivaram, and Venkatachalam, Mohan (1998). "The Role of Institutional Investors in Corporate Governance: An Empirical Investigation." *Mimeo*, October 1998.

Rexhausen, F. (1960). *Der Unternehmer und die wirtschaftliche Entwicklung*. Berlin.

Roberts, John, and Van den Steen, Eric (2000). "Shareholder Interests, Human Capital Investment and Corporate Governance." *Mimeo*, April 30, 2000.

Rock, Arthur (1992). "Strategy vs. Tactics from a Venture Capitalist." Sahlman, William A., and Stevenson, Howard H. (eds.). *The Entrepreneurial Venture*. Boston: Harvard Business School Publications: 215-221.

Rosenberg, Nathan (1976). *Perspectives on Technology*. Cambridge: Cambridge University Press.

Sahlman, William A. (1990). "The Structure and Governance of Venture-Capital Organizations." *Journal of Financial Economics*, 27: 473-521.

Sahlman, William A. (1992). "Aspects of Financial Contracting in Venture Capital." Sahlman, William A., Stevenson, Howard H. (eds.). *The Entrepreneurial Venture*. Boston: Harvard Business School Publications: 222-242.

Saint-Simon, Claude-Henri (1977). *Ausgewählte Schriften*. Ed. Lola Zahn. Berlin.

Sakakibara, Kiyonori, Koga, Tadahisa, Honjo, Yuji, and Kondo, Kazunori (2000). *Nihon ni okeru gijutsukei Benchakigyou no Keieijittai to Sougyousha ni kansuru Chousakenkyuu*. Tokyo: National Institute of Science and Technology.

Sasaki, John and Tanahashi, Hajime (2002). "Shirikon Baree Moderu toha Nanika." [What is the Silicon Valley Model?] *Mimeo*, May 2002.

Saxenian, Annalee (1994). *Regional Advantage: Culture and Competition in Silicon Valley and Route 128*. Cambridge, Mass.: Harvard University Press.

Saxenian, Annalee (1998). "Reflections of Silicon Valley and the American Economic Renaissance: Lessons Learned and Myths Dispelled." Keynote Address presented at the Conference "What We Can Learn from Silicon Valley" June 9, 1998 at the U.S. Embassy in Stockholm. Available at URL: http://www.usemb.se/Silicon, retrieved November 20, 2000.

Saxenian, Annalee (1999a). "Comment on Kenney and von Burg, 'Technology, Entrepreneurship and Path Dependence: Industrial Clustering in Silicon Valley and Route 128'." *Industrial and Corporate Change*, Vol. 8, No. 1: 105-110.

Saxenian, Annalee (1999b). *Silicon Valley's New Immigrant Entrepreneurs*. San Francisco: Public Policy Institute of California.

Say, Jean Baptiste (1840). *Cours complèt d'économie politique pratique*. Second edition. Paris: Guillaumin.

Schibsted, Evantheia (1999). "The Trible Crown Winner." *Business 2.0*, June 1999. Available at URL: http://www.business2.com, retrieved: March 21, 2000.

Schumpeter, Joseph A. (1928). "The Instability of Capitalism." *The Economic Journal*, Vol. 38, Issue 151, Sep. 1928: 361-386.

Schumpeter, Joseph A. (1935). "The Analysis of Economic Change." *The Review of Economic Statistics*, Vol. 17, Issue 4, May 1935: 2-10.

Schumpeter, Joseph A. (1942). *Capitalism, Socialism and Democracy*. New York: Harper & Row.

Schumpeter, Joseph A. (1947). "The Creative Response in Economic History." *Journal of Economic History*, Vol. 7, Issue 2, Nov. 1947: 149-159.

Schumpeter, Joseph Alois (1987). *Beiträge zur Sozialökonomik*. Edited and translated by Stephan Böhm. Wien: Böhlau. Article "Unternehmer." pp. 137-157.

Shackle, G. L. S. (1966). *The Nature of Economic Thought*. Cambridge: Cambridge University Press.

Sheard, Paul (1994). "Interlocking Shareholdings and Corporate Governance." Masahiko Aoki, and Ronald Dore (eds.). *The Japanese Firm: The Sources of Competitive Strengths*. New York: Oxford University Press: 310-349.

Sheba, Togo (1969). *Konosuke Matsushita*. Tokyo: Rengo Press.

Shieber, Jonathan (2000). "Europe Sets the Table for the Future of VC." *Venturewire*, Friday, December 15, 2000.

Shisido, Zenichi (1999). "Japanese Corporate Governance: The Hidden Problems of the Corporate Law and Their Solutions." *Working Paper*, No. 153, Columbia Law School.

Shleifer, Andrei, and Vishny, Robert W. (1997). "A Survey of Corporate Governance." *Journal of Finance*, 52: 737-783.

Siegelman, Russell (1998). "Venture Capital 101." *Mimeo*.

Smart, Geoffrey H. (1998). *Management Assessment Methods in Venture Capital: Toward a Theory of Human Capital Valuation*. Ph.D. dissertation, Claremont Graduate University.

Smith, Valerie (1997). "Varian - An Early History." *Varian Associates Corporate Information*. Available at URL: http://www.varian.com, retrieved March 7, 1998.

Snow, David (2000). "Japanese Pensions Tap U.S. Market." *Venture Capital Journal*, March 1, 2000.

Sombart, Werner (1909). "Der kapitalistische Unternehmer." *Archiv für Sozialwissenschaft und Sozialpolitik*. XXIX: 689-758.

Stanford News Service (1996). "Networking Lessons from Silicon Valley." Available at URL: http://www.stanford.edu/dept/news/pr/96/960923siliconval.html, retrieved: August 19, 1999.

Stauss, James H. (1944). "The Entrepreneur: The Firm." *Journal of Political Economy*, 52, 2: 112-127.

Stevenson, Howard H., Roberts, Michael J., Grousbeck, H. Irving, and Bhidé, Amar V. (1999). *New Business Ventures and the Entrepreneur*. Fifth Edition. Boston: Irwin/McGraw-Hill.

Storz, Cornelia (1997). *Der mittelständische Unternehmer in Japan*. Baden-Baden: Nomos.

Sturgeon, Timothy J. (2000). "How Silicon Valley Came to Be." Martin Kenney (ed.). *Understanding Silicon Valley*. Stanford: Stanford University Press: 15-47.

Suchman, Mark C. (2000). "Dealmakers and Counselors: Law Firms as Intermediaries in the Development of Silicon Valley." Martin Kenney (ed.). *Understanding Silicon Valley*. Stanford: Stanford University Press: 71-97.

Tajnai, Carolyn (1985). "Fred Terman, The Father of Silicon Valley." Computer Forum, Stanford University, May 1985. Available at URL: http://forum.stanford.edu/About/History/terman.html, retrieved: March 7, 1998.

Tajnai, Carolyn (1995). "Links Between Stanford University and Industry." Computer Forum, Stanford University. Available at URL: http://www.internetvalley.com/archives/mirrors/tajnai-links.html, retrieved: November 14, 2000.

Tajnai, Carolyn (1996). "From the Valley of Heart's Delight to the Silicon Valley: A Study of Stanford University's Role in the Transformation." Computer Forum, Stanford University, December 1996. Available at URL: http://www-forum.stanford.edu/About/History/valley_of _hearts.html, retrieved: March 7, 1998.

Taptich, Brian E. (1998). "The New Startup." *Red Herring*, October, 1998. Available at URL: http://www.redherring.com, retrieved: August 6, 1999.

Templin, Ben (1999). "Creative Financing." *Red Herring*, Supplement Guide to Professional Services 1999. Available at URL: http://www.redherring.com, retrieved: July 20, 1999.

Thomson Venture Economics (2002). *Japanese VC Survey*. September 3, 2002.

Tirole, Jean (1999). "Corporate Governance." *Mimeo*, January 5, 1999.

Toll, David (2000). "Private Equity Primer." *Mimeo*, Asset Alternatives.

Toya, Tetsuro (2000). *The Political Economy of the Japanese Financial Big Bang: Institutional Change in Finance and Public Policy Making*. Ph.D. dissertation, Stanford University.

TSE (2001). "Mothers Statistics." *Mimeo*, February 2001, Tokyo Stock Exchange.

Tsuru, Kotaro (1995). *The Japanese Market*. Tokyo: LTCB International Library Foundation.

Tuttle, Charles A. (1927). "The Function of the Entrepreneur." *The American Economic Review*, Vol. 17, Issue 1, Mar. 1927: 13-25.

Useem, Jerry (1999). "Entrepreneur of the Century." *Inc.*, 20th Anniversary Issue: 159-174.

Venture Capital Journal (VCJ). Various issues.

Venture Capital Yearbook (VCY). Various issues.

Venture Economics. Various documents available at URL: http://www.ventureeconomics.com.

Venture Enterprise Center (VEC). Various documents available at URL: http://www.venture-web.or.jp/vec.

Venture One. Various documents available at URL: http://www.ventureone.com.

Wako Securities (2000). "Aratana kigyoukachisouzou wo mezashite." *Research Report*, February 3, 2000.

Walker, Amasa (1866). *The Science of Wealth*. Boston: Little, Brown.

Walker, Francis (1887). "The Source of Business Profits." *Quarterly Journal of Economics*, 1: 265-288.

Walras, Léon (1954). *Elements of Pure Economics*. Translated by W. Jaffé. Homewood: Irwin.

Weber, Max (1930). *The Protestant Ethic and the Spirit of Capitalism*. Translated by Talcott Parsons. New York: Scribner's.

Welles, Edward O. (1999). "In Search of Equity." *Inc.*, 20th Anniversary Issue: 145-146.

Wellisz, S. (1952). "Entrepreneur's Risk, Lender's Risk, and Investment." *The Review of Economic Studies*, Vol. 20, Issue 2, 1952-53: 105-114.

Wetzel, William E. (1997). "Venture Capital." Bygrave, William D. (ed.). *The Portable MBA in Entrepreneurship*. Second Edition. New York: John Wiley.

Williamson, Oliver E. (1975). *Markets and Hierarchies*. New York: The Free Press.

Williamson, Oliver E. (1985). *The Economic Institutions of Capitalism*. New York: The Free Press.

Williamson, Oliver E. (1999). "Human Actors and Economic Organization." *Mimeo*, University of California, Berkeley, February 1999.

Wilson, John W. (1985). *The New Venturers: Inside the High-Stakes World of Venture Capital*. Menlo Park: Addison-Wesley.

Wolfe, Gary (1994). "The (Second Phase of the) Revolution Has Begun." *Wired Digital Archive*, October 1994. Available at URL: http://www.wired.com, retrieved: March 20, 1999.

World Bank (1999). "Corporate Governance: A Framework for Implementation – Overview." Washington D.C.: World Bank.

World Economic Forum (2001). "Talent Strategies for the New Economy." 2001 Annual Meeting, Session summary. Available at URL: http://www.weforum.org, retrieved: January 30, 2001.

Yoshimori, Masaru. (1995). "Whose Company Is It? The Concept of Corporation in Japan and the West" *Long Range Planning*, 28: 33-44.

Young, Margaret (2001). "Business School Students Get Gloomy View of Prospects for Venture Capital Funding." *Stanford Report*, February 28, 2001.

Zingales, Luigi (1997). "Corporate Governance." *Mimeo*, October 31, 1997 Draft. Forthcoming in the New Palgrave Dictionary of Economics and the Law.

Zook, Matthew A. (2000). "Grounded Capital: Venture Capital's Role in the Clustering of Internet Firms in the U.S." *Mimeo*, November 1, 2000.

Zucker, Lynne G., and Darby, Michael R. (1996). "Star Scientists and Institutional Transformation: Patterns of Invention and Innovation in the Formation of the Biotechnology Industry." Paper presented at a colloquium entitled "Science, Technology, and the Economy," organized by Ariel Pakes and Kenneth L. Sokoloff, held October 20-22, 1995, at the National Academy of Sciences in Irvine, CA. *Proc. Natl. Acad. Sci. USA*, Vol. 93, November 1996: 12706-12716.

Zucker, Lynne G., Darby, Michael R. and Torero, Maximo (1997). "Labor Mobility from Academe to Commerce." *NBER Working Paper*, No. 6050, May 1997, Cambridge, Mass.: NBER, 1997.

Zucker, Lynne G., Darby, Michael R., and Brewer, Marilynn B. (1996). "Intellectual Human Capital and the Birth of U.S. Biotechnology Enterprises." *Mimeo*, forthcoming in the American Economic Review.

Appendix

Biography of Frederick Emmons Terman – "Father of Silicon Valley"[436]

Frederick Emmons Terman, the first child of Lewis Madison and Anna Terman, was born in English, Indiana on June 7, 1900. Due to Lewis Terman's chronic tuberculosis, the family sought a more salubrious climate, moving to the Los Angeles area in 1905. With the elder Terman's appointment to the Stanford University Education Department in 1910, the family settled permanently in the Stanford area.

Lewis Terman, an eminent psychologist and educator, is perhaps best known for his development of the Stanford-Binet intelligence tests. His work on IQ testing was however, only one aspect of a life-long professional interest in individual giftedness and leadership. Frederick was undoubtedly influenced by some of his father's concepts, and later integrated them into his own system of identifying faculty and students of unusual promise, and encouraging the fullest realization of their potentials. Growing up in an academic environment also instilled an early and thorough understanding of university operation, later to serve well in Dr. Terman's administrative career.

Childhood at Stanford University had its less serious aspects as well. Dr. Terman recalls hiking in the Stanford foothills, fishing in Felt Lake, and swimming in Lake Lagunita. At the age of fourteen, Frederick and his neighbor, Herbert Hoover, Jr., began experimenting with "ham" radio, resulting in Dr. Terman's life-long involvement with radio.

Nine years old before he began primary school, Dr. Terman progressed rapidly and graduated from Stanford University in 1920 with a degree in Chemistry. After obtaining an additional degree in Electrical Engineering at Stanford under Professor Harris J. Ryan, Terman went to the Massachusetts Institute of Technology for graduate study under Professor Vannevar Bush. Bush emphasized the practical, industrial applications of engineering in addition to theoretical research.

Upon the completion of his doctorate in electrical engineering in 1924, Dr. Terman accepted a teaching appointment at M.I.T. Health was to play a decisive role in Frederick Terman's career as it had for his father. While visiting his family at Stanford in the summer of 1924, he had a serious attack of tuberculosis, keeping him bed-ridden for a year.

For his recovery, the California climate was preferable to Massachusetts, and the following year Dr. Terman accepted a part-time instructorship in electrical engineering at Stanford University. He continued his convalescence throughout the academic year of 1925-26, getting up only a few hours each day to teach. Despite serious illness, these years were very productive. With the intense concentration characterizing all his endeavors, Terman used the time to read extensively the existing radio engineering literature and to begin drafting his own first book.

In the academic year 1926-27, Terman began full-time teaching at Stanford, specializing in electronics. Although the electronics laboratory suffered from a severe shortage of funds, in the years between 1926 and 1941, Dr. Terman was able to build up a program distinctive in its output of ideas, people and publications.

Meanwhile, Dr. Terman's own career was flourishing. In 1937, he became a full professor and executive head of the Department of Electrical Engineering. Five of his seven books were published and were well received. More than 600,000 copies would be published in nine languages. According to Dr. Terman, his books "reflect his interest in the systematic organization of knowledge, and his desire to find simple quantitative ways to treat each topic."

He was also active in numerous professional societies, particularly the Institute of Radio Engineers. In 1941 he was elected President of the I.R.E., a notable honor signifying the growing national visibility of Dr. Terman and the Stanford electronics program.

[436] Source: Department of Special Collections (1989), "Frederick Emmons Terman Biography," Frederick Emmons Terman Papers, SC160, Stanford University Archives: Stanford, available at URL: http://www.oac.cdlib.org/dynaweb/ead/stanford/sc0160, retrieved: November 20, 2000.

Pre-WW II years were significant in his personal life as well. In 1928, he married Sibyl Walcutt, a graduate student in psychology. Their three sons, Frederick, Terrence and Lewis, were born between 1929 and 1935.

The outbreak of World War II was a turning point for Dr. Terman. He was appointed to organize and direct the Harvard Radio Research Laboratory, which was responsible for developing countermeasures against enemy radar. This research project eventually had more than 850 employees. It devised electronic radar jammers; designed tunable receivers for locating and analyzing radar signals; and manufactured billions of aluminum strips (called "chaff") which confused enemy radar reception when dropped from airplanes. The Radio Research Laboratory (operating over Europe) was credited with saving many of the allied bombers, and Dr. Terman was decorated by both the American and British governments for his wartime efforts.

At the same time that he was directing the Harvard Laboratory, Dr. Terman was educating himself in the strategies of successful university administration. He benefited by living near the treasurer of Harvard University, from whom he learned how Harvard's administrative structure and policies contributed to its pre-eminence among universities. Other issues discussed were the future of government support for university research after the war, and how such funding could best be utilized. Terman felt World War II had clearly demonstrated the importance of technological superiority in military success, and as a result, the federal government would place a new priority upon sponsoring advanced engineering research.

Terman returned to Stanford in 1946 as Dean of Engineering. In his new position of responsibility, he was able to carry out the concepts he had developed for strengthening the engineering program at Stanford. There were three basic components in his plan: the use of government research contracts; enhancement of the symbiotic relationship between local industry and the university; and distribution of funds for maximum academic benefit.

The contacts Dr. Terman had made as director of the Harvard Radio Research Laboratory were useful in obtaining the federal government contracts for Stanford. The newly established Office of Naval Research sought Dr. Terman's assistance, and with the approval of Stanford president, Donald B. Tresidder, research projects were initiated in chemistry, physics, and electronics in 1945 and 1947. Terman developed administrative guidelines to assure that sponsored research would benefit, rather than compete with, the educational mission of the University. Among the important aspects of these guidelines were that all research projects should be built around the specific interests of individual faculty members, rather than being obtained by administrators and assigned to the faculty, and that research should actually be carried out by students and faculty as an integral part of their academic programs rather than being undertaken by professional research staff as an adjunct to educational goals. The conditions established with these original sponsored projects have continued as the basis for the successful applied research programs at Stanford.

Dr. Terman had long been opposed to the "ivory tower" image of universities. He recognized the practical and mutual benefits that could accrue from interaction between industry and academia, and encouraged a closer relationship between them.

Palo Alto is often called the "birthplace of electronics" in honor of Lee DeForest's pioneering research with the audion tube in 1912, but when Dr. Terman began his teaching career in the 1920's, there were very few innovative engineering companies in the Bay Area. Terman was disturbed to find most of his best students moving to the east coast to find jobs. In the 1930's Professor Terman attempted to ameliorate the situation by helping talented students establish their own small companies. His greatest success was the Hewlett-Packard company; Terman arranged for a 8500 research assistantship to bring his former student, David Packard, back from a job at General Electric in New York to collaborate with William Hewlett, another of his inventive students. Terman was the "godfather" of this and several other student-initiated ventures that formed the nucleus of the San Francisco Bay Area's industrial development, today's "Silicon Valley."

As Dean of Engineering, Dr. Terman could effectively foster cooperation between Stanford's engineering program and local research-oriented companies. He encouraged faculty consulting, developed industrial affiliates programs through which companies could keep informed of the latest scientific developments in their fields, and initiated the Honors Cooperative Program, allowing employees of local firms to study part-time toward advanced degrees at Stanford. These arrangements proved to be mutually beneficial. Innovative industries benefited from the intellectual stimulus of a strong university, whose graduates also provided an exceptionally qualified work force. Programs like the Honors Cooperative became added recruitment incentives. In return, the Stanford Engineering School received financial support through the affiliates and cooperative programs. Potential students were attracted by the favorable employment environment as well as academic excellence. The opening of the Stanford Industrial Park in the 1950's strengthened the university-industry liaison, and the Stanford pattern has since been emulated throughout the United States.

More important to the Engineering School's development than sponsored research or industrial cooperation was Dr. Terman's program for obtaining maximum benefit from available resources. As Dean, Terman directed the fiscal policies of the School. He was firmly committed to the concept of investing in faculty, not in buildings. As an expression of this, he felt money should be directed towards hiring the finest research-oriented engineers possible. He considered it wasteful to construct new buildings, filled with expensive equipment, without top-quality scientists to use them. He also felt it was better economy to pay the high salaries necessary to attract a few leading engineers, than to use the same amount of money to hire a greater number of mediocre professors at lower salaries. He has compared his strategy to a track team, saying, "It's better to have one seven-foot jumper on your team than any number of six-foot jumpers.

He called this principle the "steeples of excellence." These steeples consist of very small groups of experts in significant fields, who by leadership in their professions, can attract grant money, as well as the finest students and junior faculty members. Terman's formula for the judicious combining of federal money with industrial support propelled the Stanford Engineering School from a merely regional institution into national prominence.

With his appointment as Provost of Stanford University in 1955, Dr. Terman assumed broader administrative responsibilities. Although President J. E. Wallace Sterling, historian, and Frederick Terman, engineer, had different academic backgrounds, they shared similar administrative and educational philosophies. Like Terman, Sterling believed institutional superiority was based upon the outstanding achievement of individual faculty members. Highest priority was placed upon hiring and retaining the finest scholar-teachers, and faculty search, selection, and tenure polices were made more rigorous and competitive at all levels. As can be seen in Series III of this collection, Dr. Terman and his Provost's Office staff kept meticulously detailed data on the operations of every department throughout the University, including average class sizes, number of student contacts for each faculty member, Ph.D. output per professor, faculty salaries and anticipated retirement dates. Dr. Terman often had a fuller knowledge of the workings of a department than did its chairman. These statistics were invaluable for strengthening and streamlining the academic programs in all areas of Stanford. During the Sterling-Terman administration, the University experienced unprecedented growth in national academic prominence and prestige.

Although Dr. Terman retired as Provost in 1965, he has continued to serve as a part-time consultant to the President, and has designed and carried out several studies on school and department budgets, faculty planning, benefits and retirement. Dr. Terman has continued to be active in many professional societies, holding elective offices or committee appointments in the Institute of Radio Engineers, the American Institute of Electrical and Electronics Engineers, the Institute of Electrical and Electronics Engineers, the National Academy of Engineering, and Sigma Xi.

In keeping with his belief that the United States must maintain technological superiority in a highly competitive world, he has served as a consultant or advisor for the Institute of Defense Analysis, the Defense Science Board, the President's Scientific Advisory Committee, and the Navy, Air Force, and Signal Corps.

Since his retirement in 1965, he has devoted particular attention to the development of higher education in science and engineering, both in the United States and abroad. Among these project have been the Southern Methodist Foundation for Science and Engineering, the Korean Institute for Advanced Science, and a U.S. Office of Education mission to the U.S.S.R.

Dr. Terman once said, "I most enjoy helping to build something up, taking an unformulated enterprise and making it into what it could become." Today Stanford University, and the surrounding communities of technical scholars, bear witness to the continuing influence of that idea.

SAMPLE TERM SHEET

[COMPANY]

MEMORANDUM OF TERMS FOR PRIVATE PLACEMENT OF EQUITY SECURITIES

July 1999

This memorandum summarizes the principal terms with respect to the proposed Series A Preferred Stock financing of Company, a California corporation.

Capitalization

The Company's capitalization after the offering:

	Authorized	Outstanding	Percentage
Common Stock	______(1)	______(2)	______%
Series A Preferred Stock	______	______	______%
Totals:	______	______	100.0%

(1) Includes ______ shares of Common Stock reserved for issuance under the Company's 1998 Stock Plan.
(2) Includes options exercisable for ______ shares of Common stock.

Proposed Private Placement

The Company proposes a private placement of shares on the following terms:

Type of Security:	Series A Preferred Stock ("Preferred")
Number of Series A Shares Offered:	Up to __________
Price Per Series A Share:	$ _________
Total Amount of Offering:	Up to $ ________
Manner of Offering:	The sale of Preferred shares will occur in one or more closings.

Rights, Preferences and Privileges of Series A Preferred Stock

Dividend Provisions:	The holders of Preferred shall be entitled to receive non-cumulative dividends at the rate of [6-8] % of original issue price per share per annum, when and if declared by the Board of Directors, payable in preference to dividends paid on the Common Stock ("Common"). The holders of Preferred will not participate in dividends paid to the holders of Common.
Liquidation Preference:	In the event of any liquidation or winding up of the Company, the holders of Preferred shall be entitled to receive, in preference to the holders of Common, an amount equal to original price per share (adjusted for any stock splits, stock dividends, stock combination or recapitalization), plus declared and unpaid dividends. Thereafter, the holders of Common shall be entitled to receive all remaining assets of the Company.
	A merger, reorganization or sale of substantially all of the assets of the Company, in which the Company's shareholders immediately prior to the transaction possess less than 50% of the voting securities of the surviving entity (or parent, if any) immediately following the transaction, shall be deemed to be a liquidation for purposes of the liquidation preference.
Conversion Rights:	Each share of Preferred may be converted at the holder's option, at any time, into one share of Common, subject to adjustments as provided below.
Automatic Conversion:	Each Preferred will be automatically converted into Common, at the then applicable conversion rate, upon (i) the closing of a firmly underwritten public offering of the Company's stock, at a

price of _____ (which equals at least [3-5] times original price) and an aggregate offering price of not less than $ ____ ("IPO"), or (ii) the consent of the holders of [1/2-2/3%] of the then outstanding Preferred.

Anti-dilution Provisions:	The conversion price of the Preferred shall be subject to a [broad/narrow base weighted average] adjustment if the Company issues additional equity securities (other than the reserved 1998 stock plan shares and Common issuable upon conversion of the Preferred) at a purchase price less than the applicable conversion price. The conversion price will also be subject to proportional adjustment for stock splits, stock dividends, stock combinations and recapitalizations.
Voting Rights:	Except as required by law or as provided below, the Preferred shall be entitled to vote on all matters, on an as-converted basis, together with the Common Stock as a single class.
Protective Provisions:	So long as at least _____ shares of Preferred are outstanding, the Company shall not, without first obtaining the approval of the holders of at least a majority of the then outstanding shares of Preferred: (a) effect a merger, reorganization or sale of assets of the Company, (b) alter or change the rights of the Preferred in an adverse manner, (c) increase the authorized number of shares of Common Stock, Preferred or any Series of Preferred, (d) create any new class or series, or any other security convertible into equity securities, having a preference over or on parity with the Preferred, or (e) declare or pay any dividend.
Board of Directors:	As of the closing, the Board of Directors

	of the Company shall consist of _____ directors, with holders of Preferred having the rights to elect _____ directors and the holders of common having the right to elect the remaining directors, one of which will be an independent director nominated by the Founders and reasonably satisfactory to the Investors.
[Redemption:	The Company shall [have the right to/at the Investors' request], at any time after 4 years after the Closing, redeem the outstanding Preferred at a price of original price per share (adjusted for any stock splits, stock dividends, stock combination or recapitalization) plus any declared but unpaid dividends.]
<u>Registration Rights</u>	
Demand Rights:	Investors holding at least 50% of the Preferred or Common issued upon conversion of the Preferred, or a combination thereof, may request at any time after [the later of] ____________ __, 20__ [or six months after completion of the IPO], that the Company file a registration statement for their shares and shares of other participating holders having an aggregate offering price of not less than $ _____, and the Company will use its best efforts to cause such shares to be registered. The Company shall not be obligated to cause more than 2 registration(s) under this Demand Rights Provision.
"Piggyback" Rights:	The Investors shall be entitled to "piggyback" registration rights on all registrations of the Company, subject to underwriter cutback of 100% in case of an IPO and ___% of the offering in subsequent transactions. The Founders will have piggyback rights subordinate to the Investors.

S-3 Rights:	The Investors shall be entitled to Form S-3 registration rights at such times as the Company is a registrant entitled to use Form S-3, provided that the aggregate offering price exceeds $ _______ and that the Investors shall be entitled to only one registration every 12 month period.
Expenses:	All registration expenses of the demand registrations and piggyback registrations (exclusive of underwriting discounts and commissions) shall be borne by the Company, including fees and disbursements of one special counsel for the selling shareholders, and subject to exceptions for withdrawn registrations.
Lock-up:	Each Investor will agree to a lock-up of 180 days after the closing of the IPO, [subject to execution of similar lock-ups by the Company's officers, directors and 1% shareholders.]
Transfer of Rights:	The registration rights may be transferred provided (i) the transferee acquires at least _____ shares of Preferred (adjusted for any stock splits and the like), and (ii) the Company is given written notice thereof.
<u>Information Rights</u>:	So long as an Investor holds not less than ___% of the Preferred or of the Common issued upon conversion of such Preferred, or a combination thereof, the Company will furnish the Investor with unaudited [monthly/quarterly] and audited annual financial statements and with an annual plan, and will grant the Investors customary visitation and inspection rights. These rights will expire upon the closing of an IPO.
<u>Right of First Offer</u>:	The Investors shall have a right of first offer to purchase their pro rata portion of

equity securities, on an as-converted basis, in the event of any proposed issuance by the Company, excluding shares issued pursuant to acquisitions, equipment leasing arrangements, employee stock plans and other customary exceptions. These rights will expire upon completion of an IPO.

<u>Co-Sale Agreement</u>: As of the closing date, Founders will have entered into a co-sale agreement with the Company and each Investor purchasing not less than __________ shares of Preferred, pursuant to which those Investors shall have the right to participate in any sales by Founders of __% or more of Common. Certain customary carve-outs will apply.

<u>Founders' Stock</u>: The Founders will grant the Company an option to repurchase a portion of their Common at cost upon termination of their employment with the Company for any or no reason. [The repurchase option shall apply to 50% of the Common Stock held by the Founders,] which shares shall vest on a monthly basis over a period of four years from the Closing.

<u>Employee Agreements</u>: Each officer and key employee of the Company will enter into an Employee Agreement with respect to proprietary information and inventions in a form reasonably acceptable to the Company and the Investor.

<u>The Purchase Agreement</u>: The investment shall be made pursuant to a Stock Purchase Agreement reasonably acceptable to the Company and the Investors, which Agreement shall contain, among other things, appropriate representations and warranties of the Company and appropriate conditions of closing which shall include, among other things,

	qualification of the shares under applicable Blue Sky laws, the filing of a Certificate of Amendment of Articles of Incorporation establishing the rights and preferences of the Preferred and an opinion of counsel.
<u>Expenses</u>:	If the financing closes, the Company will pay the reasonable fees and expenses of special counsel for the Investors, up to a maximum of $_________.
<u>Closing</u>:	The closing of the transaction is expected to occur on or before ____________ __, 1999.

Ebay employment contract from http://techdeals.biz.findlaw.com/agreements/ebay/whitman.html
Retrieved October 23 2000

eBay
2005 HAMILTON AVENUE, SUITE 350
San Jose, CA 95125

PHONE 408 369-4830
FAX 408 369-4839
WWW.eBAY.COM

January 16, 1998

Ms. Margaret C. Whitman
204 Warren Street
Brookline, MA 02146

Dear Meg:

eBay, Inc. (the "Company" or "eBay") is pleased to offer you a position as Chief Executive Officer, at a salary, payable twice per month, which is equivalent to a yearly salary of $175,000.00. In addition, you will be eligible for an annual bonus up to $100,000.00, solely at the discretion of the Board of Directors. eBay will also compensate you for reasonable out-of-pocket expenses incurred for the relocation of your family and your belongings.

You will also be entitled to the benefits that eBay customarily makes available to employees in positions comparable to yours and it will be recommended to the Board of Directors that you be granted an option for the purchase of 800,000 shares of the Company's Common Stock. The option will be granted under the Company's 1996 Stock Option Plan and, assuming you remain an employee, will vest with respect to 25% of the shares subject to the option one year after the commencement of your employment and, at the end of each month thereafter, with respect to an additional 1/48 of the shares subject to the option; provided, however, that if your employment is terminated by the Company other than for "Cause"'. During your first year of employment, the option will vest, at the end of each month, with respect to 1/48 of the shares subject to the option. No other acceleration of vesting will occur in connection with any termination of your employment or any acquisition of eBay. At least 100,000 of the shares underlying the stock option must be purchased for cash at the option exercise price, as soon as possible after the grant is approved; these shares will be subject to a repurchase option in favor of the Company to the extent they are "Unvested".

If your employment is terminated by the Company other than for "Cause" at any time during your employment, you will continue to receive salary compensation for an additional six months and, if at the end of such period you remain unemployed, you will be eligible for additional salary compensation for the lesser of (i) six months, or (ii) until you find other employment.

The Company asks that you complete the enclosed "Employee Information and Inventions Agreement" prior to commencing employment. In part, this Agreement requests that a departing employee refrain from using or disclosing eBay's Confidential Information (as defined in the Agreement) in any manner which might be detrimental to or conflict with the business interests of eBay or its employees. This Agreement does not prevent a former employee from using his or her general knowledge and experience no matter when or how gained in any new field or position. If you should have any questions about the "Employee Confidential Information and Inventions Agreement," please call me.

Under federal immigration laws, the Company is required to verify each new employee's identity and legal authority to work in the United States. Accordingly, please be prepared to furnish appropriate documents satisfying those requirements; this offer of employment is conditioned on submission of satisfactory documentation.

We hope that you and eBay will find mutual satisfaction with your employment. All of us at eBay are very excited about your joining our team and look forward to a beneficial and fruitful relationship. Nevertheless, employees have the right to terminate their employment at any time with or without cause or notice, and the Company reserves for itself an equal right. We both agree that any dispute arising with respect to your employment, the termination of that employment, or a breach of any covenant of good faith and fair dealing related to your employment, shall be conclusively settled by final and binding arbitration in accordance with the Voluntary Labor Arbitration Rules of the American Arbitration Association (AAA) at the AAA office in San Jose.

This letter and the "Employee Confidential Information and Inventions

Agreement" contain the entire agreement with respect to your employment. The terms of this offer may only be changed by written agreement, although the Company may from time to time, in its sole discretion, adjust the salaries and benefits paid to you and its other employees. Should you have any questions with regard to any of the items indicated above, please call me. Kindly indicate your consent to this employment agreement by signing and returning a copy of this letter and a completed "Employee Confidential Information and Inventions Agreement" to me by the close of business January 16, 1998. Upon your signature below, this will become our binding agreement with respect to your employment and its terms merging and superseding in their entirety all other or prior agreements and communications by you and eBay as to the specific subjects of this letter.

Very truly yours,

/s/ Pierre Omidyar

Pierre Omidyar
Chief Executive Officer

ACCEPTED:

/s/ Margaret C. Whitman 1/16/98

Margaret Whitman Date
"CAUSE"

For the purposes of this offer, the term "Cause" means (i) the conviction of any felony or any crime involving moral terpitude or dishonesty; (ii) participation in a fraud or act of dishonesty against the Company which adversely affects the Company in a material way; (iii) willful breach of the Company's policies which adversely affects the Company in a material way; (iv) causing intentional damage to the Company's property or business; (v) conduct which constitutes gross insubordination or incompetence; (vi) habitual neglect of duties; or (vii) conduct which demonstrates gross unfitness to serve; provided that the action or conduct described in clauses (iii), (v) and (vii) above will constitute "Cause" only if such action or conduct continues after the Company has provided Employee with written notice thereof and a reasonable opportunity (to be not less than 30 days nor more than 90 days) to cure the same. For the above purposes, a termination by the Company without Cause includes a termination of employment by the Employee within 30 days following any of the following events: (x) the assignment of any duties to Employee inconsistent with, or reflecting a materially adverse change in, Employee's position, duties, responsibilities or status with the Company, or the removal of Employee from, or failure to reelect Employee to, any of such positions; or (y) the relocation of the Company's principal executive offices, or relocating Employee's principal place of business, in excess of fifty (50) miles from the Company's current executive offices.

Survey Questionnaires

1. Founder Questionnaire

Research Project "Venture Governance" – Questionnaire

ベンチャー・ガバナンス研究プロジェクト

I. 会社/Company Information:

会社名/Company Name:

住所/Address:

ホームページ/URL: http://

業種/Industry:

商品／サービス/Products/Services Offered:

会社創立年月日/Date of Establishment: 年/Year 月 /Month 日/Day

従業員数/Number of Employees:

II. 個人/Personal Information:

氏名/Name:

役職名/Position Title:

メール/E-mail:

会社との関係/Your relationship with the company (適当なところを全部チェックして下さい/Please check all appropriate fields.)

設立者/Founder

社長/Chief Executive Officer

投資家/Investor

a) 融資提供者/provider of debt finance

b) 資本提供者/provider of equity

会社員/Employee

技術の提供者/Provider of Technology

供給者/Supplier

顧客/Customer

アドバイサー/その他/Advisor/Other

本日の年月日/Date: 年/Year 月/Month 日/Day

III. 研究質問/Research Questions

a) 設立者への質問/Founder Section

会社創立前の職業/What did you do prior to establishing this company?

以前の仕事について/How would you describe the following aspects of your previous position?

	大変悪い Very Bad			大変良い Very Good	無回答 N.A.
報償/Compensation.	○	○	○	○	○
労働時間/Working Time.	○	○	○	○	○
同僚との関係/Relationship with Co-workers.	○	○	○	○	○
上司との関係/Relationship with Superiors.	○	○	○	○	○
会社戦略への影響度/Ability to influence the direction of the company.	○	○	○	○	○
成功報償の程度/Ability to share in the success of the company.	○	○	○	○	○
全般的な業績/Overall quality of your previous company	○	○	○	○	○

会社設立にあたって重要だった点について/How important were the following factors in your decision to establish this company?

	重要でない Not important			大変重要 Very Important
自分の仕事のスタイルと価値観に合った組織を作ること/Design an organization that suits my own work style and values.	○	○	○	○
社員より高い収入を得ること/Make more money than as an employee.	○	○	○	○
最も興味を持つ分野で仕事をすること/Work in the area that I find most interesting.	○	○	○	○
上司を持ったないこと/Have nobody who tells me what to do.	○	○	○	○
お金持ちになること/Have a chance to become really rich.	○	○	○	○
社員より仕事が楽になること/Do less or more enjoyable work than as an employee.	○	○	○	○
他の人から尊敬されること/Gain the respect of others.	○	○	○	○

ビジネスのアイデアを進める上で重要だった点/How important were the following factors in developing your business idea?

	重要でない Not important			大変重要 Very Important
同じような仕事をする/Do the same business that I did in my previous position.	○	○	○	○
大学での研究分野の技術を商業化する/Commercialize an invention that I developed in an	○	○	○	○

前の仕事で開発した技術を商業化する/Commercialize a technology that I developed in my previous position.				
一般的な新技術を用する/Make use of a new technology that is generally available.				
未開拓のマーケットニーズを開拓する/Satisfy a market need that nobody had identified so far.				
他の会社のビジネス·モデルを真似する/Copy the business model of another company.				
現存のマーケットに入って最も効率的な組織を作る/Enter an existing market and design an organization that is more efficient that incumbent competitors.				

設立時に考えたリスクにつて/How did you perceive the following risks at the time of establishment?

	低い Not high			大変高い Very high
技術／サービスが失敗するというリスク/Risk that the product/service technology fails.				
マーケットが小さ過ぎるというリスク/Risk that the market for the product/service is too small.				
利益が出ないというリスク/Risk that the company will not be profitable.				
倒産するというリスク/Risk that the company will become bankrupt.				
会社が倒産した後に次のいい仕事が見つけられるかというリスク/Personal career risk of not finding a good job if the company fails.				
個人資産の ____ %を失うというリスク、/Personal financial risk of loosing <-% of personal assets.				

設立時に考えられた可能性について/How did you perceive the following possibilities at the time of establishment?

	低い Not high			大変高い Very high
生涯続けられるような会社の可能性/Possibility of creating a company that I can lead for the rest of my professional career.				
収入の増加とともにライフスタイルを変えられる可能性/Possibility of changing my lifestyle by earning more money.				
お金持ちになって、早期退職は可能になる可能性/Possibility of becoming very rich, and be able to retire early.				
三年以内に株式を公開出来る可能性/Possibility of leading the company to a public offering within 3 years.				
十年以内に株式を公開出来る可能性/Possibility of leading the company to a public offering within 10 years.				
会社所有者として止まって尊敬された安定性がある会社を作る可能性/Build a respected and sustainable company and remain its sole owner.				

通常業務が始まった年月日/When would you date the beginning of normal business operations?

年/Year [ ] 月/Month [ ] 日/Day [ ]

業務開始に関連して以下のような活動をいつ完了しましたか/When, in relation to the above date, did you accomplish the following activities?

	無し Never	上記日付前 Prior	上記日付後 After	いつごろ Approximate Date
社外融資の確保/Secure external finance	○	○	○	年/Year [ ] 月/Month [ ]
最初の顧客の確保/Secure first customers	○	○	○	年/Year [ ] 月/Month [ ]
従業員の確保/Secure employees	○	○	○	年/Year [ ] 月/Month [ ]
技術やノウハウの確保/Secure technology/know how	○	○	○	年/Year [ ] 月/Month [ ]
会社の法的登記/Legally establish the company	○	○	○	年/Year [ ] 月/Month [ ]
ビジネスプランの作成/Prepare a business plan	○	○	○	年/Year [ ] 月/Month [ ]
弁護士の確保/Retain an attorney	○	○	○	年/Year [ ] 月/Month [ ]
経理制度の確立/Establish an accounting system	○	○	○	年/Year [ ] 月/Month [ ]
第三者資本資金の導入/Obtain external equity financing	○	○	○	年/Year [ ] 月/Month [ ]
第三者負債資金の導入/Obtain external debt financing	○	○	○	年/Year [ ] 月/Month [ ]
ビィジョンの作成/Write a mission statement	○	○	○	年/Year [ ] 月/Month [ ]
従業員の採用/Hire an employee	○	○	○	年/Year [ ] 月/Month [ ]
人事担当者の採用/Hire a full-time personnel specialist	○	○	○	年/Year [ ] 月/Month [ ]
マーケティングプランの作成/Develop a marketing plan	○	○	○	年/Year [ ] 月/Month [ ]
製品／サービスの発表/Announce a product	○	○	○	年/Year [ ] 月/Month [ ]
特許申請の手続き/File a patent application	○	○	○	年/Year [ ] 月/Month [ ]
最初の商品／サービスの販売/Sell first product	○	○	○	年/Year [ ] 月/Month [ ]

設立時に考えていた成長戦略について/What kind of growth strategy did you envision at the time of establishment?

ブレークイーブンは何ヶ月あとだと予想していましたか/After how many months did you expect to reach break-even?

期待キャッシュフローに関して以下の科目から最も適切なものを選んで下さい/Please choose the most appropriate description of your expected Cash Flow development from the below options.(グラフの例を参照して下さい/see example graph)

キャッシュアウトフロー/Cash Out-Flow	経常キャッシュフローからの投資及び経費 Investment/expenses from operating cash flow	内部創出キャッシュインフローより投資/High up-front investment 技術／設備投資 in technology/ capital equipment	 マーケティング／宣伝 in marketing/ advertising
キャッシュインフロー/Cash In-Flow	○	○	○
一定の成長率 Steady Sales Growth ○			
鈍化する成長率 Declining Sales Growth ○			
急激な成長率 Increasing Sales Growth ○			

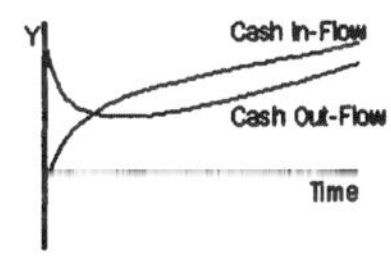

b) 社長への質問/Chief Executive Officer (設立者社長/Founder-CEO)

現在株式保有していますか/Do you currently hold shares in the equity of your company? もしあれば何パーセントぐらいですか/If so, what percentage of total shares outstanding?

%

待遇と報酬全般、そしてその会社業績との関連について記入して下さい/Please fill in the following table describing the structure of your overall compensation, and its relation to the performance of the company.

会社業績 Overall Performance of the Company	全体報酬の上限と下限 Range of Overall Compensation	報酬全体の割合/Share of Overall Compensation as 固定給 Fixed Salary	 ボーナス Bonus	 ストックオプション Stock Options

一番いい場合 Best Case	%	%	%	%
予想どうりの場合 Expected	100 %	%	%	%
最悪の場合 Worst Case	%	%	%	%

現在の貴社の資本比率はどのぐらいですか/What is your company's current ratio of debt to equity?

負債/Debt : 資本/Equity = ___ : 1

会社の資金供給者構造について次の表に記入して下さい/Please fill in the following table regarding the financing structure of your company.

資本/Equity	設立者/Founders	%
	ベンチャーキャピタル会社/Venture Capital Companies	%
	産業企業/Corporate Investors	%
	個人投資家/Individual Investors	%
	合計/Total	100 %
負債/Debt	金融機関/Banks, etc.	%
	ベンチャーキャピタル会社/Venture Capital Companies	%
	個人投資家/Individual Investors	%
	その他/Others	%
	合計/Total	100 %

もしあなたがベンチャーキャピタル会社から資金提供を受けるとしたらその財務構造はどのようになりますか。そしてベンチャーキャピタル会社の特別な権利についてはどのようになりますか。/If you have received venture capital financing, please describe the financing structure and superminority rights, if applicable.

経営戦略の意志決定について次のような質問をお答え下さい/Please answer the following questions regarding your decision-making on strategic management issues?

	決してない Never	ときどき Sometimes	いつも Always
自分で決める/I decide on my own.	○	○	○

社員全員と相談して合意を作り出す/I consult everybody in the company and create a consensus.			
最も関係する者と相談する/I consult the people who are most concerned.			
取締役と相談する/I consult board members.			
社外アドバイサーと相談する/I consult outside professional advisors.			
顧客と相談する/I consult customers.			
友人と相談する/I discuss issues with friends.			
投資家から指示を貰う/I receive instructions from investors.			
取締役らから指示を貰う/I receive instructions from board members.			

日常業務の意志決定について次のような質問をお答え下さい/Please answer the following questions regarding your decision-making on day-to-day management issues?

	決してない Never	ときどき Sometimes	いつも Always
自分で決める/I decide on my own.			
社員全員と相談して合意を作り出す/I consult everybody in the company and create a consensus.			
最も関係する者と相談する/I consult the people who are most concerned.			
取締役と相談する/I consult board members.			
社外アドバイサーと相談する/I consult outside professional advisors.			
顧客と相談する/I consult customers.			
友人と相談する/I discuss issues with friends.			
投資家から指示を貰う/I receive instructions from investors.			
取締役らから指示を貰う/I receive instructions from board members.			

貴社の顧客について次の質問にお答え下さい/Please answer the following questions regarding your company's customers:

現在の顧客数/How many customers does your company currently have? [ ] 一年後の顧客数の予想/What do you think will be the number of customers one year from now? [ ] 個人消費者の割合/What percentage of your customers are private individuals ([ ] %), 法人顧客の割合/what percentage are companies, etc. ([ ] %). 上位二十%の顧客は売上高に占める割合/The 20 % largest customers make up for [ ] % of total revenues. 社長就任以前からの知り合いの顧客数/How many of your customers did you know before joining this company? ______. 貴社に投資している顧客はいますか/Do you have customers who also invested in your company? ______.

顧客にとっては次のどの点が重要だと思いますか/How important, do you think, are the following aspects to your customers?

	重要でない Not important			大変重要 Very Important
素早く生産及び配達/Quick production and delivery.	○	○	○	○
低価格/Low Price	○	○	○	○
高信頼性/Reliability	○	○	○	○
ブランドイメージ/Image/Brand	○	○	○	○
テーラーメイドの商品及びサービス/Customized Production/Service	○	○	○	○
娯楽性/Pleasure/Entertainment	○	○	○	○

貴社の取引先について次のような質問をお答えて下さい/Please answer the following questions regarding your company's suppliers of goods, services, and technology:

現在、取引先は何社ぐらいあるか/How many suppliers does your company currently have? ______ 一年後に何社ぐらいになっているか/What do you think will be the number of suppliers one year from now? ______ 正常な支払期間/What are your standard terms of payment? ______. 上位二十%の取引先が全体の購入コストに占める割合/The 20 % largest suppliers make up for ______ % of total procurement costs. 社長就任以前からの知り合いの取引先の数/How many of your suppliers did you know before joining this company? ______. 貴社に投資している顧客はいますか/Do you have suppliers who also invested in your company? ______.

購入決定で次のどの点が重要ですか/How important are the following aspects in your purchasing decision?

	重要でない Not important			大変重要 Very Important
素早く生産及び配達/Quick production and delivery.	○	○	○	○
低価格/Low Price	○	○	○	○
高信頼性/Reliability	○	○	○	○
ブランドイメージ/Image/Brand	○	○	○	○
テーラーメイドの商品及びサービス/Customized Production/Service	○	○	○	○
娯楽性/Pleasure/Entertainment	○	○	○	○

従業員に関してお答えて下さい/Please answer the following questions regarding your company's employees:

現在の従業員数/How many people are currently employed by your firm?

[ ] 正社員数/full time [ ] パートタイマ数/part time [ ] その他（インターンなど）/others (intern, without salary, etc.). [ ] 臨時社員数/temporary employees

契約及びパートタイム社員は次の部署でどのように使われていますか/Which best describes your company's use of contract and part time workers?

	契約社員/Independent Contractors			パートタイマ/Part Timers		
	使わない Never used	時々使う Sometimes used	いつも使う Regularly used	使わない Never used	時々使う Sometimes used	いつも使う Regularly used
管理職/Senior Management	○	○	○	○	○	○
事務管理職/Other Administrative & Managerial	○	○	○	○	○	○
技術/Engineering & Science	○	○	○	○	○	○
営業＆マーケティング/Sales & Marketing	○	○	○	○	○	○
事務職/Clerical	○	○	○	○	○	○
熟練労働/Skilled labor	○	○	○	○	○	○
未熟練労働/Unskilled labor	○	○	○	○	○	○

どのような方法で採用しますか/Which of the following recruitment channels do you use?

	社内登用 Promote from within	新聞広告 Advertise in the newspaper	ウェブサイト広告 Advertise on the web site	現社員の紹介 Get referrals from current employees	取引先からの紹介 Get referrals from business contacts	大学からの採用 Recruit at schools or colleges	人材紹介会社の利用 Use employment agencies or search firms
管理職/Senior Management	☐	☐	☐	☐	☐	☐	☐
事務管理職/Other Administrative & Managerial	☐	☐	☐	☐	☐	☐	☐
技術/Engineering & Science	☐	☐	☐	☐	☐	☐	☐
営業＆マーケティング/Sales & Marketing	☐	☐	☐	☐	☐	☐	☐
事務職/Clerical	☐	☐	☐	☐	☐	☐	☐
熟練労働/Skilled labor	☐	☐	☐	☐	☐	☐	☐
未熟練労働/Unskilled labor	☐	☐	☐	☐	☐	☐	☐

各職種採用時にあなたの会社の最も重要と思う基準について書いて下さい/How important are the following criteria in determining whom your company hires for various positions? (最も重要なものにはMを選んで下さい、最も重要ではないものにはLを選んで下さい/Please enter M for the most important criterion and L for the least important criterion for each of the occupational groups).

	会社及びグループへの適応度 Company or Group Fit	学歴／証明書 Credentials	ビジネス経験 Industry/Business Experience	専門技能 Specialized Skills	全体的なやる気及び向上心 Overall Motivation or Drive	無回答 N.A.
管理職/Senior Management						
事務管理職/Other Administrative & Managerial						
技術/Engineering & Science						
営業&マーケティング/Sales & Marketing						
事務職/Clerical						
熟練労働/Skilled labor						
未熟練労働/Unskilled labor						

報酬制度について記入して下さい/Which best describes your company`s compensation structure?

	固定給 Fixed Salary	個人業績に基づくボーナス Individual Performance-based Bonus	ストックオプション Stock Options	時間給 Hourly Wage
管理職/Senior Management	使わない/Never	使わない/Never	使わない/Never	使わない/Never
事務管理職/Other Administrative & Managerial	使わない/Never	使わない/Never	使わない/Never	使わない/Never
技術/Engineering & Science	使わない/Never	使わない/Never	使わない/Never	使わない/Never
営業&マーケティング/Sales & Marketing	使わない/Never	使わない/Never	使わない/Never	使わない/Never
事務職/Clerical	使わない/Never	使わない/Never	使わない/Never	使わない/Never
熟練労働/Skilled labor	使わない/Never	使わない/Never	使わない/Never	使わない/Never
未熟練労働/Unskilled labor	使わない/Never	使わない/Never	使わない/Never	使わない/Never

年俸の昇給を決定する基準について答えて下さい/How important are the following criteria in determining increases in annual compensation? (最も重要なものにはMを選んで下さい、最も重要ではないものにはLを選んで下さい/Please enter M for the most important criterion and L for the least important criterion for each of the occupational groups).

	グループの業	一般給与相場との

	Individual Performance	績 Group Performance	Firm Performance	Rank	Seniority	整合性 Adjusting to Market Wager
管理職/Senior Management						
事務管理職/Other Administrative & Managerial						
技術/Engineering & Science						
営業&マーケティング/Sales & Marketing						
事務職/Clerical						
熟練労働/Skilled labor						
未熟練労働/Unskilled labor						

この調査に参加していただきどうも有り難うございました。終わったら以下のボックスをチェックして「Submit」ボタンを押してください。

Thank you for taking the time to fill in this questionnaire. When you are done, please check the below box and push the "submit" button.

☐ 終わった/Done!

Submit　　Reset

質問やコメントはこちらにクリック下さい！For questions and comments please click here!

2. Non-Founder CEO Questionnaire

Research Project "Venture Governance" - Questionnaire

ベンチャー・ガバナンス研究プロジェクト

I. 会社/Company Information:

会社名/Company Name:

住所/Address:

ホームページ/URL: http://

業種/Industry:

商品／サービス/Products/Services Offered:

会社創立年月日/Date of Establishment: 年/Year 月 /Month 日/Day

従業員数/Number of Employees:

II. 個人/Personal Information:

氏名/Name:

役職名/Position Title:

メール/E-mail:

会社との関係/Your relationship with the company (適当なところを全部チェックして下さい/Please check all appropriate fields.)

設立者/Founder ☐

会社員/Employee ☐

社長/Chief Executive Officer ☐

技術の提供者/Provider of Technology ☐

投資家/Investor

供給者/Supplier ☐

a) 融資提供者/provider of debt finance ☐

顧客/Customer ☐

b) 資本提供者/provider of equity ☐

アドバイサー/その他/Advisor/Other

本日の年月日/Date: 年/Year 月/Month 日/Day

III. 研究質問/Research Questions

b) 社長/Chief Executive Officer (設立者ではない社長/Non-Founder CEO)

現職前の仕事について/What did you do prior to assuming the CEO position at this company?

以前の仕事について/How would you describe the following aspects of your previous position?

	大変悪い Very Bad			大変良い Very Good	無回答 N.A.
報償/Compensation.	○	○	○	○	○
労働時間/Working Time.	○	○	○	○	○
同僚との関係/Relationship with Co-workers.	○	○	○	○	○
上司との関係/Relationship with Superiors.	○	○	○	○	○
会社戦略への影響度/Ability to influence the direction of the company.	○	○	○	○	○
成功報償の程度/Ability to share in the success of the company.	○	○	○	○	○
全般的な業績/Overall quality of your previous company	○	○	○	○	○

どのようにこのポジションを受けましたか/How and when did you get in contact with this company?

この会社に入るにあたって重要だった点について/How important were the following factors in your decision to join this company?

	重要でない Not important			大変重要 Very Important
自分の仕事のスタイルと価値観に合った組織を作ること/Design an organization that suits my own work style and values.	○	○	○	○
前の仕事より高い収入を得ること/Make more money than in my previous position.	○	○	○	○
最も興味を持つ分野で仕事をすること/Work in the area that I find most interesting.	○	○	○	○
上司を持ったないこと/Have nobody who tells me what to do.	○	○	○	○
お金持ちになること/Have a chance to become really rich.	○	○	○	○
前の仕事より仕事が楽になること/Do less or more enjoyable work than as an employee.	○	○	○	○

他の人から尊敬されること/Gain the respect of others.				

会社に入る時に考えたリスクにつて/How did you perceive the following risks at the time of joining this company?

	低い Not high			大変高い Very high
技術／サービスが失敗するというリスク/Risk that the product/service technology fails.				
マーケットが小さ過ぎるというリスク/Risk that the market for the product/service is too small.				
利益が出ないというリスク/Risk that the company will not be profitable.				
倒産するというリスク/Risk that the company will become bankrupt.				
会社が倒産するあるいは辞めさせられる場合に次のいい仕事が見つけられるかというリスク/Personal career risk of not finding a good job if the company fails or getting fired.				
個人資産の ☐ %を失うというリスク、/Personal financial risk of loosing <-% of personal assets.				

会社に入る時に考えられた可能性について/How did you perceive the following opportunities at the time of joining this company?

	低い Not high			大変高い Very high
生涯続けられるような会社の可能性/Possibility of creating a company that I can lead for the rest of my professional career.				
収入の増加とともにライフスタイルを変えられる可能性/Possibility of changing my lifestyle by earning more money.				
お金持ちになって、早期退職は可能になる可能性/Possibility of becoming very rich, and be able to retire early.				
三年以内に株式を公開出来る可能性/Possibility of leading the company to a public offering within 3 years.				
十年以内に株式を公開出来る可能性/Possibility of leading the company to a public offering within 10 years.				

会社に入る時に考えていた成長戦略について/What kind of growth strategy did you envision at the time of joining the company?

ブレークイーブンは設立時の何ヶ月あとだと予想していましたか/After how many months did you expect to reach break-even?

☐

期待キャッシュフローに関して以下の科目から最も適切なものを選んで下さい/Please choose the most appropriate description of your expected Cash Flow development from the below options.(グラフの例を参照して下さい/see example graph)

経常キャッシュフローからの投資及　　内部創出キャッシュインフローより投資/High up-front investment

ロー/Cash Out-Flow	び経費 Investment/expenses from operating cash flow	技術/設備投資 in technology/ capital equipment	マーケティング/宣伝 in marketing/ advertising
キャッシュインフロー/Cash In-Flow	○	○	○

一定の成長率/Steady Sales Growth ○

鈍化する成長率/Declining Sales Growth ○

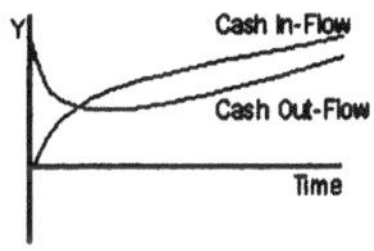

急激な成長率/Increasing Sales Growth ○

現在株式保有していますか/Do you currently hold shares in the equity of your company? もしあれば何パーセントぐらいですか/If so, what percentage of total shares outstanding?

[ ] %

待遇と報酬全般、そしてその会社業績との関連について記入して下さい/Please fill in the following table describing the structure of your overall compensation, and its relation to the performance of the company.

会社業績 Overall Performance of the Company	全体報酬の上限と下限 Range of Overall Compensation	報酬全体の割合/Share of Overall Compensation as 固定給 Fixed Salary	ボーナス Bonus	ストックオプション Stock Options
一番いい場合 Best Case	[ ] %	[ ] %	[ ] %	[ ] %
予想どうりの場合 Expected	100 %	[ ] %	[ ] %	[ ] %
最悪の場合 Worst Case	[ ] %	[ ] %	[ ] %	[ ] %

現在の貴社の資本比率はどのぐらいですか/What is your company's current ratio of debt to equity?

負債/Debt : 資本/Equity = [ ] : [1]

会社の財務構造について次の表に記入して下さい/Please fill in the following table regarding the financing structure of your company.

資本/Equity	設立者/Founders	[ ] %
	ベンチャーキャピタル会社/Venture Capital Companies	[ ] %
	産業企業/Corporate Investors	[ ] %
	個人投資家/Individual Investors	[ ] %
	合計/Total	100 %
負債/Debt	金融機関/Banks, etc.	[ ] %
	ベンチャーキャピタル会社/Venture Capital Companies	[ ] %
	個人投資家/Individual Investors	[ ] %
	その他/Others	[ ] %
	合計/Total	100 %

もしあなたがベンチャーキャピタル会社から資金提供を受けるとしたらその財務構造はどのようになりますか。そしてベンチャーキャピタル会社の特別な権利についてはどのようになりますか。/If you have received venture capital financing, please describe the financing structure and superminority rights, if applicable.

[ ]

経営戦略の意志決定について次のような質問をお答え下さい/Please answer the following questions regarding your decision-making on strategic management issues?

	決してない Never	ときどき Sometimes	いつも Always
自分で決める/I decide on my own.	○	○	○
社員全員と相談して合意を作り出す/I consult everybody in the company and create a consensus.	○	○	○
最も関係する者と相談する/I consult the people who are most concerned.	○	○	○
取締役と相談する/I consult board members.	○	○	○

社外アドバイサーと相談する/I consult outside professional advisors.	○	○	○
顧客と相談する/I consult customers.	○	○	○
友人と相談する/I discuss issues with friends.	○	○	○
投資家から指示を貰う/I receive instructions from investors.	○	○	○
取締役らから指示を貰う/I receive instructions from board members.	○	○	○

日常業務の意志決定について次のような質問をお答え下さい/Please answer the following questions regarding your decision-making on day-to-day management issues?

	決してない Never	ときどき Sometimes	いつも Always
自分で決める/I decide on my own.	○	○	○
社員全員と相談して合意を作り出す/I consult everybody in the company and create a consensus.	○	○	○
最も関係する者と相談する/I consult the people who are most concerned.	○	○	○
取締役と相談する/I consult board members.	○	○	○
社外アドバイサーと相談する/I consult outside professional advisors.	○	○	○
顧客と相談する/I consult customers.	○	○	○
友人と相談する/I discuss issues with friends.	○	○	○
投資家から指示を貰う/I receive instructions from investors.	○	○	○
取締役らから指示を貰う/I receive instructions from board members.	○	○	○

貴社の顧客について次の質問にお答え下さい/Please answer the following questions regarding your company's customers:

現在の顧客数/How many customers does your company currently have? ☐ 一年後の顧客数の予想/What do you think will be the number of customers one year from now? ☐ 個人消費者の割合/What percentage of your customers are private individuals (☐ %), 法人顧客の割合/what percentage are companies, etc. (☐ %). 上位二十%の顧客が売上高に占める割合/The 20 % largest customers make up for ☐ % of total revenues. 社長就任以前からの知り合いの顧客数/How many of your customers did you know before joining this company? ☐ . 貴社に投資している顧客はいますか/Do you have customers who also invested in your company? ☐ .

顧客さんにとってはつぎのどの点が重要だと思いますか/How important, do you think, are the following aspects to your customers?

	重要でない Not important			大変重要 Very Important
素早く生産及び配達/Quick production and delivery.				
低価格/Low Price				
高信頼性/Reliability				
ブランドイメージ/Image/Brand				
テーラーメイドの商品及びサービス/Customized Production/Service				
娯楽性/Pleasure/Entertainment				

貴社の取引先について次のような質問をお答えて下さい/Please answer the following questions regarding your company's suppliers of goods, services, and technology:

現在、取引先は何社ぐらいあるか/How many suppliers does your company currently have? [ ] 一年後に何社ぐらいになっているか/What do you think will be the number of suppliers one year from now? [ ] 正常な支払期間/What are your standard terms of payment? [ ]. 上位二十%の取引先が全体の購入コストに占める割合/The 20 % largest suppliers make up for [ ] % of total procurement costs. 社長就任以前からの知り合いの取引先の数/How many of your suppliers did you know before joining this company? [ ]. 貴社に投資している顧客はいますか/Do you have suppliers who also invested in your company? [ ].

購入決定で次のどの点が重要ですか/How important are the following aspects in your purchasing decision?

	重要でない Not important			大変重要 Very Important
素早く生産及び配達/Quick production and delivery.				
低価格/Low Price				
高信頼性/Reliability				
ブランドイメージ/Image/Brand				
テーラーメイドの商品及びサービス/Customized Production/Service				
娯楽性/Pleasure/Entertainment				

従業員に関してお答えて下さい/Please answer the following questions regarding your company's employees:

現在の従業員数/How many people are currently employed by your firm?

☐ 正社員数/full time ☐ パートタイマ数/part time ☐ その他（インターンなど）/others (intern, without salary, etc.). ☐ 臨時社員数/temporary employees

契約及びパートタイム社員は次の部署でどのように使われていますか/Which best describes your company's use of contract and part time workers?

	契約社員/Independent Contractors			パートタイマ/Part Timers		
	使わない Never used	時々使う Sometimes used	いつも使う Regularly used	使わない Never used	時々使う Sometimes used	いつも使う Regularly used
管理職/Senior Management	○	○	○	○	○	○
事務管理職/Other Administrative & Managerial	○	○	○	○	○	○
技術/Engineering & Science	○	○	○	○	○	○
営業＆マーケティング/Sales & Marketing	○	○	○	○	○	○
事務職/Clerical	○	○	○	○	○	○
熟練労働/Skilled labor	○	○	○	○	○	○
未熟練労働/Unskilled labor	○	○	○	○	○	○

どのような方法で採用しますか/Which of the following recruitment channels do you use?

	社内登用 Promote from within	新聞広告 Advertise in the newspaper	ウェブサイト広告 Advertise on the web site	現社員の紹介 Get referrals from current employees	取引先からの紹介 Get referrals from business contacts	大学からの採用 Recruit at schools or colleges	人材紹介会社の利用 Use employment agencies or search firms
管理職/Senior Management	☐	☐	☐	☐	☐	☐	☐
事務管理職/Other Administrative & Managerial	☐	☐	☐	☐	☐	☐	☐
技術/Engineering & Science	☐	☐	☐	☐	☐	☐	☐
営業＆マーケティング/Sales & Marketing	☐	☐	☐	☐	☐	☐	☐
事務職/Clerical	☐	☐	☐	☐	☐	☐	☐
熟練労働/Skilled labor	☐	☐	☐	☐	☐	☐	☐
未熟練労働/Unskilled labor	☐	☐	☐	☐	☐	☐	☐

各職種採用時にあなたの会社の最も重要と思う基準について書いて下さい/How important are the following criteria in determining whom your company hires for various positions? (最も重要なものにはMを選んで下さい、最も重要ではないものにはLを選んで下さい/Please enter M for the most important criterion and L for the least important criterion for each of the occupational groups).

	会社及びグループへの適応度 Company or Group Fit	学歴／証明書 Credentials	ビジネス経験 Industry/Business Experience	専門技能 Specialized Skills	全体的なやる気及び向上心 Overall Motivation or Drive	無回答 N.A.
管理職/Senior Management						
事務管理職/Other Administrative & Managerial						
技術/Engineering & Science						
営業&マーケティング/Sales & Marketing						
事務職/Clerical						
熟練労働/Skilled labor						
未熟練労働/Unskilled labor						

報酬制度について記入して下さい/Which best describes your company`s compensation structure?

	固定給 Fixed Salary	個人業績に基づくボーナス Individual Performance-based Bonus	ストックオプション Stock Options	時間給 Hourly Wage
管理職/Senior Management	使わない/Never	使わない/Never	使わない/Never	使わない/Never
事務管理職/Other Administrative & Managerial	使わない/Never	使わない/Never	使わない/Never	使わない/Never
技術/Engineering & Science	使わない/Never	使わない/Never	使わない/Never	使わない/Never
営業&マーケティング/Sales & Marketing	使わない/Never	使わない/Never	使わない/Never	使わない/Never
事務職/Clerical	使わない/Never	使わない/Never	使わない/Never	使わない/Never
熟練労働/Skilled labor	使わない/Never	使わない/Never	使わない/Never	使わない/Never
未熟練労働/Unskilled labor	使わない/Never	使わない/Never	使わない/Never	使わない/Never

年俸の昇給を決定する基準について答えて下さい/How important are the following criteria in determining increases in annual compensation? (最も重要なものにはMを選んで下さい、最も重要ではないものにはLを選んで下さい/Please enter M for the most important criterion and L for the least important criterion for each of the occupational groups).

	個人の業績	グループの業	会社の業績	職位	就業年数	一般給与相場

	績					との整合性
	Individual Performance	Group Performance	Firm Performance	Rank	Seniority	Adjusting to Market Wager
管理職/Senior Management						
事務管理職/Other Administrative & Managerial						
技術/Engineering & Science						
営業＆マーケティング/Sales & Marketing						
事務職/Clerical						
熟練労働/Skilled labor						
未熟練労働/Unskilled labor						

この調査に参加していただきどうも有り難うございました。終わったら以下のボックスをチェックして「Submit」ボタンを押してください。

Thank you for taking the time to fill in this questionnaire. When you are done, please check the below box and push the "submit" button.

☐ 終わった/Done!

Submit Reset

質問やコメントはこちらにクリック下さい！For questions and comments please click here!

3. *Investor Questionnaire*

Research Project "Venture Governance" – Questionnaire

ベンチャー・ガバナンス研究プロジェクト

I. 会社(調査対象)/Company Information(Survey Company):

会社名/Company Name:

住所/Address:

ホームページ/URL: http://

業種/Industry:

商品／サービス/Products/Services Offered:

会社創立年月日/Date of Establishment: 年/Year 月 /Month 日/Day

従業員数/Number of Employees:

II. 投資家/Investor Information:

氏名/Name:

役職名/Position Title:

メール/E-mail:

会社との関係/Your relationship with the company (適当なところを全部チェックして下さい/Please check all appropriate fields.)

設立者/Founder

社長/Chief Executive Officer

投資家/Investor

a) 融資提供者/provider of debt finance

b) 資本提供者/provider of equity

会社員/Employee

技術の提供者/Provider of Technology

供給者/Supplier

顧客/Customer

アドバイサー/その他/Advisor/Other

本日の年月日/Date: 年/Year 月/Month 日/Day

適当なリンクを選んで下さい/Please select the appropriate link!

資本投資家

Equity Investor

負債提供者

Provider of Debt Finance

III. 研究質問/Research Questions

c) 投資家/Investor Section

資本投資家/Equity Investor

あなたの投資の特徴と会社の業績との関連について次の表を記入して下さい/Please fill in the following table with regard to the characteristics of your investment, and its relation to the performance of the company.

会社業績 Overall Performance of the Company	全体投資実績の上限と下限 Range of Overall Return	予想投資実績/Expected Investment Performance Expected Rate of Return (IRR)	株 From Stock	ストックオプション From Stock Options
一番いい場合 Best Case	[ ] %	[ ] %	[ ] %	[ ] %
予想どうりの場合 Expected	100 %	[ ] %	[ ] %	[ ] %
最悪の場合 Worst Case	[ ] %	[ ] %	[ ] %	[ ] %

最悪の場合投資額の何%ぐらいを失うと思いますか/What percentage of your investment amount do you expect to loose in the worst thinkable case?

[ ] %

会社の経営参加について次の科目に答えて下さい/Please answer the following questions regarding your involvement in the management of the company.

	通常 On an ongoing basis	必要のある場合 If demanded/necessary
経営戦略について助言をしますか/Do you provide advice on strategic management issues?	決してしない/Never	決してしない/Never
日常業務について助言をしますか/Do you provide advice on day-to-day management issues?	決してしない/Never	決してしない/Never
経理税金関係の助言をしますか/Do you provide accounting and tax advice?	決してしない/Never	決してしない/Never
アドバイサーを紹介しますか/Do you introduce advisors to the company?	決してしない/Never	決してしない/Never
顧客を紹介しますか/Do you introduce customers to the company?	決してしない/Never	決してしない/Never
取引先を紹介しますか/Do you introduce suppliers to the company?	決してしない/Never	決してしない/Never
新入社員を紹介しますか/Do you introduce employees to the company?	決してしない/Never	決してしない/Never

投資家を紹介しますか/Do you introduce other investors to the company?	決してしない/Never	決してしない/Never

貴社の取締役ですか/Are you a member of the company`s board of directors?

貴社の経営人にどのぐらいの頻度で会いますか/How often do you meet with the senior management of the company?

貴社の施設をどのくらい訪問しますか/How often do you visit the company's facilities?

会社の業績とあなた自身の権利によって以下のような活動することがありますか/Please comment on the likelihood of the following action being taken, depending on the company's performance and your control rights.

	うまく行っている場合 If things go well	問題がある場合 If the company is in trouble
新入社員採用の許可を与えることがありますか/Do you exercise a right of approval for appointment of new employees?	実行する/Likely	実行する/Likely
管理職の指名の許可を与えることがありますか/Do you exercise a right of approval for appointment of senior management positions?	実行する/Likely	実行する/Likely
投資の決定の許可を与えることがありますか/Do you exercise a right of approval for large investments?	実行する/Likely	実行する/Likely
現職の管理職を辞めさせる権利を使えますか/Do you exercise a right to replace current management?	実行する/Likely	実行する/Likely
設立者を辞めさせる権利を使えますか/Do you exercise a right to replace the founder-manager?	実行する/Likely	実行する/Likely
経理を監査しますか/Do you exercise a right to check the company's books	実行する/Likely	実行する/Likely

終わったらこちらにクリックして下さい/If you are done, please click here!

負債提供者/Provider of Debt Finance

あなたの投資の特徴と会社の業績との関連について次の表を記入して下さい/Please fill in the following table with regard to the characteristics of your investment, and its relation to the performance of the company.

会社業績 Overall Performance of the Company	全体投資実績の上限と下限 Range of Overall Return	予想投資実績/Expected Investment Performance Expected Rate of Return (IRR)	セキュリティ/ローン From Security/Loan	ストックオプション From Stock Options

一番いい場合 Best Case	[ ] %	[ ] %	[ ] %	[ ] %
予想どうりの場合 Expected	100 %	[ ] %	[ ] %	[ ] %
最悪の場合 Worst Case	[ ] %	[ ] %	[ ] %	[ ] %

最悪の場合投資額の何%ぐらいを失うと思いますか/What percentage of your investment amount do you expect to loose in the worst thinkable case?

[ ] %

会社の経営参加について次の科目に答えて下さい/Please answer the following questions regarding your involvement in the management of the company.

	通常 On an ongoing basis	必要のある場合 If demanded/necessary
経営戦略について助言をしますか/Do you provide advice on strategic management issues?	決してしない/Never	決してしない/Never
日常業務について助言をしますか/Do you provide advice on day-to-day management issues?	決してしない/Never	決してしない/Never
経理税金関係の助言をしますか/Do you provide accounting and tax advice?	決してしない/Never	決してしない/Never
アドバイサーを紹介しますか/Do you introduce advisors to the company?	決してしない/Never	決してしない/Never
顧客を紹介しますか/Do you introduce customers to the company?	決してしない/Never	決してしない/Never
取引先を紹介しますか/Do you introduce suppliers to the company?	決してしない/Never	決してしない/Never
新入社員を紹介しますか/Do you introduce employees to the company?	決してしない/Never	決してしない/Never
投資家を紹介しますか/Do you introduce other investors to the company?	決してしない/Never	決してしない/Never

貴社の取締役ですか/Are you a member of the company`s board of directors?

[ ]

貴社の経営人にどのぐらいの頻度で会いますか/How often do you meet with the senior management of the company?

[ ]

貴社の施設をどのくらい訪問しますか/How often do you visit the company's facilities?

会社の業績とあなた自身の権利によって以下のような活動することがありますか/Please comment on the likelihood of the following action being taken, depending on the company's performance and your control rights.

	うまく行っている場合 If things go well	問題がある場合 If the company is in trouble
新入社員採用の許可を与えることがありますか/Do you exercise a right of approval for appointment of new employees?	実行する/Likely	実行する/Likely
管理職の指名の許可を与えることがありますか/Do you exercise a right of approval for appointment of senior management positions?	実行する/Likely	実行する/Likely
投資の決定の許可を与えることがありますか/Do you exercise a right of approval for large investments?	実行する/Likely	実行する/Likely
現職の管理職を辞めさせる権利を使えますか/Do you exercise a right to replace current management?	実行する/Likely	実行する/Likely
設立者を辞めさせる権利を使えますか/Do you exercise a right to replace the founder-manager?	実行する/Likely	実行する/Likely
経理を監査しますか/Do you exercise a right to check the company's books	実行する/Likely	実行する/Likely

この調査に参加していただきどうも有り難うございました。終わったら以下のボックスをチェックして「Submit」ボタンを押してください。

Thank you for taking the time to fill in this questionnaire. When you are done, please check the below box and push the "submit" button.

☐ 終わった/Done!

Submit Reset

質問やコメントはこちらにクリック下さい！For questions and comments please click here!

4. Employee Questionnaire

Research Project "Venture Governance" – Questionnaire

ベンチャー·ガバナンス研究プロジェクト

I. 会社/Company Information:

会社名/Company Name: ______

住所/Address: ______

ホームページ/URL: http:// ______

業種/Industry: ______

商品／サービス/Products/Services Offered: ______

会社創立年月日/Date of Establishment: 年/Year ___ 月/Month ___ 日/Day ___

従業員数/Number of Employees: ___

II. 個人/Personal Information:

氏名/Name: ______

役職名/Position Title: ______

メール/E-mail: ______

会社との関係/Your relationship with the company (適当なところを全部チェックして下さい/Please check all appropriate fields.)

設立者/Founder ☐	会社員/Employee ☐
社長/Chief Executive Officer ☐	技術の提供者/Provider of Technology ☐
投資家/Investor	供給者/Supplier ☐
a) 融資提供者/provider of debt finance ☐	顧客/Customer ☐
b) 資本提供者/provider of equity ☐	アドバイザー/その他/Advisor/Other ______

本日の年月日/Date: 年/Year ___ 月/Month ___ 日/Day ___

III. 研究質問/Research Questions

d) 会社員への質問/Employee

この会社に入る前にの職業/What did you do prior to joining this company?

以前の仕事について/How would you describe the following aspects of your previous position?

	大変悪い Very Bad			大変良い Very Good	無回答 N.A.
報償/Compensation.	○	○	○	○	○
労働時間/Working Time.	○	○	○	○	○
同僚との関係/Relationship with Co-workers.	○	○	○	○	○
上司との関係/Relationship with Superiors.	○	○	○	○	○
会社戦略への影響度/Ability to influence the direction of the company.	○	○	○	○	○
成功報償の程度/Ability to share in the success of the company.	○	○	○	○	○
全般的な業績/Overall quality of your previous company	○	○	○	○	○

どのようにこのポジションを受けましたか/How and when did you get in contact with this company?

この会社に入るにあたって重要だった点について/How important were the following factors in your decision to join this company?

	重要でない Not important			大変重要 Very Important
自分の仕事のスタイルと価値観に合った会社で働く/Work in an organization that suits my own work style and values.	○	○	○	○
前の仕事より高い収入を得ること/Make more money than in my previous position.	○	○	○	○
最も興味を持つ分野で仕事をすること/Work in the area that I find most interesting.	○	○	○	○
自立的に働くことが出来る/Be able to work independently.	○	○	○	○
お金持ちになること/Have a chance to become rich.	○	○	○	○
前の仕事より仕事が楽になること/Do less or more enjoyable work than as an employee.	○	○	○	○

他の人から尊敬されること/Gain the respect of others.	○	○	○	○

現在株式保有していますか/Do you currently hold shares in the equity of your company? もしあれば何パーセントぐらいですか/If so, what percentage of total shares outstanding?

[ ] %

待遇と報酬全般、そしてその会社業績との関連について記入して下さい/Please fill in the following table describing the structure of your overall compensation, and its relation to the performance of the company.

会社業績 Overall Performance of the Company	全体報酬の上限と下限 Range of Overall Compensation	報酬全体の割合/Share of Overall Compensation as 固定給 Fixed Salary	ボーナス Bonus	ストックオプション Stock Options
一番いい場合 Best Case	[ ] %	[ ] %	[ ] %	[ ] %
予想どうりの場合 Expected	100 %	[ ] %	[ ] %	[ ] %
最悪の場合 Worst Case	[ ] %	[ ] %	[ ] %	[ ] %

会社に入る時に考えたリスクにつて/How did you perceive the following risks at the time of joining this company?

	低い Not high			大変高い Very high
技術／サービスが失敗するというリスク/Risk that the product/service technology fails.	○	○	○	○
マーケットが小さ過ぎるというリスク/Risk that the market for the product/service is too small.	○	○	○	○
利益が出ないというリスク/Risk that the company will not be profitable.	○	○	○	○
倒産するというリスク/Risk that the company will become bankrupt.	○	○	○	○
会社が倒産する場合あるいは辞めさせられる場合に次のいい仕事が見つけられるかというリスク/Personal career risk of not finding a good job if the company fails or getting fired.	○	○	○	○
個人資産の [ ] %を失うというリスク、/Personal financial risk of loosing <-% of personal assets.	○	○	○	○

会社に入る時に考えられた可能性について/How did you perceive the following possibilities at the time of joining this company?

	低い Not high			大変高い Very high
生涯続けられるような会社の可能性/Possibility of workin in this company for the rest of my professional career.	○	○	○	○
収入の増加とともにライフスタイルを変えられる可能性/Possibility of changing my lifestyle by earning more money.	○	○	○	○
お金持ちになって、早期退職は可能になる可能性/Possibility of becoming very rich, and be able to retire early.	○	○	○	○
会社の成長としたがって昇進する可能性/Possibility of being promoted as the company grows.	○	○	○	○
自分の業績で昇進する可能性/Possibility of being promoted due to my personal performance.	○	○	○	○

この調査に参加していただきどうも有り難うございました。終わったら以下のボックスをチェックして「Submit」ボタンを押してください。

Thank you for taking the time to fill in this questionnaire. When you are done, please check the below box and push the "submit" button.

☐ 終わった/Done!

Submit　　Reset

質問やコメントはこちらにクリック下さい！For questions and comments please click here!

ベンチャー·ガバナンス研究プロジェクト **Venture Governance Research Project** Aggregate Results

Participants:
Founders, CEOs, Employees, and Investors of 10 Venture capital-backed Internet Startups in Tokyo.

Survey Period:
November 1999 - June 2000

a) 設立者への質問 以前の仕事について	**a) Founder Section** How would you describe the following aspects of your previous position?	大変悪い Very Bad			大変良い Very Good	無回答 N.A.
報償	Compensation.		10%	40%	50%	
労働時間	Working Time.	40%	10%	10%	40%	
同僚との関係	Relationship with Co-workers.			10%	90%	
上司との関係	Relationship with Superiors.	10%		10%	80%	
会社戦略への影響度	Ability to influence the direction of the company.	20%	30%	10%	40%	
成功報償の程度	Ability to share in the success of the company.	40%		40%	20%	
全般的な満足	Overall quality of your previous company		10%	40%	50%	

会社設立にあたって重要だった点について	How important were the following factors in your decision to establish this company?	重要でない Not important			大変重要 Very Important
自分の仕事のスタイルと価値観に合った組織を作ること	Design an organization that suits my own work style and values.			10%	90%
社員より高い収入を得ること	Make more money than as an employee.	50%	30%	20%	
最も興味を持つ分野で仕事をすること	Work in the area that I find most interesting.			20%	80%
上司を持ったないこと	Have nobody who tells me what to do.	30%	30%	20%	20%
お金持ちになること	Have a chance to become really rich.	10%	10%	40%	40%
社員より仕事が楽になること	Do less or more enjoyable work than as an employee.	80%			20%
他の人から尊敬されること	Gain the respect of others.	30%	50%	10%	10%

ビジネスのアイデアを進める上で重要だった点	How important were the following factors in developing your business idea?	重要でない Not important			大変重要 Very Important
同じような仕事をする	Do the same business that I did in my previous position.	38%	25%	25%	13%
大学での研究分野の技術を商業化する	Commercialize an invention that I developed in an academic context.	88%			13%
前の仕事で開発した技術を商業化する	Commercialize a technology that I developed in my previous position.	63%		38%	
一般的な新技術を用する	Make use of a new technology that is generally available.	25%		38%	38%
未開拓のマーケットニーズを開拓する	Satisfy a market need that nobody had identified so far.	13%			88%
他の会社のビジネス·モデルを真似する	Copy the business model of another company.	50%		38%	13%
現存のマーケットに入って最も効率的な組織を作る	Enter an existing market and design an organization that is more efficient than incumbent competitors.	38%	13%	13%	38%

設立時に考えたリスクにつて	How did you perceive the following risks at the time of establishment?	低い Not high			大変高い Very high
技術 / サービスが失敗するというリスク	Risk that the product/service/technology fails.	44%	11%	44%	
マーケットが小さ過ぎるというリスク	Risk that the market for the product/service is too small.	50%	30%		20%
利益が出ないというリスク	Risk that the company will not be profitable.	20%		30%	50%
倒産するというリスク	Risk that the company will become bankrupt.	20%	10%	40%	30%
会社が倒産した後に次のいい仕事が見つけられるかというリスク	Personal career risk of not finding a good job if the company fails.	100%			
個人資産のX%を失うというリスク。	Personal financial risk of loosing X% of personal assets.	40%	20%		40%

ベンチャー・ガバナンス研究プロジェクト	Venture Governance Research Project	Aggregate Results			
設立時に考えられた可能性について	How did you perceive the following possibilities at the time of establishment?				
		低い Not high			大変高い Very high
生涯続けられるような会社の可能性	Possibility of creating a company that I can lead for the rest of my professional caree	44%	22%	22%	11%
収入の増加とともにライフスタイルを変えられる可能性	Possibility of changing my lifestyle by earning more money.	20%	20%	40%	20%
お金持ちになって、早期退職は可能になる可能性	Possibility of becoming very rich, and be able to retire early.	20%	10%	40%	30%
三年以内に株式を公開出来る可能性	Possibility of leading the company to a public offering within 3 years.	10%	10%	10%	70%
十年以内に株式を公開出来る可能性	Possibility of leading the company to a public offering within 10 years.	30%	10%	10%	50%
会社所有者として止まって尊敬された安定性がある会社を作る可	Build a respected and sustainable company and remain its sole owner.	75%	25%		
通常業務が始まった年月日	When would you date the beginning of normal business operations?				
業務開始に関連して以下のような活動をいつ完了しましたか	When, in relation to the above date, did you accomplish the following activities?				
		無し Never	上記日付前 Prior	上記日付後 After	
社外融資の確保	Secure external finance	50%	38%	13%	
最初の顧客の確保	Secure first customers	13%	38%	50%	
従業員の確保	Secure employees		38%	63%	
技術やノウハウの確保	Secure technology/know how		88%	13%	
会社の法的登記	Legally establish the company		75%	25%	
ビジネスプランの作成	Prepare a business plan		75%	25%	
弁護士の確保	Retain an attorney	25%	25%	50%	
経理制度の確立	Establish an accounting system		13%	88%	
第三者資本資金の導入	Obtain external equity financing	25%	13%	63%	
第三者負債資金の導入	Obtain external debt financing	100%			
ビィジョンの作成	Write a mission statement	25%	63%	13%	
従業員の採用	Hire an employee		13%	88%	
人事担当者の採用	Hire a full-time personnel specialist	88%		13%	
マーケティングプランの作成	Develop a marketing plan	13%	75%	13%	
製品 / サービスの発表	Announce a product	25%	25%	50%	
特許申請の手続き	File a patent application	38%		63%	
最初の商品 / サービスの販売	Sell first product	13%	13%	75%	
経営戦略の意志決定について次のような質問をお答え下さい	Please answer the following questions regarding your decision-making on strategic management issues?				
		決してない Never	ときどき Sometimes	いつも Always	
自分で決める	I decide on my own.	33%	44%	22%	
社員全員と相談して合意を作り出す	I consult everybody in the company and create a consensus.	30%	60%	10%	
最も関係する者と相談する	I consult the people who are most concerned.		40%	60%	
取締役と相談する	I consult board members.		60%	40%	
社外アドバイサーと相談する	I consult outside professional advisors.		100%		
顧客と相談する	I consult customers.	70%	30%		
友人と相談する	I discuss issues with friends.	50%	50%		
投資家から指示を貰う	I receive instructions from investors.	40%	60%		
取締役らから指示を貰う	I receive instructions from board members.	30%	70%		

ベンチャー・ガバナンス研究プロジェクト Venture Governance Research Project

Aggregate Results

日常業務の意志決定について次のような質問をお答え下さい	Please answer the following questions regarding your decision-making on day-to-day management issues?	決してない Never	ときどき Sometimes	いつも Always
自分で決める	I decide on my own.		56%	44%
社員全員と相談して合意を作り出す	I consult everybody in the company and create a consensus.	11%	78%	11%
最も関係する者と相談する	I consult the people who are most concerned.	11%	56%	33%
取締役と相談する	I consult board members.	11%	78%	11%
社外アドバイサーと相談する	I consult outside professional advisors.	11%	78%	11%
顧客と相談する	I consult customers.	44%	44%	11%
友人と相談する	I discuss issues with friends.	22%	67%	11%
投資家から指示を貰う	I receive instructions from investors.	33%	56%	11%
取締役らから指示を貰う	I receive instructions from board members.	22%	67%	11%

顧客にとっては次のどの点が重要だと思いますか	How important, do you think, are the following aspects to your customers?	重要でない Not important			大変重要 Very important
素早く生産及び配達	Quick production and delivery.	10%		10%	80%
低価格	Low Price	10%	10%	10%	70%
高信頼性	Reliability			10%	90%
ブランドイメージ	Image/Brand	10%	10%	20%	60%
テーラーメイドの商品及びサービス	Customized Production/Service	10%	20%	30%	40%
娯楽性	Pleasure/Entertainment	20%	10%	40%	30%

購入決定で次のどの点が重要ですか	How important are the following aspects in your purchasing decision?	重要でない Not important			大変重要 Very important
素早く生産及び配達	Quick production and delivery.			33%	67%
低価格	Low Price	13%	13%	38%	38%
高信頼性	Reliability				100%
ブランドイメージ	Image/Brand	25%	13%	38%	25%
テーラーメイドの商品及びサービス	Customized Production/Service	13%	25%	13%	50%
娯楽性	Pleasure/Entertainment	63%	25%	13%	

契約及びパートタイム社員は次の部署でどのように使われていますか	Which best describes your company's use of contract and part time workers?	契約社員 Independent Contractors			パートタイマ Part Timers		
		使わない Never used	時々使う Sometimes	いつも使う Regularly used	使わない Never used	時々使う Sometimes	いつも使う Regularly used
管理職	Senior Management	90%	10%		78%	11%	11%
事務管理職	Other Administrative & Managerial	50%	50%		44%	56%	
技術	Engineering & Science	40%	40%	20%	22%	44%	33%
営業＆マーケティング	Sales & Marketing	30%	40%	30%	44%	33%	22%
事務職	Clerical	56%		44%	20%	20%	60%
熟練労働	Skilled labor	86%	14%		50%	33%	17%
未熟練労働	Unskilled labor	63%	13%	25%	43%	14%	43%

ベンチャー･ガバナンス研究プロジェクト　Venture Governance Research Project　Aggregate Results

どのような方法で採用しますか
Which of the following recruitment channels do you use?

		社内登用 Promote from within	新聞広告 Advertise in the newspaper	ウェブサイト広告 Advertise on the web site	現社員の紹介 Get referrals from current employees	取引先からの紹介 Get referrals from business contacts	大学からの採用 Recruit at schools or colleges	人材紹介会社の利用 Use employment agencies or search firms
管理職	Senior Management	30%	10%	40%	80%	60%		60%
事務管理職	Other Administrative & Managerial	40%	10%	40%	60%	30%		40%
技術	Engineering & Science		20%	50%	70%	50%	10%	60%
営業＆マーケティング	Sales & Marketing	10%	30%	60%	70%	30%	10%	70%
事務職	Clerical	10%	30%	40%	80%	20%	20%	30%
熟練労働	Skilled labor		10%	20%	40%	10%		30%
未熟練労働	Unskilled labor		10%	20%	40%	10%	10%	10%

各職種採用時にあなたの会社の最も重要と思う基準について書いて下さい
How important are the following criteria in determining whom your company hires for various positions?

(最も重要なものにはMを選んで下さい、最も重要ではないものにはLを選んで下さい
Please enter M for the most important criterion and L for the least important criterion for each of the occupational groups).

Most important

		会社及びグループへの適応度 Company or Group Fit	学歴／証明書 Credentials	ビジネス経験 Industry/ Business Experience	専門技能 Specialized Skills	全体的なやる気及び向上心 Overall Motivation or Drive	無回答 N.A.
管理職	Senior Management	13%		63%	25%		
事務管理職	Other Administrative & Managerial			38%	38%	25%	
技術	Engineering & Science				100%		
営業＆マーケティング	Sales & Marketing			13%	13%	75%	
事務職	Clerical	25%		13%	13%	50%	
熟練労働	Skilled labor				100%		
未熟練労働	Unskilled labor	33%				67%	

(最も重要なものにはMを選んで下さい、最も重要ではないものにはLを選んで下さい
Please enter M for the most important criterion and L for the least important criterion for each of the occupational groups).

Least important

		会社及びグループへの適応度 Company or Group Fit	学歴／証明書 Credentials	ビジネス経験 Industry/ Business Experience	専門技能 Specialized Skills	全体的なやる気及び向上心 Overall Motivation or Drive	無回答 N.A.
管理職	Senior Management		75%		25%		
事務管理職	Other Administrative & Managerial		88%		13%		
技術	Engineering & Science		88%	13%			
営業＆マーケティング	Sales & Marketing		88%		13%		
事務職	Clerical		100%				
熟練労働	Skilled labor		100%				
未熟練労働	Unskilled labor		100%				

ベンチャー･ガバナンス研究プロジェクト　Venture Governance Research Project　Aggregate Fesults

報酬制度について記入して下さい　Which best describes your company's compensation structure?

		固定給 Fixed Salary			個人業績に基づくボーナス Individual Performance-based Bonus		
		使わない Never	時々使う Sometimes	通常使う Regularly	使わない Never	時々使う Sometimes	通常使う Regularly
管理職	Senior Management			100%	30%	20%	40%
事務管理職	Other Administrative & Managerial			100%	40%	30%	20%
技術	Engineering & Science			100%	50%	30%	20%
営業＆マーケティング	Sales & Marketing		10%	90%	30%	30%	40%
事務職	Clerical	10%	10%	80%	60%	20%	10%
熟練労働	Skilled labor	33%		67%	67%		33%
未熟練労働	Unskilled labor	50%		50%	50%		

		ストックオプション Stock Options			時間給 Hourly Wage		
		使わない Never	時々使う Sometimes	通常使う Regularly	使わない Never	時々使う Sometimes	通常使う Regularly
管理職	Senior Management	10%	20%	70%	100%		
事務管理職	Other Administrative & Managerial	11%	33%	56%	89%	11%	
技術	Engineering & Science	11%	33%	56%	67%	22%	11%
営業＆マーケティング	Sales & Marketing	22%	22%	56%	89%		11%
事務職	Clerical	38%	38%	25%	56%	22%	22%
熟練労働	Skilled labor	50%		50%	50%	50%	
未熟練労働	Unskilled labor	50%		50%		50%	50%

ベンチャー·ガバナンス研究プロジェクト　Venture Governance Research Project　Aggregate Results

年俸の昇給を決定する基準について答えて下さい.
How important are the following criteria in determining increases in annual compensation?

(最も重要なものにはMを選んで下さい、最も重要ではないものにはLを選んで下さい
Please enter M for the most important criterion and L for the least important criterion for each of the occupational groups).

Most important

		個人の業績 Individual Performance	グループの業績 Group Performance	会社の業績 Firm Performance	職位 Rank	就業年数 Seniority	一般給与相場との整合性 Adjusting to Market Wager
管理職	Senior Management	38%	13%	50%			
事務管理職	Other Administrative & Managerial	38%	13%	38%			
技術	Engineering & Science	86%					14%
営業＆マーケティング	Sales & Marketing	50%		25%			
事務職	Clerical	50%		25%			
熟練労働	Skilled labor	100%					
未熟練労働	Unskilled labor	50%		50%			

(最も重要なものにはMを選んで下さい、最も重要ではないものにはLを選んで下さい
Please enter M for the most important criterion and L for the least important criterion for each of the occupational groups).

Least important

		個人の業績 Individual Performance	グループの業績 Group Performance	会社の業績 Firm Performance	職位 Rank	就業年数 Seniority	一般給与相場との整合性 Adjusting to Market Wager
管理職	Senior Management					88%	13%
事務管理職	Other Administrative & Managerial					88%	13%
技術	Engineering & Science				13%	75%	13%
営業＆マーケティング	Sales & Marketing				13%	75%	13%
事務職	Clerical	14%				71%	14%
熟練労働	Skilled labor					67%	33%
未熟練労働	Unskilled labor					100%	

ベンチャー・ガバナンス研究プロジェクト Venture Governance Research Project

Aggregate Results

c) 投資家 (資本投資家) / Investor Section (Equity Investor):

会社の経営参加について次の科目に答えて下さい / Please answer the following questions regarding your involvement in the management of the company.

		通常 On an ongoing basis			必要のある場合 If demanded/necessary		
		決してしない Never	時々する Sometimes	いつもする Regularly	決してしない Never	時々する Sometimes	いつもする Regularly
経営戦略について助言をしますか	Do you provide advice on strategic management issues?	25%		75%			100%
日常業務について助言をしますか	Do you provide advice on day-to-day management issues?	25%		75%	25%		75%
経理税金関係の助言をしますか	Do you provide accounting and tax advice?	25%		75%	25%		75%
アドバイサーを紹介しますか	Do you introduce advisors to the company?	33%	33%	33%		50%	50%
顧客を紹介しますか	Do you introduce customers to the company?	25%	25%	50%	33%		67%
取引先を紹介しますか	Do you introduce suppliers to the company?	25%	25%	50%	33%		67%
新入社員を紹介しますか	Do you introduce employees to the company?	25%	25%	50%	33%		67%
投資家を紹介しますか	Do you introduce other investors to the company?	25%	50%	25%		50%	50%

会社の業績とあなた自身の権利によって以下のような活動することがありますか / Please comment on the likelihood of the following action being taken, depending on the company's performance and your control rights.

		うまく行っている場合 If things go well			問題がある場合 If the company is in trouble		
		実行する Likely	可能性がある Possible	可能性が無い Unthinkable	実行する Likely	可能性がある Possible	可能性が無い Unthinkable
新入社員採用の許可を与えることがありますか	Do you exercise a right of approval for appointment of new employees?			100%	25%	50%	25%
管理職の指名の許可を与えることがありますか	Do you exercise a right of approval for appointment of senior management positions?		75%	25%	25%	75%	
投資の決定の許可を与えることがありますか	Do you exercise a right of approval for large investments?	25%	25%	50%	50%	50%	
現職の管理職を辞めさせる権利を使えますか	Do you exercise a right to replace current management?			100%		75%	25%
設立者を辞めさせる権利を使えますか	Do you exercise a right to replace the founder-manager?			100%		50%	50%
経理を監査しますか	Do you exercise a right to check the company's books	75%	25%		75%	25%	

ベンチャー·ガバナンス研究プロジェクト　Venture Governance Research Project　Aggregate Results

d) 会社員への質問	Employee Section					
以前の仕事について	How would you describe the following aspects of your previous position?	大変悪い Very Bad			大変良い Very Good	無回答 N.A.
報償	Compensation.	13%		75%	13%	
労働時間	Working Time.	25%	38%	13%	25%	
同僚との関係	Relationship with Co-workers.			25%	75%	
上司との関係	Relationship with Superiors.	13%	38%	25%	25%	
会社戦略への影響度	Ability to influence the direction of the company.	13%	63%	13%	13%	
成功報償の程度	Ability to share in the success of the company.	38%	38%	25%		
全般的な業績	Overall quality of your previous company	25%	25%	25%	13%	13%
この会社に入るにあたって重要だった点について	How important were the following factors in your decision to join this company?	重要でない Not important			大変重要 Very Important	
自分の仕事のスタイルと価値観に合った会社で働く	Work in an organization that suits my own work style and values.			25%	75%	
前の仕事より高い収入を得ること	Make more money than in my previous position.	13%	50%	38%		
最も興味を持つ分野で仕事をすること	Work in the area that I find most interesting.			13%	88%	
自立的に働くことが出来る	Be able to work independently.		13%	25%	63%	
お金持ちになること	Have a chance to become rich.			88%	13%	
前の仕事より仕事が楽になること	Do less or more enjoyable work than as an employee.	50%	25%	25%		
他の人から尊敬されること	Gain the respect of others.	13%	13%	75%		
会社に入る時に考えたリスクにつて	How did you perceive the following risks at the time of joining this company?	低い Not high			大変高い Very high	
技術 / サービスが失敗するというリスク	Risk that the product/service technology fails.	25%	13%	63%		
マーケットが小さ過ぎるというリスク	Risk that the market for the product/service is too small.	63%	38%			
利益が出ないというリスク	Risk that the company will not be profitable.	13%	13%	50%	25%	
倒産するというリスク	Risk that the company will become bankrupt.	25%	38%	38%		
会社が倒産する場合あるいは辞めさせられる場合に次のいい仕事が見つけられるかというリスク	Personal career risk of not finding a good job if the company fails or getting fired.	63%	13%	13%	13%	
個人資産のx%を失うというリスク、	Personal financial risk of loosing x% of personal assets.	63%	38%			
会社に入る時に考えられた可能性について	How did you perceive the following possibilities at the time of joining this company?	低い Not high			大変高い Very high	
生涯続けられるような会社の可能性	Possibility of working in this company for the rest of my professional career.	25%	50%	13%	13%	
収入の増加とともにライフスタイルを変えられる可能性	Possibility of changing my lifestyle by earning more money.	13%	13%	25%	50%	
お金持ちになって、早期退職は可能になる可能性	Possibility of becoming very rich, and be able to retire early.	13%	38%	25%	25%	
会社の成長としたがって昇進する可能性	Possibility of being promoted as the company grows.		38%	38%	25%	
自分の業績で昇進する可能性	Possibility of being promoted due to my personal performance.		50%	13%	38%	

MIX
Papier aus verantwortungsvollen Quellen
Paper from responsible sources
FSC® C105338

If you have any concerns about our products,
you can contact us on
ProductSafety@springernature.com

In case Publisher is established outside the EU,
the EU authorized representative is:
Springer Nature Customer Service Center GmbH
Europaplatz 3, 69115 Heidelberg, Germany

Printed by Libri Plureos GmbH
in Hamburg, Germany